TAKING BACK OUR STREETS

FIGHTING CRIME IN AMERICA

WILLIE L. WILLIAMS LAPD

WITH BRUCE B. HENDERSON

A LISA DREW BOOK

SCRIBNER

A LISA DREW BOOK/SCRIBNER
1230 Avenue of the Americas
New York, NY 10020

SCRIBNER and design are trademarks of Simon & Schuster Inc.

Set in Bodoni Book

DESIGNED BY ERICH HOBBING

Manufactured in the United States of America

10   9   8   7   6   5   4   3   2   1

Library of Congress Cataloging-in-Publication Data
Williams, Willie L.
Taking back our streets : fighting crime in America / Willie L. Williams.
p.   cm.
"A Lisa Drew Book."
Includes index.
1. Williams, Willie L. 2. Police chiefs—California—Los Angeles—Biography. 3. Los Angeles
(Calif.) Police Dept.—Officials and employees—Biography. 4. Crime—United States—Preven-
tion. I. Henderson, Bruce B., date. II. Title.
HV7911.W494A3   1996
363.2'092—dc20
[B]   95-26814
CIP

ISBN 0-684-80277-5

To the "wind beneath my wings," my wife, Evelina, who has always supported me and been there when it counted.

And to my mother, Helen Williams, and my children, Lisa, Willie 3rd, and Eric 1st.

And also to the memory of the late Francis Walker, Captain, Philadelphia Police Department, who taught me the meaning of studying and preparing for the future.

W.L.W.

To my children, Chelsea, Nathan, Grant, and Evan. May our society be made safer for them, their children, and all the other children to come.

And to Theresa Ann Sanders, who knows why.

B.B.H.

TAKING
BACK
OUR
STREETS

THE BEATING

IT ALL BEGAN with a traffic violation.

At 12:40 A.M. on March 3, 1991, a California Highway Patrol (CHP) unit cruising westbound on Interstate 210 in the northeastern corner of Los Angeles's San Fernando Valley observed a white car approaching from behind traveling at a high rate of speed. The white car, a Hyundai, slowed abruptly as it passed the patrol car.

Pulling an old state-trooper trick, the patrol car left the freeway at the next off-ramp and reentered from the adjoining on-ramp. The CHP unit soon caught up with the Hyundai, speeding again, now using three lanes to dart in and out of slower-moving traffic.

The CHP unit, its red lights flashing and siren wailing, followed the Hyundai as it spun down an off-ramp, ran a stop sign at the bottom, and continued on surface streets at speeds of up to 80 mph, running a red light.

The speeding driver was Rodney G. King, a twenty-five-year-old black man who was about to become famous worldwide. One passenger in his car, Bryant Allen, reportedly urged King to pull over. The other passenger, Freddie Helms, would later tell authorities that he was asleep during the entire chase. (Helms subsequently died in an unrelated traffic accident.)

Los Angeles Police Department (LAPD) patrol car unit 16A23, assigned to Officers Laurence M. Powell and Timothy Wind, joined the chase as the LAPD's primary pursuit car. A Los Angeles Unified School District Police car that happened to be nearby also took part in the pursuit.

With several pursuing squad cars behind it, the Hyundai stopped at a red light at the corner of Osborne Street and Foothill Boulevard. When the light turned green, the Hyundai proceeded through the intersection, pulled over to the curb, and stopped.

The time was 12:50 A.M.

LAPD unit 16A23 radioed a "Code 6" to indicate that the pursuit had concluded. Approximately sixty seconds later, the following report from the scene was radioed to the LAPD radio transmission officer (RTO): "Foothill and Osborne—there appears to be sufficient units here."

The RTO immediately broadcast a "Code 4," notifying all units that additional assistance was not needed at the scene.

During the pursuit, LAPD officers Theodore J. Briseno and Rolando Solano were designated the LAPD's secondary pursuit car. When they heard the Code 6, they could see the flashing red lights off in the distance and proceeded to the scene. They pulled up as King was exiting his car in response to directions from a CHP officer.

Sgt. Stacey Koon also pulled up just as the pursuit ended. Koon, a fifteen-year department veteran, was a field supervisor responsible for monitoring the activities of LAPD's Foothill Division patrol officers.

At the termination of the pursuit, a CHP officer, following standard "felony-stop" procedures, used a loudspeaker to order the occupants out of the Hyundai. Passengers Allen and Helms exited on the right-hand side. King opened the driver's door and seemed to be struggling as he tried to unbuckle his seat belt.

After King stepped from the car, CHP officer Melanie Singer approached him. She intended to order the suspect into the "felony-kneeling" position and to take him into custody. However, LAPD Sergeant Koon told her to stay back. "We'll handle it," Koon said.

King was ordered to lie flat on his stomach on the ground. Some reports indicate that King responded by getting down on all fours and slapping the ground, apparently refusing to lie down.

Sergeant Koon ordered the officers to "stand clear." At that point and while King was still on the ground, Koon fired his Taser electric stun gun once, then again. An officer at the scene later reported that the Taser hits—electric darts shot at a suspect—appeared to affect King because the suspect shook and yelled for several seconds.

At that moment, George Holliday, a plumbing-supply salesman, awakened by the commotion, stepped onto his second-floor deck across the street with his new Sony video camera in hand. From this vantage point, he began filming.

When Holliday's grainy but startlingly clear videotape begins, King is on the ground. He rises and moves toward Officer Powell, who is standing close by. It is unclear whether the movement was intended as an attack or an attempt to get away. Several Taser wires can be seen dangling from King's back. As King moves forward, Powell hits him hard with his two-foot-long baton. The blow lands squarely on King's skull, and he drops to the ground.

Powell hits King several more times with his baton. King then rises to his knees. Powell and Wind, who earlier that evening at roll call had participated in a training session in the parking lot of the Foothill Station on the proper use of the baton, strike King again and again with their batons while he is on the ground.

Sergeant Koon would later acknowledge that he ordered the baton blows, directing Officers Powell and Wind to hit King with "power strokes."

Meanwhile, on the other side of the car, passengers Allen and Helms had both complied with officers' commands after they exited the Hyundai to lie flat on the ground in the "prone-out" position. They were handcuffed, and a school district police officer kept his service revolver pointed at them as they lay on the ground. Allen and Helms both heard screams from King but could not see anything because they were ordered not to look up, but to keep their heads on the ground.

After fifty-six baton blows and six kicks to Rodney King's

head and body by four LAPD officers, more officers swarmed in and placed him in handcuffs and leg restraints.

King was dragged on his stomach to curbside to await the arrival of the fire department's rescue ambulance.

CHAPTER ONE

WHEN I FIRST SAW the videotape of the Rodney King incident, I was in Washington, D.C., attending a national conference of mayors and police chiefs. As I watched the group of Los Angeles police officers repeatedly strike the suspect with their nightsticks in quick frames shown on the television news, I had two thoughts: *What had this guy done to make those officers so mad?* and *I'm glad this isn't my department.*

At the time, I had been in law enforcement for twenty-seven years, the last three years as commissioner of the Philadelphia Police Department, the fourth-largest municipal police force in the country.

Until more details of the Los Angeles incident were released, I withheld judgment. Like all veteran police officers, I had spent years on the streets and had fought and wrestled with my share of suspects. That's part of the job, and you like your superiors to give you the benefit of the doubt. I had also investigated many complaints against police officers throughout the years and knew there were always two sides to a story. What had happened before the camera started filming? Had he shot at the police officers? Did they have some other reason to believe the suspect might be armed? How much of the total confrontation were we seeing? Had it gone on for thirty seconds or five minutes?

As head of a police department, I knew how important it was to give your people on the street the benefit of the doubt in such cases. At the same time, you had to ask the hard questions and hold people accountable for their actions. Presumably, that process was now taking place within the Los Angeles Police Department.

Though I held off from immediately concluding it was excessive force, I wondered, like a lot of people who saw the videotape, what in the world had occurred that would trigger such a serious assault against a defendant by numerous police officers.

The officers involved and their department, the Los Angeles Police Department, needed to answer some difficult questions being asked about what exactly had happened that night.

Rodney King received twenty stitches at the hospital, including five inside his mouth. He had numerous skull fractures, a broken cheekbone, and a broken right ankle. Blood and urine samples taken five hours after King's arrest showed that his blood-alcohol level was 0.075 percent, indicating that at the time of his arrest he was legally drunk (0.08 percent) under California law. The tests showed traces of marijuana, but no sign of PCP or other hallucinogenics or any other illegal drugs.

As details emerged in the following days and weeks, it became clear that the police officers involved in this incident may have badly overreacted and engaged in excessive force. What was involved here were *traffic violations*—speeding, failure to stop, running a red light—and some lack of cooperation from a drunk suspect once he emerged from the car. Simply put, the punishment did not appear to fit the crime.

It seemed shocking that the situation on the street that night, which did not involve an armed suspect or even a felony suspect, had so escalated despite there being such a large number of officers on the scene. In all, there were twenty-three officers from the LAPD, including four "training officers" responsible for supervising probationary officers during their first year after graduation from the police academy, and an LAPD patrol sergeant. There were also four officers from two other police agencies. Yet things had gotten so out of hand that a man was severely beaten and hospitalized. It was inexcusable, and I found myself embarrassed as a professional police officer.

I was concerned about the condition of the injured man and wondered, too, if any of the officers had been injured in the incident. I also thought about the repercussions of what would surely be a public relations nightmare. What was going to happen to the Los Angeles Police Department? LAPD was unquestionably a good "cop shop," long regarded by many in law enforcement as the best police force in the country. And what would be the impact on the ethnically diverse community of Los Angeles, considered America's new melting pot for the eighties and nineties? What kind of message did such police misconduct send to people of color not only in Los Angeles, but in every major city in the country? Indeed, what message went out to other nations, friends and foes alike, about the state of American policing?

I knew firsthand how an incident like this could precipitate great changes in a big-city police department. We had had our crisis in Philadelphia almost six years earlier. . . .

It had happened on a hot, muggy day. At 5:37 P.M., on May 13, 1985, a Philadelphia police lieutenant leaned from the open door of a state police helicopter and dropped a satchel containing three and a half pounds of military explosive on the roof of a row house in West Philadelphia. This followed the firing of ten thousand rounds of ammunition by police in under ninety minutes at the house, which was known to contain children. The house had been the location of a twelve-hour siege with a radical, "back to nature," mostly black group called MOVE, which had alienated the local neighbors, threatened violence, and been involved eight years earlier in a violent confrontation with police. The ensuing fire from this fiery explosion led to the deaths of eleven people—including five children—destroyed sixty-one homes, and displaced hundred of residents in a predominately black, middle-class neighborhood.

On that sad day in Philadelphia history, I was a captain assigned to the Twenty-second Police District in another part of the city. I could only hear radio police reports and watch occasional news updates as the disaster played out just ten blocks away from where my widowed mother lived. It turned out that the home of a good friend of mine, who had allowed police to use his house during the action, burned down.

I was horrified by what I saw and heard. At one point, a terribly loud automatic weapon was being fired at the MOVE house. One of my officers, who had been in the military, identified it as a .50-caliber machine gun. I had no idea we even had such a weapon in our arsenal.

Like many other police officers in the City of Brotherly Love that day, I had felt shame and anger. I kept wondering, over and over, *Why weren't we better prepared?* The decision to drop the bomb, both reckless and ill-conceived, had been authorized at the scene by the police commissioner. After the bomb had ignited and the fire started, many of us at the Twenty-second district station house had asked, "Where is the fire department?" It later came out—investigative hearings were aired live on Philadelphia television—that the police commissioner held back the firefighters as a "tactical decision," which may have added to the unconscionable cost of further life and property.

It had been a morality lesson for the city of Philadelphia and its police department—one that I would always remember. *A police department must never be an island unto itself. Nothing good ever comes from police harboring an us-against-them mentality.*

The independent investigation that followed gave the city's leaders and residents the unique opportunity to evaluate and reform police procedures. It also led to the hiring of my predecessor, Kevin Tucker, the city's first outside police commissioner in fifty years. (In the East, the head of a police department is usually called *police commissioner.* In the West, *police chief* is more commonly used.) Tucker began a program to rebuild the Philadelphia Police Department into a national model for community policing, a partnership between the police and the public working together in a joint effort to prevent crime and promote safety. In this way, police work with citizens, identifying their concerns and soliciting their help. Such a major change in the Philadelphia Police Department would never have come about without the MOVE debacle.

The Rodney King incident did not soon go away. Nor should it have. The impact of the beating—its shocking images burned in our collective psyche through countless airings on television— has been compared to the Scottsboro case in 1931 and the Serpico case in 1967. Rightly called "sickening" by then-president George Bush, it was condemned by virtually all segments of our society.

The command level of the Los Angeles Police Department, I would later learn, was divided over the incident. One view was to be cautious, tell the public that the case would be evaluated right away, and come up with a strong, speedy public response. And then another part of the organization was very conservative in nature and felt nothing wrong had happened. The guy didn't stop and when he finally did, he didn't do what he was supposed to do. LAPD chief Daryl Gates called the beating an "exception," leaving the impression that little was going to be done. He, and the department, lost the opportunity to take a strong stand. From then on, their damage-control efforts were as useless as the *Titanic's*.

Shocking as the incident was, it had apparently not surprised many Los Angeles residents. A *Los Angeles Times* poll taken two weeks later found that 68 percent of all respondents—59 percent of whites, 87 percent of African-Americans, and 80 percent of Hispanics—stated that incidents of LAPD brutality were either "very common" or "fairly common." Clearly, most of the city's residents saw the LAPD as a police department with an attitude.

Los Angeles ended up with its own independent investigation of the police department, conducted by a blue-ribbon panel led by Warren Christopher, later U.S. secretary of state. Members of the panel, which came to be known as the Christopher Commission, were appointed by Mayor Tom Bradley and Chief Gates. The ten-member commission—seven members were selected by the mayor and three by Gates—was composed of six lawyers, two professors, a college president, and a corporation chairman. Supported by a staff of 103 lawyers and 10 accountants, the commission held public hearings at various locations around the city and interviewed people inside and outside the department.

Had the cover pages to the Christopher Commission Report, released in July 1991, and the Philadelphia Police Study that followed the MOVE tragedy been switched, one could review the major findings and recommendations of each report without realizing they were pertaining to a city on the opposite coast. (The MOVE report found Mayor W. Wilson Goode, Police Commissioner Greg Sambor, the city's managing director and the fire commissioner "grossly negligent" in handling the crisis. "Dropping a bomb on an occupied row house was unconscionable and should have been rejected out-of-hand," the commission concluded.)

Like the Philadelphia Police Study, the Christopher Commission Report demanded reform of the police department, with an urgent call to "stop the use of excessive force and curb racism and bias" within the ranks. The report cited the difficulties the public encountered in attempting to file complaints against LAPD officers.

In the wake of the Christopher Commission report, pressure mounted on longtime LAPD chief Daryl Gates to resign. But Gates refused. Since the LAPD chief had long been a civil service position, little could be done to expedite his departure. Since there was no mandatory retirement age for the LAPD chief, Gates was de facto "chief for life." (Because of Gates, the commission recommended that future LAPD chiefs be non–civil service so as to make them more accountable and easier to replace.) However, later that summer, a beleaguered Gates announced his decision to retire the following year (1992).

Had it not been for the Rodney King beating, the Christopher Commission would never have been formed, and there would have been no coordinated hue and cry from the community and its officials for reform of the LAPD. In all likelihood, Gates would not have retired anytime soon, and I would not have found myself in early 1992 contending for the job of Los Angeles police chief.

When I had first wondered about the aftermath of the Rodney King incident, I could not have dreamed how it would trigger events that would impact so greatly not only on the city in which it had happened but also on my own life and career.

Born in Philadelphia forty-eight years before, I had never lived anywhere else. In high school, I had been pretty good in math and I gave serious thought to becoming an accountant. But what really interested me was aerial photography. I took the Air Force test in my senior year with four friends. All of us passed and my friends went in after graduation, but I was turned down due to my chronic asthma. I tried the air wing of the Navy but was turned away for the same reason. When I registered for the draft, my asthma caused me to be labeled 4-F. I remember that as my first crushing blow in life.

I was the oldest of seven children born to a working-class family. I think life was a financial struggle for my parents with so many children—my father never made more than $5,000 a year—and I don't remember us ever taking a vacation, yet ours was a happy home. The work ethic was deeply instilled in us by our parents. From nine years of age on, I always had an after-school job—newspaper route, drugstore, the local deli. Upon graduation from high school, I found this note on the kitchen table from my father, who often worked two jobs as a meat cutter and carpenter to make ends meet: "Willie, you graduated Thursday. This is Monday. It's time to go to work." I did, eventually getting a full-time job in the meat plant where my father worked, and where I had worked part-time during school and nearly lost my left hand two years earlier in an industrial accident. A year later, I applied for a job with the city and was hired as a clerk/messenger. Part of my job was delivering interoffice mail and dropping off city-job notices—the form that all cities circulate regarding what positions are open. Not wanting to remain a clerk/messenger for long, every Saturday I took another city test. I took the test for cashier, clerk/typist, you name it. One day I saw the notice for police officer—it paid $5,000 a year, twice as much as I was then making. I took the test, scored in the low 90s, and got called two months later for the physical and psychological testing. I was hired on February 10, 1964, and immediately entered the police academy.

I had met my future wife, Evelina, in 1963 at the beach in Wildwood, New Jersey, about eighty miles from Philadelphia. The following week, I called her up for a date. I remembered her saying how much she liked baseball, so I invited her to a Phillies-Dodgers game. She accepted, although much later she told me she had met another fellow at the beach that same day whose name was Bill, and she didn't know which one of us was calling. But she figured a baseball game was harmless.

I asked for her thoughts on my becoming a police officer about the time I joined the department—I wasn't yet old enough to vote or legally drink. I don't remember her saying much one way or the other. Of course, we were only dating then—we didn't marry until two years later. Years later, I would find out that she worried more about some assignments than others—like when I was a sergeant in narcotics for two years (1974–75). That was a dangerous job, and we had to deal with a lot of lowlifes. I replaced a sergeant who was killed in the line of duty. Evelina worried more then than at any other time.

My police career wasn't exactly a lightning rise to the top. I flunked my first promotional test because I hadn't studied for it. Not long after that, I was given a short lecture by Frank Walker, who became one of the few black captains in the Philadelphia Police Department.

"You can drive around in a patrol car for the next twenty years," Walker told me, "or you can study and prepare yourself for the tests so you can supervise and manage the people in those cars. Your choice."

At the time, there were lawsuits by some minority officers

over the makeup of the department's promotional exams, but Walker dismissed the challenges as distractions.

"Don't worry about whether the tests are fair or unfair," he counseled. "You can't do anything about that. But if you are willing to work, I can teach you how to study for and pass the tests they give."

On my free time, I would go to Walker's house, spread out my books in the kitchen, the living room, even on the back porch in the summer, and study. Several other young black officers became part of this study group and remain good friends to this day, including Harvey Crudup, whose climb up the ranks would parallel mine, and Richard Neal, who would replace me as Philadelphia police commissioner.

After Harvey and I decided that we were going to move up in the Philadelphia Police Department, every time we passed each other on the street we'd pull out a flash card with a question. If the other person knew the answer, we'd get mad because we hadn't made it difficult enough. Through this friendly competition, we pushed each other hard. I made detective before Harvey, he made sergeant before me. I made lieutenant before Harvey, he made captain before me. I made inspector before Harvey, he made deputy commissioner. Then, after twenty-two previous assignments that included patrol, detectives, narcotics, juvenile, gangs, sex crimes, and administration, I made commissioner. I'm not sure either of us would have made it without the other.

I had another mentor in Morrie Green. A sergeant when I first met him, he would also eventually rise to the rank of captain. Morrie did more than encourage me to study. If it was a quiet night, he would call me in and let me hit the books in a back room. Morrie and Frank were not inclined to give up on you as long as you were trying. When I did well on my next promotional test, I think they were almost as happy as me. I returned to this unofficial study group midcareer, after failing my first captain's test. The second time I passed.

By 1991, Evelina and I had been married for twenty-six years. She was also a longtime City of Philadelphia employee, having worked in the department of license and inspections for fourteen years. Our three grown children were settling into their own lives and we were hoping for grandchildren in the future.

Having become a Philadelphia police officer at the age of twenty, I had grown up not only in this town—which has the lowest crime rate among the ten largest cities in the United States—but also in its police department. Did I really want to leave at this point in my life?

That summer (1991), I received a call from someone in the L.A. city personnel department asking if I knew any qualified individuals who might be interested in the LAPD post. At the time, I was serving as president of the National Organization of Black Law Enforcement Executives. I promised to contact some likely candidates and otherwise spread the word. At the time, I had been giving thought to some career possibilities in the private sector. (My predecessor had gone to work for a prominent local bank in a management position.) I intended to retire from the Philadelphia Police Department while I still had some years left in me, and when I did, I had no plans to continue in law enforcement. Later that summer, however, I received another phone call from Los Angeles, this time asking me if I would be interested in applying for the position.

Initially, I didn't think so much about the challenge of what would lie ahead in Los Angeles as chief of police of the famous Los Angeles Police Department—even after Rodney King, it was still viewed by professionals as the top law enforcement agency in the United States. Instead, I thought about what it would be like to make such a big break and leave my hometown.

The more I thought about it and talked to my family about it, the more the idea of managing the LAPD seemed to present a unique opportunity for capping my law enforcement career. It would provide some personal and professional growth, and I had always enjoyed a new challenge.

I didn't make a final decision about trying for the LAPD chief's job until I was sure that my wife was comfortable with moving away from our family and hometown. Evelina had been with me since I had made $5,000 a year as a beat patrolman, and I planned to be with her long after I retired from police work. After receiving her 100 percent support for this career move, I decided to go for it.

I knew it would not be easy to reshape and reform the Los Angeles Police Department. I would be assuming command of the third-largest police department in the nation's second-largest city—a department with the lowest officer-to-citizen ratio of any major U.S. city, where crime was continuing to increase. Yes, the city's leaders and citizens were clamoring for action in the wake of Rodney King and the Christopher Commission Report. As Confucius said, "The definition of crisis is opportunity." There was surely a window of opportunity at present, but the kind of changes that were needed were far-reaching and cultural in nature. I knew they could not happen overnight—true reform would take years. Would the community be as supportive three years down the road, or would other seemingly more pressing issues become paramount? They intended to hire a new police chief and give him the responsibility for making law enforcement in Los Angeles more fair and just, but would they be willing to provide him with the tools he would need to carry out that mission—namely, political, financial, and public support? No aspect of municipal government is ever a snap to reform, and a major police department, with its strong paramilitary traditions, is considerably more difficult to change than the Department of Water and Power or the Recreation Department. Also, as a career police officer, I had an idea that if someone were to poll the ranks of the LAPD, they would likely support the status quo. That could turn out to be a real problem, as a police department can only be changed from the inside out.

I understood that managing the LAPD at this juncture in its history would be the biggest professional challenge of my life.

The 9,800-member LAPD, at the time (1992), had 7,600 sworn officers, 2,200 civilian employees, a territory of over 450 square miles, and an annual budget of nearly $1 billion. Its promise "To Protect and To Serve" 3.5 million citizens—and another 600,000 people who visit and work in the city daily—is stenciled on the doors of its patrol cars for all to see.

The day I arrived in Los Angeles for a job interview, I didn't know a single officer of any rank (other than Daryl Gates) or civilian employee in the department. If the Board of Police Commissioners and the city wanted a chief who knew the LAPD and Los Angeles, or even one who could find his way around on the local freeways, I was not their man. But if Los Angeles was seeking someone who had experience carrying out the recommendations of an independent commission and who accepted the mandate of the community and its leaders to change the way the LAPD operates—using a blueprint for reform that took into account what type of policing the residents themselves wanted— then I would have a chance. The job would not be easy; there would be an enormous amount of work for members of the department and the community at large to do together. The good news was that it could be done. We had proven that in Philadelphia.

Findings like these from the Christopher Commission were close to my heart:

- "The LAPD should develop programs to deemphasize force and promote restraint, to foster with the department a different attitude toward the population it serves and to assist the public to gain greater trust in the department."
- "We recommend a new standard of accountability. Los Angeles should have a police department whose Chief is accountable to civilian officials for the department's performance, and where ranking officers are responsible for the conduct of those they lead. Ugly incidents will not diminish until ranking officers know they will be held responsible for what happens in their sector, whether or not they personally participate."

I was well aware that such isolation led to a lack of communication and loss of understanding, as well as deteriorating support from the very community that a police force is supposed to serve. The result can be a police department out of control.

An independent investigatory body like the Christopher Commission was not charged with reviewing the good work done by the conscientious and hardworking men and women of the police department who risked their lives on a daily basis. A highly publicized incident like the Rodney King beating casts a long and indiscriminate shadow on an entire department. That was the inevitable fallout, and I knew that morale within the department would suffer as a result. The new chief would have to be ready to help the LAPD aspire to higher professional standards without undoing all the good police work already being done. It would be a precarious tightrope to walk.

The field of more than thirty candidates who applied for the LAPD chief's position in the fall of 1991 was narrowed to twelve before interviewing began. In lieu of a written test, oral interviews were conducted by a citizens panel. The applicants were graded, and eventually the field was cut to six candidates—five from inside the LAPD and myself.

To be selected from the final list from which the new chief would be hired, an outside candidate had to out score every insider. In addition, all the inside candidates were given one bonus point. In true scores, the number-three person among the top twelve candidates was a Hispanic deputy chief of the Los Angeles Sheriff's Department. Since he was surpassed by one inside candidate, he did not make the final six. I finished first with a score of 98 percent. My closest competitor, a deputy chief in the department, scored two points behind me, and after receiving an added bonus point, ended up one point behind.

One of the first calls of congratulations I received when the six finalists were announced came from a very gracious Chief Gates.

The Los Angeles Police Commission then began its own

round of interviews and background investigations of us. The commission was free to hire anyone on the list.

In all, I went through more than nine hours of interviews with the Los Angeles Police Commission during two days of questioning. I was asked how I thought I would fit in and learn about the department and manage it. They wanted to know how I proposed to lead the LAPD into a new era: "If you get the job, how will you build your management team?" "How are you going to select your senior staff?"

I was asked how I would fit in as an outsider. "How are you going to learn about the department when even the terminology is completely different?" In Philadelphia we used words, not code numbers, on the radio. In Los Angeles, if there is a robbery, it is broadcast as a "two-eleven [211]." In Philadelphia, we call it a "robbery." A "four-five-nine [459]" in Los Angeles is called a "disturbance" back East. Now, an argument can be made that it's just as easy to say it in plain English as it is to use a code number. But I didn't take that position with the Los Angeles Police Commission. "I'll learn the code numbers," I promised.

The citizens panel as well as the police commissioners asked probing questions about the findings of the Christopher Commission. They wanted to know my thoughts and philosophies about many of its more than 150 recommendations. By then, I knew the focus of the report inside out and backward.

I had had a copy of the Christopher Commission report delivered to my office in downtown Philadelphia within ten days of its publication—several months before I gave any thought to the LAPD job. I distributed summaries of the report to my senior staff officers so we would all know what had gone so terribly wrong, and to make sure it didn't happen in Philadelphia. I had also ordered that the videotape of the Rodney King beating be played at training classes for veterans and recruits alike. Portions of the tape have since been used as an example of "how not to apprehend a suspect" at hundreds of police academies around the country. Many law enforcement professionals viewed the videotape of the King beating the same way a physician examines a bad wound. A doctor doesn't see blood and guts, but rather trauma and an opportunity to do some good and save a life.

There were some corollaries between law enforcement in Philadelphia and Los Angeles. At one time the Philadelphia Police Department had been seen by some as insulting to the minority community. Excessive-use-of-force complaints were fairly common. Along with other reforms that had begun with Commissioner Tucker, the department had taken strong measures to eliminate use-of-force problems. Since then, police had largely regained the respect of the community. It occurred to me, if Los Angeles and Philadelphia could share so many of the same problems, might they also share the same solutions?

While it was obvious that no one would be hired for the LAPD job who didn't embrace the bulk of the findings of the Christopher Commission Report, I didn't hesitate to point out to my interviewers where I objected.

For example, I disagreed with the idea of having a citizens police review board to review all citizens complaints against the LAPD and make decisions regarding department discipline.

I had opposed a move for a citizens panel in Philadelphia because I felt that the senior manager of the department—the police commissioner—should be held directly accountable for discipline in the organization. "You can't delegate discipline to a citizens panel and expect an equally high degree of accountability from the chief," I explained to the L.A. Police Commission.

In Los Angeles, there was a Board of Police Commissioners made up of citizens. Together, they formed the civilian policy-making board for the police department. The commission could review and draw conclusions and make comments on how discipline was administered, but the final authority rested, by city charter, with the chief of police. In other words, the chief was *accountable.* If you took this vital task away and created a new level of civilian review, the chief would be less accountable, seriously weakening management of the department.

"Maybe I'm going against the community grain," I admitted, "but I think this would be going the wrong way. I would ask you to hold me, as chief of police, accountable."

Other tough questions were asked. How was I going to know who would help or hurt me within the department since I didn't know a soul? How could I know who the pro-Gates or anti-Gates people were? I answered that I would try to turn these possible stumbling blocks into advantages.

For instance, I went in with a blank slate, no personal allegiances within the department implied or required. I promised not to rush to fill senior staff vacancies, but would instead work with the top commanders already in place. It would be a valuable assessment period for us all. (I didn't fill any senior staff positions for six months. In fact, had I done so when I first took over, I may have made some very different choices.)

The L.A. Police Commissioners and staff came to Philadelphia, talked to the city's managing director, the city personnel department, the police union, and some major newspaper and television representatives. By the time they were finished, they knew my management and personal style, which was quite different from that of the outgoing LAPD chief and the chiefs before him. They also had a good idea of what had been overcome and accomplished in Philadelphia. Our police force had been made more responsive to the community's needs and wants and turned into a better-trained and more effective law enforcement agency.

Late in the evening on April 14, 1992, I was telephoned by the president of the L.A. Police Commission and offered the job. I was asked to come to Los Angeles the next day to discuss terms of my employment.

Two days later, on April 16, the mayor of Los Angeles announced that I would become the new Los Angeles police chief. I was to be the first outsider to head the LAPD in more than forty years. It would be the second time in my career that the press would label me the "first black police chief in city history." Frankly, that characterization bothered me more than it should have. I had already discovered the "first" label to be both a help and a hindrance. But the fact that I am of African-American heritage is secondary to how I perform as a police officer and chief of police.

Under a city charter amendment approved by the Los Angeles voters that same year, the L.A. police chief would no longer be a civil service position. (Also, voters allowed for demoting a police employee for the first time.) I was hired as a probationary employee (for one year) prior to this change in the city charter. I had, along with the other final candidates, been advised that as chief we would relinquish civil service status in the event voters passed the charter amendment, since we would still be probationary. As I had not been civil service in Philadelphia, I had no problem with the change. When the voters approved the charter amendment, I became one of only a few department heads in Los Angeles city government who were "exempt" from civil service regulations. (Similar charter amendments that took away civil service protection from other city department managers—making it easier for the mayor to appoint and replace them—were approved by Los Angeles voters in 1995.)

I was appointed to a five-year term and can be reappointed by the police commission to one additional five-year term. After that, as in Philadelphia and many other cities, all future L.A. police chiefs would serve at the pleasure of the mayor, who will make his selection from a list of three candidates provided to him by the police commission. If the mayor rejects the three names, he may ask for another list of three. In other words, the mayor will be able to appoint any one of the top six candidates for police chief, who, like me, may serve a maximum of two five-year terms.

I was to "retire" from the Philadelphia Police Department on May 15 and assume my new duties in June.

I made a couple of trips to Los Angeles before I was sworn in. During one, in late April 1992, I visited Parker Center, the

LAPD's eight-story headquarters at Los Angeles and First Streets, named after legendary ex-chief (1950–66) William H. Parker, who molded the LAPD—with a long prior history of corruption and scandal—into a professional, corruption-free, paramilitary police force that was widely admired and emulated across the country.

Chief Gates, a Parker protégé who as a young officer served as Chief Parker's driver, was preparing to meet with the city council over a proposed reduction of three hundred police officers, and he asked me to join him. We walked across the street together to council chambers. It was quite an introduction to my new city—appearing before the council in opposition to a proposed manpower reduction for an organization that I hadn't yet taken over.

If anyone on the city council thought that the new chief was going to come in and take whatever came down the pike for a time because he was so happy to have the job, they found out otherwise. Alongside Gates, I argued as forcefully as possible, "We can't take these cuts."

The cuts did not happen, though not due to our testimony, but rather because of the dramatic events that were about to engulf the city of Los Angeles.

During that visit, I heard talk around the city and in Parker Center, too, regarding the trial of the four LAPD officers accused in the Rodney King beating. The trial was expected to conclude soon in nearby Simi Valley, a predominantly white suburb of L.A. I did not discuss the subject with Gates. The LAPD was still his to manage.

I would not know until later that there was no contingency plan at all on the part of the LAPD to respond to any kind of anarchy or riot situation resulting from the verdict in this trial. Apparently, some senior commanders had expressed the opinion that there could be problems, but their warnings weren't heeded. In fact, a group of top LAPD staff were allowed to attend a three-day retreat in Oxnard, more than an hour's drive northwest of Los Angeles, even though the verdicts were expected any day.

Before leaving L.A., I was asked by someone in the news media whether I planned to attend the annual Cinco de Mayo celebration downtown. This May Fifth celebration, with much food, song, and frivolity, commemorates Mexico's victory over French forces in a long-ago battle. I found out, the hard way, that it's pronounced Cinco de "Miyo." To a reporter covering the event I said "Mayo," and that night on the eleven o'clock news I heard that "the new police chief from the East Coast who hasn't even assumed his duties yet" had committed his "first faux pas." I had to chuckle. *If that's the worse mistake I make*, I thought, *I'll take it.*

I returned to Philadelphia to wrap up my affairs. A search was under way to replace me, and I had given the mayor a short list of individuals within the Philadelphia Police Department whom I could recommend for the top job. (It is generally regarded as part of the job for a police chief or commissioner to groom a pool of candidates within the department who will be qualified to succeed him.)

On Wednesday, April 29, 1992, at 12:45 P.M., notice was given to the L.A. media that the Simi Valley jury had concluded its deliberations and verdicts would be announced in two hours.

In spite of the advance notice, LAPD's field detectives— whose normal workday ended at 3:30 P.M.—were not held over in the event they might be needed. Had they been, there would have been an extra twelve hundred veteran officers on duty throughout the city, doubling the number routinely on patrol. Instead, the detectives went home.

Events took place in the following chronology:*

---

*Chronology of events documented in the Webster/Williams Report, October 21, 1992, authored by Judge William H. Webster, former FBI director, and Hubert Williams, former public-safety director of Newark, New Jersey, serving as special advisers to the L.A. Board of Police Commissioners on the civil disorder in Los Angeles.

3:10 P.M. Not-guilty verdicts are announced in the case against the four LAPD officers charged in the King beating.

3:20 P.M. Angry crowds gather at Fifty-fifth and Normandie in South Central L.A. as well as at the site of the Rodney King beating.

4:00 P.M. Television stations broadcast Mayor Tom Bradley's announcement of shock and dismay over the verdicts.

4:15 P.M. First looting occurs at Florence and Normandie.

5:00 P.M. Chief Gates makes public appearance and states, "We are prepared for this."

5:45 P.M. Rioters at Florence and Normandie attack cars and motorists with crowbars, bottles, and rocks. LAPD's Seventy-seventh Street watch commander orders police dispatchers not to send units to the area.

6:20 P.M. Chief Gates turns over command of the department to a deputy chief before going to Brentwood for a political fund-raiser to defeat Proposition F, the Christopher Commission reforms, set for the June ballot.

6:45 P.M. An eighteen-wheel cement truck enters the intersection of Florence and Normandie. Moments later, the driver, a white man named Reginald Denny, is pulled from the cab of the truck and beaten.

The Los Angeles riots had begun.

At that moment, I was three thousand miles away.

I arrived home shortly after 9 P.M. (EST) that evening. From my office at the Philadelphia Police Department headquarters, I had already given the press a statement in reaction to the verdicts from Los Angeles. At the time, scattered acts of civil unrest were being reported in L.A. Keeping a stiff upper lip with the media, I said that I hoped people would accept the verdicts as part of the American judicial system.

Deep down, however, as a police officer and as someone who had lived through the riots of the 1960s, in my own city and across the country, I had an uneasy feeling. I had been on the police force six months when Philadelphia experienced its one and only urban riot. What amazed me at the time was how it had started: over a rumor of a black woman being beaten by a police officer during a traffic stop. Only it was a false rumor. *The incident never happened.* Yet word spread like wildfire up and down streets that were soon filled with shouting, angry, defiant people. By today's standards, I guess the three-day riot that ensued was tame—no shooting, no fires, nobody got killed. Instead, bottle-throwing and major looting. As a young patrolman, I came away with the opinion that whatever event "starts" a riot is really just the match touching the fuse. The underlying atmosphere for unrest has to already exist; it serves as the explosive charge.

When I came home, I found my wife glued to the television, which was carrying coverage live from Los Angeles. There was little we could do to console one another. Like many Americans that night, we watched the real-life drama unfold live as a television-station helicopter hovered above Florence and Normandie showing in agonizing detail the assault on the truck driver. Shocked and dismayed at the full-scale rioting in Los Angeles, we followed the coverage all night.

At one point, I had a brief conversation with a member of the L.A. Board of Police Commissioners, who reported that fires, arson, and looting were spreading over South Central Los Angeles and parts of the Wilshire business district. I found out that the department was still trying to bring in all off-duty personnel and get them in uniform and out on the streets. I did not try to phone anyone in the LAPD, as I knew they had their hands full.

After midnight my time, I watched as television cameras showed a mass of angry protesters ransacking near Los Angeles City Hall, then moving across the street and setting fire to a guard post in front of Parker Center.

Never in my life had I seen a police facility or any part of one burned down. Though it was only a guard shack, that fire—combined with the indiscriminate roaming of lawless mobs throughout the city—symbolized for me a complete breakdown in civil order.

I was both horrified and mesmerized by the images broadcast from Los Angeles. My God, this was my new city!

At ten o'clock that night Chief Gates returns from the fund-raiser and views the city first from a helicopter, then by automobile. He cannot find any police patrols.

The next morning, all the major networks and several local news outlets in L.A. besieged my office in person and by phone wanting to know what the incoming LAPD police chief was going to do about the mess in Los Angeles.

"Why aren't you in Los Angeles now?" I was asked.

"Wait a minute," I protested. "I'm not the chief yet. There's only one LAPD chief and it's Daryl Gates."

The job's not even mine for six weeks, I thought. *How can they consider me responsible for dealing with the riots?*

It didn't take long for me to understand that I was going to have to deal with it. If there had been a need for a reform police chief before the riots, there was an even greater need now.

I would soon realize how much added responsibility would be mine to shoulder beyond managing the recovery and reconstruction of the Los Angeles Police Department. An entire city needed healing.

What in the world had I gotten myself into?

CHAPTER TWO

WE HAD A GENERAL tactical plan in Philadelphia for dealing with riots, although nothing specifically tailored for the trial in California of the four police officers involved in the Rodney King beating.

With Los Angeles on fire that first week of May 1992, some Philadelphians feared similar outbreaks of looting and violence. By the second and third days of the L.A. riots, in fact, cities such as Las Vegas and Atlanta were reporting such fallout. I put the department on special deployment—increasing police presence on the streets—so that we would be ready just in case.

I had intended to be in Los Angeles for what turned out to be the week of the riots—Evelina and I were to continue our house-hunting—but I canceled the trip to remain at the helm of the Philadelphia Police Department.

Around 7 P.M. on Friday, May 1—by then, the streets of Los Angeles were being patrolled by the National Guard and a city-wide curfew was in effect—one of my commanders telephoned with distressing news. A Philadelphia police officer had shot and killed a man in our predominantly Latino Twenty-fifth Police District. Initial reports indicated it was a justifiable shooting. Still, we knew that the Twenty-fifth—one of the poorest sections of town—was a powder keg, with as much potential as South Central L.A. to be a municipal war zone. If rioting was to break out in Philadelphia, this could be the place, and a police shooting could supply the spark.

It was in the Twenty-fifth a year or two earlier where a drug dealer, killed in a fight, had been turned into a hero by his peers and given a lavish funeral. Unbelievably, his mother ended up taking over the drug operation. Finally, with support from fed-up residents and working with federal law enforcement agencies, we were able to shut down the entire operation and send the kingpins—including the drug-dealing mother—to prison.

Early reports indicated that the latest incident, which involved a white officer and a black suspect, was an "in policy" shooting—one that conformed to the department's shooting policy—and that there were cooperative witnesses. Still, I ordered extra officers into the surrounding area to heighten deployment. I did not want the immediate scene flooded with extra uniformed personnel, but for our people to stay back two or three blocks. If things were quiet—as reports indicated they were—I didn't want to aggravate the situation or bring attention to it. I hoped this show of measured force would accomplish two things: signal the residents that we were prepared to maintain calm and order, and send out a strong message that anyone who broke the law would go to jail.

An integral part of our Crisis Response Plan involved the Neighborhood Advisory Councils, formed in 1987 as part of our citywide community-policing program. These councils, formed in each of the city's nearly two dozen police districts, met regularly and prepared annual reports, making local police commanders more directly accountable to the citizens and the businesses they served. These working partnerships provided linkage between the community and the police, leading to improved communications between the two. Through the years, solid relationships built upon mutual trust had been forged in the neighborhoods.

We now put our plan to the test.

Within a couple of hours of the shooting, the police captain of the Twenty-fifth District phoned the head of the local neighborhood council to provide her with details of the incident. A man who had been drinking came up to an officer sitting in a patrol wagon, shouting, "This is for Rodney King!" and waving a handgun. Fearing for his life, the officer had pulled his gun and shot. A number of civilian witnesses verified the incident as a justifiable shooting.

While a number of neighborhood council members went out to the scene to talk to witnesses and police, others lit up a "phone tree." Soon, scores of local residents were making calls to pass along factual information, squelch rumors, and keep everyone calm.

It was still quiet on the streets several hours later when I drove through the Twenty-fifth, even though the media was on the scene en masse. Reporters and television crews were milling around, as if waiting for a riot to start.

We had, then, a section of the city where we could easily have had a major disturbance on the heels of the rioting in L.A. We did not, I am convinced, because of the goodwill we had placed on deposit with the community. That allowed us, when the crisis came, to reach in and make a withdrawal to keep things calm.

I can think of no better example of the way community policing should work.

I arrived in Los Angeles three weeks after the riots. It was one of several visits I would make to the city prior to assuming my new job.

Met at the airport by an LAPD driver, I joined an official tour that included members of the L.A. Board of Police Commissioners and other city leaders to view the hardest-hit areas.

By then, the National Guard had departed, and the LAPD was back policing the shaken city. The widespread devastation was unimaginable. I had seen buildings on several blocks burnt to the ground after the MOVE fire, but the ruins here went on for miles.

I got out of the car and walked amid the debris. The smell of smoke and soot filled my nostrils. On many of the major commercial streets of South Central Los Angeles, 50 percent or more of the buildings were damaged or destroyed, leaving behind scorched shells of twisted metal. On some blocks no more than one or two structures appeared untouched by fire. Supermarkets and neighborhood stores were almost nonexistent. The scene might have been a bombed-out city in any war-torn country, only it wasn't.

The enemy is among us, I thought sadly, *burning our homes, looting our businesses, killing our neighbors. If they succeed, we have lost—not just the police, but every resident in every town in America will have lost.*

While riding along one nearly leveled street, I recognized, a short distance away, the outline of the main chapel of the First African Methodist Episcopal Church, spared from the flames. I had met here with community and church leaders on the day my appointment was announced—one of the several places I had visited that special day with a small caravan of officials and, following close behind, the ever-present media. I remembered how lively and upbeat my visit had been that day to one of the oldest black churches in Los Angeles. Now, a few weeks later, the church stood amid a sea of urban wreckage.

"Chief, what are you going to do about this?" I was asked by a news reporter covering the tour.

I looked at him curiously. "I wasn't hired to build new buildings or bring jobs back to the city."

Little did I know: In the succeeding months, questions like these from the media and citizens alike became common as a sizable vacuum developed in city government. The mayor soon announced that he would not run for re-election, and other top city officials decided that it was an opportune time to retire.

Though not exactly in my official job description, it did become my responsibility to help instill enough confidence in the city and its police department so that tourists and displaced businesses would return and investments would be made to build new facilities on ruins now filled with twisted steel.

The people of Los Angeles paid heavily for the worst American insurrection of the twentieth century. In five days of rioting, at least 42 people lost their lives, another 1,850 people were injured, more than 700 businesses were burned, and some $1 billion in property and equipment was damaged or destroyed. As a result, some 400,000 jobs were lost and unemployment jumped to 10.5 percent in the city.

Although the rioting spread to many areas in the city, hardest hit was South Central L.A.—formerly largely African-American but heavily Hispanic in the 1990s—and a nearby area composed mainly of small businesses known as Koreatown. (Los Angeles has the largest Korean population outside of Korea. It also has the largest Hispanic population outside of Latin America.)

In the old days, the Los Angeles Police Department was viewed as being able to invade a small hostile country, if need be. But with the riots came the widespread public perception that the LAPD couldn't protect its own citizens when push came to shove on the streets. The public's view—thanks to the Rodney King incident and the initial slow response of police to the rioting—was that the LAPD had abandoned the public it was charged to protect. This feeling was so extensive that only 35 percent of those residents polled by a news organization after the riots had confidence in the LAPD to perform its job. People who lived outside Los Angeles shared similar concerns; tourism dropped off 50 percent and many worried that it might never come back.

In a well-publicized incident, the watch commander in the Seventy-seventh Street Division ordered his badly outnumbered personnel to retreat when the initial violence broke out at the intersection of Florence and Normandie. This lieutenant did not necessarily make a mistake. In fact, his decision might have saved lives. However, the failure of some senior commanders to regroup and redeploy their manpower and return rapidly to the scene of growing violence—truck driver Reginald Denny was beaten nearly to death at this intersection—was a critical error.

Unquestionably, the department was not prepared for what it

faced in the aftermath of the not-guilty verdicts in the Rodney King trial. It was reported during the rioting that different police commanders, often of the same rank, decided on their own whether they would or would not commit their personnel and resources to a particular assignment. In the crucial early hours, the LAPD had an utterly disorganized response to the rioting. No unified command was in place and there was no comprehensive plan to respond to any type of anarchy or riot. The fault lay with the LAPD's leaders whose job was strategic planning, not with the rank and file on the street.

More than five thousand arrests for crimes that included murder, assault, arson, theft, burglary, and looting were made in the four geographic bureaus of the LAPD during the six days of rioting. And just who made all those arrests?

The men and women who make up the thin, blue ranks of the Los Angeles Police Department, that's who.

I took over as the fiftieth chief of the Los Angeles Police Department at 12:01 A.M. on Sunday, June 28, 1992.

Five hours later, an earthquake shook awake much of southern California. Answering my bedside phone shortly after the jolt—which caused minimal damage and no injuries—I discovered that with the chief's job came another responsibility: chairman of the city's Emergency Operations Board. Somehow, no one had gotten around to telling me.

I had taken the oath of office the previous Friday—two days earlier—in a private ceremony inside the condo my wife and I had rented not far from downtown. (We eventually bought a hillside home in the San Fernando Valley, about a forty-five-minute drive from downtown.) This was done to ensure continuity of command, since Chief Gates retired at midnight on Saturday, June 27, 1992. The short ceremony was witnessed by the city clerk and the president of the Los Angeles Police Commission, Stanley K. Sheinbaum.

With my wife next to me, I placed my left hand on our family

Bible, raised my right hand, took the oath of office, and swore to protect the people of Los Angeles.

Later that day, I had gone to Parker Center. I made a point of waiting in an empty office until Gates had said his good-byes and departed. When I stepped into the sixth-floor hallway, it was still lined with dozens of officers and staff workers who had said their farewells and apparently weren't sure what to do next. It was obviously a reflective and sad moment for them, as they quietly filed past me. About the same time, Gates was meeting the press downstairs for the last time as chief of police, I walked in to see my new office.

Sometime later, on my way out of the building, I was stopped by the same reporters and asked to comment. I spoke off the cuff about renewing, reorganizing, and rebuilding the Los Angeles Police Department.

"We will be addressing concerns about police abuse, misuse of force, and about sexism and racism," I promised. "We're going to look at our training, too. There are a lot of areas we are going to address. We're going to take a whole fresh look at this department from A to Z."

Before the riots, I privately didn't think that being police chief in Los Angeles was going to be much more difficult than it had been in Philadelphia. In coming to L.A., I saw myself stepping in as outsider Kevin Tucker had when he took command in Philadelphia. While the role was a different one for me, I felt prepared. Also, I was comfortable with the agenda given me: to reform the Los Angeles Police Department where necessary and to institute citywide community policing. But after the riots, that agenda was greatly extended. There was far more demand for significant change within the department. In fact, rightly or wrongly, the recovery of the city of Los Angeles was clearly linked to changes in its police department.

I was ready to get to work, but there was still another ceremony. On Tuesday, June 30, I repeated the oath of office at the LAPD police academy in Elysian Park before a group of officials that included the mayor, district attorney, city attorney, city council members, county supervisors, and judges. There were thirty television camera crews from local stations as well as national networks and some even from overseas. My swearing-in was broadcast live on every local TV station in Los Angeles, and it even made the national news. The only way I can explain this kind of media attention to the swearing-in of a city police chief is that Rodney King and the riots had thrown such an intense spotlight on the LAPD that even such a routine event was considered big news.

Hundreds of LAPD officers and civilian personnel were present, along with about forty friends and thirty family members, including Evelina, our sons, Will and Eric, daughter Lisa, my sixty-eight-year-old mother, Helen, who made the trip from Texas, and aunts, uncles, and cousins from Philadelphia, California, New York, New Jersey, Connecticut, Texas, and South Carolina.

When I had first been briefed on the plans for the ceremony, I was told that only senior personnel from the rank of captain and above were going to be invited. I had asked why the rank and file were not included and was told there wasn't enough room inside the auditorium. I suggested that the event be moved outdoors, which it was, so that everyone in the department who wished to attend would be welcome. I was pleased to see in the audience several hundred blue-uniformed officers of all ranks.

We were gathered on a warm, sunny morning—the type of California day I had so gleefully anticipated that before leaving Philadelphia I had confidently given my cashmere overcoat to my son Will. The LAPD all-volunteer orchestra was playing, the color guard looked sharp, there were a lot of snappy salutes, and a squad of six LAPD helicopters did a flyby not far above the heads of the twelve hundred spectators.

The outdoor extravaganza had a shade too much pomp and circumstance for me, but it was an upbeat moment that the department needed. It suggested an end to the recent painful past and a smooth bridge to the future. (Daryl Gates did not attend. I later read that he had spent the morning at the dentist. However, in a videotaped farewell message to the department that aired at roll calls, he said he had "high hopes" that the change in leadership would help improve morale.)

We were all here to take the next step together and gather in a breath of fresh air and appreciate this moment under a brilliant sun that came out as if on cue.

I had spent two weeks writing perhaps the most important speech of my life. I wanted to get across that I was here as chief to address the needs and concerns that were important to the sworn officers and civilian employees of the department, and that I stood ready to pull together and work with them. I also intended to emphasize that I recognized my position was chief of police for the 3.5 million people who lived in the city of Los Angeles. I wanted the audience to know that I understood I was expected to address community issues and to move forward, without losing sight of the mandates for change from the Christopher Commission Report.

I hoped to set a tone that I knew what it was like to run an organization. I was the new chief in Los Angeles, but I wasn't a new chief of police. I would speak up to ensure the department had the financial base and the resources to do some of the things that were necessary. I wasn't going to just sit back, happy with my new job. I fully planned to hit the ground running.

When I stepped to the podium, I wasn't at all nervous. I knew what I wanted to do, and I knew what I could do.

"Our city and its police department have both undergone one of the most difficult periods of their history," I began. The events of the past sixteen months—following the Rodney King beating— were "the triggering devices that set off an explosion of emotions, pent-up fears, bias, unfulfilled expectations, and needs.

"We cannot begin the healing and stabilization process until, and when, we make peace with ourselves and each other. As Martin Luther King said, 'True peace is not merely the absence of tension; it is the presence of justice.'

"We must begin today the process of talking with each other and not just at each other. We cannot remove the tensions which hang in the air like dark, looming storm clouds if we are afraid to meet our neighbors, new as well as old. Tension cannot be removed, nor will we see justice prevail, if we continue to back across the street or lock our doors or speed up our cars whenever we come upon one who is a stranger."

The stabilization and healing process, I explained, would require that both citizens and police, politicians and the press, adults as well as children, friends and foes alike, stop attacking each other, looking only for those points of imperfection in each of us.

"To the citizens of Los Angeles, I ask your support in the stabilization process. Each citizen who lives in our city, as well as those who work here, have a stake in the future of the LAPD. We need your support. Don't just point out and talk about the negatives, but also shout about all the good work and service our officers deliver every day. Thousands of unsung men and women need your vocal assurance that you care. You most certainly can and must continue to hold us accountable to be fair, honest, non-biased, expedient, and efficient in not only our patrol-service delivery but in every other aspect of management in the police department. To the citizens of Los Angeles, I promise as your police chief to be your spokesperson as well as your protector."

To the rank and file of the LAPD, I promised to stop the "rocking ship" and steer it through the "very difficult waters that lie just ahead of us."

It was time, I continued, to begin a thorough evaluation of our capacity to deliver basic police services as well as to examine the quality of those services currently being delivered. I promised to begin an analysis of our staffing needs in the face of rising crime, as well as rising calls for service and other demands on our scarce resources. Our deployment plan would be examined to ensure that it met not only our current population needs but was situated to meet tomorrow's needs as well.

"As your police chief, I will talk to as well as listen to each of you, from our newest recruit, to our civilian employees, to the senior command. We must create an atmosphere for frank and open discussions in the many areas we are responsible for.

"As we begin a new recruitment process, we must keep in mind that just as our city is culturally and ethnically diverse, so should our police department reflect the city it serves. Through recruitment, training, assignments, and promotions, we will establish a long-term goal of improving the diversity within the LAPD from the top to the lowest rank."

There was no doubt in my mind that my experience in implementing community policing in Philadelphia was a major reason I was hired to manage the LAPD. Citing the LAPD's "organizational culture that emphasizes crime control over crime prevention and that isolates the police from the communities and the people they serve," the Christopher Commission had strongly urged citywide implementation of community policing. Up to then, community policing had been tried in Los Angeles only recently on an experimental basis in a few areas.

I now promised publicly to make community policing a hallmark of my administration. "Community policing does not require more money or more people to be successful," I explained, addressing some of the lingering claims leveled by critics of this partnership between the police and community. "What it does require is a confirmation by our officers and citizens to work together to meet our mandate to serve and protect.

"Community policing is not soft on crime. To the contrary, civic empowerment helps citizens and the police reclaim the streets and their neighborhoods.

"With community policing, those of us managing the department, from the chief on down, will listen to you. We will listen to the rank and file, as well as to the citizens of the city. This will soon become the operational as well as philosophical style of policing in Los Angeles."

That was my final promise of the day to my new city about its police department—a department roundly criticized by the Christopher Commission for being "too militaristic" and "failing to embrace the community."

I intended to see that it was kept.

Even on a day of such ceremony, open conflict among city leaders rose to the surface. In their remarks to the gathering, the mayor and police commission president publicly disagreed over whether the city had the ability to provide additional money to the hard-pressed department for more officers and better equipment.

"Don't come soon to ask for more money," Mayor Bradley had said from the dais on the academy's grassy athletic field, turning his head to look squarely at me. "It simply isn't there."

Accentuating the mayor's comment, the labor contract under which LAPD's officers worked was due to expire within hours—at midnight to be exact. The mayor and city council insisted that there was no money for salary increases, and negotiations hadn't gone well. Understanding how damaging a prolonged labor standoff could be to the morale of the already besieged department, I could only hope for a speedy resolution. Instead, we were to endure the most horrendous and protracted labor strife in LAPD history—which wouldn't be settled for *two years*.

Following Mayor Bradley to the podium, police commission president Stanley Sheinbaum disagreed with the mayor. "I will tell you that the money is there," he said to loud applause. "It just takes the intelligence and the wisdom of the people in government to get it to us."

It's already starting, I thought. The swearing-in ceremonies were not yet over and my new mayor and police commission president were already publicly disagreeing.

After the ceremony, in my first official press conference as LAPD chief, I promised to "fight very publicly and loudly" over any cuts in the department. In fact, there were no cuts in the department's budget that year, due in part to strong public sentiment following the riots—people would not stand for less policing. But neither did the department receive any new dollars or resources.

My earlier fears about lack of fiscal and political support seemed to have materialized—and this on my first official day as the new police chief. I would describe my mood that day as I met with the press at the academy as surprisingly somber. The best I could do for now, I admitted, was to hold the line. Programs I had talked about to the Board of Police Commissioners during my interviews would be put on hold. And what about the Christopher Commission's findings?—many of the 150 reforms required additional money and manpower.

I recalled to the L.A. press after my swearing-in the day four years earlier when I had been sworn in as commissioner of the Philadelphia Police Department. "My first day on the job, the mayor announced layoffs of nearly two hundred police officers because of a reduction in the budget, and that same day we had three drive-by shootings."

You could say I was used to rude awakenings.

Across the country, a Philadelphia police officer responding to a domestic disturbance in a minority neighborhood was shot just below his bulletproof vest. The critically wounded officer was white. The armed suspect, who was black, was chased by police before being shot and killed.

Had the same incident occurred in Los Angeles, the *Los Angeles Times* speculated on the day of my swearing-in ceremony, "it could have set off another furor such as that after the not-guilty verdicts in the King beating."

In my hometown, however, people remained calm. Rather than waiting for rumors to spread through the streets or for the media's interpretation of the shootings, the department sent officers wearing suits and ties into the neighborhood to knock on doors and explain the circumstances of the incident to the residents. "It was perhaps community-based policing in its rawest form," the *Times* reported, "[and] perhaps one of the most telling examples of the Willie Williams legacy."

Labeling it my "legacy" was a little too dramatic, but I was

proud of Philadelphia—of its residents and its police department—for having worked so well together to defuse a tragic
incident by not allowing it to be used as an excuse for widespread violence. This did not mean, however, that there wasn't
more work to do—police officers in Philadelphia, as elsewhere,
still made mistakes, and the department was far from perfect.

Whenever police and residents band together to keep the
peace on our cities' streets, it is a powerful force to be reckoned
with.

The style of my predecessor and a long line of LAPD chiefs
before him was that the chief ruled supreme. He made all the
rules and set the direction for the department almost single-
handedly. Staff from the most senior commanders down followed
his orders with few questions asked.

Most certainly, I did not fit the LAPD-chief prototype. Besides
relying on an entirely different management style, I was an outsider, an easterner, and an African-American. While Daryl Gates
might have fit comfortably into the mold left behind by Chief Bill
Parker, there was no such cast for me. Just how different a chief of
police I would be for the LAPD was brought home to me when I
held my first staff meeting the day after my swearing-in.

Waiting for me in a conference room at Parker Center were
some very senior people, men (not a single woman and only one
minority) who had cut their teeth in law enforcement in the
1950s and 1960s and had seen it all.

Nobody said anything unless I asked a question, after which I
got a direct answer. There were no lively discussions, no pointed
suggestions, no helpful critiques.

I wasn't comfortable with the stilted atmosphere. I wanted people to feel free to raise issues and bat them around. I was accustomed to working with a staff that was not shy about stating their
opinions and did so without fear of castigation. I would rather have
my senior staff a little too noisy than stricken to silence.

At the same time, a sense of impatience filled the air. I had a feeling people were trying to figure out what I wanted done right away and that they were thinking, "If the chief will just tell us what to do, we'll do it."

Cops are really good at following orders. We are absolutely great at that just about anywhere in the country. We are trained that our objective is to follow orders that lead to swift action in solving a problem. When you are dealing with a crime in progress, you want a quick fix, not consensus building.

It can, however, be tough for someone who made rank in a paramilitary organization to answer questions like "How can we make things better?" or "What do you think?" or "What are the pros and cons?" or "Let's have some discussion." To these type of queries, even the most senior police commander can turn as stiff as a board.

I want to hear proposals from my staff all the time. That's my preferred style of management. It was what I did in Philadelphia, and it was what I intended to do in Los Angeles. It is a philosophy practiced every day in the private sector by the most successful companies.

Even when I wasn't convinced immediately that something would work, I liked to say, "Go ahead and try it and let me know how it works out. If it doesn't work, come back and we'll figure something else out."

I sensed it would take some members of the LAPD's senior staff a long time—perhaps years—before they would get comfortable with my very different style of management. I also knew that a number of these top commanders might never accept me or the other changes that would start taking place. I figured if I was lucky, maybe half of them would be immediately and genuinely interested in changing and reforming the "new" LAPD.

I wasn't born with my management style, and it sure wasn't something I picked up studying for any police promotional exam. Nor did I learn it as I came up through the ranks. As a patrolman, I remember thinking that whatever the sergeant said was akin to the word of God. As for the lieutenant, you steered clear of him—if you had to talk to the lieutenant, it meant you were in big trouble.

In 1986, shortly after Kevin Tucker became police commissioner with a mandate to reform the Philadelphia Police Department, he sent forty-four midlevel administrators to Harvard for a management training program. This was a major commitment on the part of the city, as tuition was some $20,000 each. (The following year, the department sent another group of forty-four to Harvard.) I was one of the original forty-four. At the time, I was a police inspector commanding the civil affairs division.

No one had ever heard of police administrators going to Harvard to polish their skills. The local press dubbed us the "Harvard 44." I'm not sure I want to know what some of our fellow officers might have called us behind our backs. Rightly or wrongly, we were singled out to be the change agents in the Philadelphia Police Department.

The fact that we were all midlevel in the department was the key. If you are setting out to change an institution, you can't rely solely on the senior-most personnel who got to the top under the old ways. While some senior staff are open to change, Tucker knew that many of his senior commanders were not the least bit interested in changing anything about the Philadelphia Police Department. Not afraid to alienate obstructionists, he reached around and over them to identify, groom, and promote his "change agents" and place them in key slots, enlisting in the cause those individuals who were on their way up and had a stake in the department's future. Of course, this takes time, which is why making widespread changes in a big-city police department takes, at minimum, four, five, and six years.

A lot of us were somewhat dubious about going to Harvard. We felt honored and proud, but what exactly would going off to the granddaddy of all Ivy League schools accomplish in terms of our law enforcement careers?

After graduating from high school I had not returned to school until sixteen years later when the police department sent me to

Northwestern University (1977–78) near Chicago for a ten-month police management program. That experience encouraged me to enroll in college at night upon my return to Philadelphia and to earn my two-year associate of arts degree in business administration at age thirty-nine. (Because my family couldn't afford it, none of my brothers or sisters went to college right after high school either. Like me, five of them enrolled in night school as adults, and four eventually received degrees.)

And yet, here I was sitting in a classroom at Harvard University, the alma mater of the likes of John F. Kennedy, other former U.S. presidents, and countless business and government leaders.

For three weeks at Harvard we didn't open a book in class. Our professors were mostly Harvard faculty, with a sprinkling from Yale and Cornell. We attended class from eight-thirty in the morning to six o'clock in the evening. We had group projects during the day, with the forty-four of us sitting around in a big circle talking openly about tough issues that had never before been discussed in the Philadelphia Police Department. We had lots of reading to do on our own at night. It was definitely work—we were not in Massachusetts that cold, icy winter for a vacation.

In class, we considered various business and community models, discussing how the private sector resolved a wide range of problems. We learned about "interrelationships"—how one problem is so often tied to another. It made sense, but I kept wondering, *When are we going to talk about police work?*

After about three days, a light came on for me. I suddenly saw what we were doing here. We were relating the corporate world to the Philadelphia Police Department. This was a novel approach. Up until then, we had been groomed to believe that our problems were so different from the rest of the world's that nobody else could possibly tell us how to do our job better. If they tried to, that meant, given the prevailing us-against-them mind-set so ingrained in many police departments, that they were against us.

What we began to realize was that whether you looked at Nabisco or RCA or Westinghouse, when it came to problem solving, the underlying issues and general solutions were often the same. Conflicts between employees and managers . . . a company failing to keep its eyes on its customers . . . a manufacturer not having product ready when there was a demand for it . . . a service industry not having enough properly trained personnel—all these situations could easily be related to daily police work.

Surely, Commissioner Tucker must have known that an advanced course that taught career law enforcement personnel the finer points of corporate management would dovetail with implementation of community policing.

The Harvard course reminded us that there is nothing mystical about wearing a badge and gun belt. We are a service industry. The public pays us for a specific job: to keep the peace and arrest the bad guys. They're pleased when we do our job and disappointed when we do not. The real boss is not the sergeant or the lieutenant or the chief of police but, rather, Mary and John Q. Public.

Up to then, none of our senior commanders in the department would have allowed any of us midlevel people to open our mouth and talk about the problems within the department and conflicts with the community. If we had, we would have been banished to the far reaches of the department, never to be seen again.

What we learned at Harvard we kept thinking about and talking about when we came home. This was really the first step of the change process and our move toward community policing. Of course, ample numbers of Philadelphia police officers knew how to treat the public right a long time before "community policing"—and the same can be said for Los Angeles. Yet in minority neighborhoods, we had to work to overcome our image as oppressors. When he had led the Philadelphia Police Department (1969–71) the opinionated and often reactionary Frank Rizzo thought—erroneously, I believe—that a strong police presence alone could prevent a riot. "The streets of Philadelphia are safe," Rizzo used to say. "It's only the people who make them unsafe." In Kevin Tucker, and later me, Philadelphia had found the antithesis of Frank Rizzo.

Returning with our new skills and philosophies, we started to apply what we had learned, gleaning further insights from our successes and mistakes. I was soon put in charge of creating the department's first career-development strategy for police officers. The idea was to continually develop the careers of officers from the time they graduated from the academy until they retired. Nothing like that had ever been done before. A rookie went to the academy for six months, graduated, and then didn't get much more official training for the next thirty years—not the best way to end up with well-trained police officers.

We came home from Harvard understanding that it was just as vital for a police department to engage in long-range strategic planning as it is for any corporation. (While I was commissioner, the Philadelphia Police Department released its first five-year strategic plan, covering 1991–96. At the time, such a plan was unusual for police departments, although today it is more common.)

Though it did not happen overnight, change did come to the Philadelphia Police Department—helped along as the "change agents" steadily advanced in rank.*

I had seen with my own eyes in Philadelphia how a misguided management style within a police department could cost lives. The tactical decision to drop the explosive device that killed those men, women, and children during the MOVE standoff was made in haste by the police commissioner on the recommenda-

*The original "Harvard 44" were mostly inspectors and captains, with a few lieutenants. Of the group, there were seven African-Americans, one Hispanic, and two women—reflecting at the time the ethnic and gender makeup of the department. There were then no women above lieutenant. Most of the "Harvard 44" stayed with the department, while some moved on. Several are chiefs in suburban departments outside Philadelphia; one became chief of the school police in Philadelphia; one was appointed chief of police at Rutgers University; three are currently deputy police commissioners of Philadelphia. The current Philadelphia police commissioner was in the second Harvard group. Among the women sent to Harvard, at least three became captains. Since 1987, most of the group that remained with the department have been promoted at least two ranks.

tion of a couple of low-level people at the scene, leaving two or three tiers of senior managers out of the loop. In other words, that crucial decision was made without consulting the msot experienced people in the department.

It is easier to fly by the seat of your pants and lock into your opinion than to make yourself listen to other people and consider their opinions. But if you don't listen to the advice of others, and then make a wrong decision, you are doubly wrong. Wrong for the bad decision you made, and wrong for not listening to others, who may have steered you in the right direction. We are much better off listening and getting all the options, then making a decision and living with the decision once we have made it.

Some police chiefs want to listen to their staff for ten minutes and, boom-boom, go with something right then. In my view, there are few things that you have to make an instant decision on—if one is necessary, I don't have any problem making it. However, by nature, I am a consensus builder. I am able to do this about half the time. The other half of the time I know I am going to have to make the call myself, but before doing so I try to hear from the best minds on a particular subject. The more input you have, the better and sounder and more lasting the decision you have to make will be, particularly if it is something that is going to grow over time.

Whether you make a decision based on consensus or not, if you don't first avail yourself of the opportunity to listen to those senior people around you for ten minutes or ten hours, and you go off half-cocked and make a bad decision, then you don't deserve to be a chief of police. You are going to be doomed to failure. You may survive a small incident, or even a series of minor incidents, but sooner or later you are going to push the wrong button at the wrong time, and the end result will cost you your job. That's what happened to Greg Sambor, the Philadelphia police commissioner who made the decision to drop the MOVE bomb. And that's what happened to Daryl Gates, in the way he handled the Rodney King incident. Before the riots, of course, the decision had already been made to get a new LAPD chief. But had that decision not already been made, it would certainly have been in the aftermath of the riots, due to the confusion and diffusion in the upper ranks of the LAPD and lack of planning and overall leadership within the department.

The management style in place at the Los Angeles Police Department when I took over was a concern to me. Few senior staff members were willing to state an opinion without the chief giving his own opinion first. Everyone seemed to be waiting for a stamp of approval before they acted. "Why should I stick my neck out?" was the prevailing attitude.

After successive hits from the Rodney King incident and the riots, morale among the cops on the beat had plummeted as they attempted to reconcile the public's loss of confidence in them with their own strong feelings of being outgunned, ill-equipped, and otherwise unable to do their jobs.

Morale among the senior commanders had also suffered. When I arrived, the three top staff positions—assistant chiefs— were vacant, two having decided to retire after the riots and the third position having been vacant for two years. Among the remaining staff, a lot of finger-pointing was still going on and blaming of each other for what had gone wrong during the riots. And there were clear pro-Gates and anti-Gates factions at the highest ranks.

Due to civil service restrictions, I was prohibited from bringing any top staff people to Los Angeles. In fact, I did not have a single non–civil service appointment I could make in the LAPD—in contrast to the commissioner of the New York Police Department, who can make a couple hundred non–civil service appointments above the rank of captain. Eventually, I would raise the ire of the LAPD command staff by supporting a proposal for all ranks above captain—this would involve about three dozen commanders, deputy chiefs, and assistant chiefs— to serve at the pleasure of the chief. In other words, a captain promoted to commander or deputy chief would serve in the higher capacity while maintaining civil service seniority and protection at captain. At any time, the appointee could be returned by the chief to the rank of captain.

Some people argue that doing away with civil service at the upper ranks would automatically lead to cronyism. I don't think so. No chief is going to surround himself with a lot of incompetent people. When they are unable to do the job, it will reflect badly on the chief. When you appoint your own people, you're going to be real sure to elevate smart, motivated, and effective people who will reflect well on you. In this way, a chief has the ability to build a team of people who think and act alike and understand a clear focus. And, importantly, accountability would be greatly increased. Why shouldn't a new chief be able to put together his or her own senior staff?

The LAPD and the Philadelphia Police Departments are the only two large police departments in the United States that are still civil service from the lowest to the highest ranks. In Los Angeles, all but the chief are civil service, and in Philadelphia, the commissioner and three deputy commissioners are the only non–civil service employees. In L.A., police became civil servants back in the 1930s after a period of police corruption. It was seen as a way to keep the department clean by creating a professional law enforcement organization. By all accounts, the LAPD had remained largely free of corruption since.

I do not believe that a police department needs to be entirely civil service from top to bottom to remain corruption-free. Civil service makes for entrenched employees within a very structured organization—both of which, by nature, can be extremely resistant to change. Ninety-five percent of our local, state, and federal government is managed across the country by non–civil service employees, and the vast majority of them are honest and hardworking.

Even if I could have brought in all my top people from the outside, I would not have. Instead of having one person learning the lay of the land, there would have been a dozen or more. At the same time, it's good to have people at your side who understand you and whom you can trust to send out as emissaries within and outside the department to verbalize and carry out your policies. This is the key to managing and gaining control of a police department.

In Philadelphia, after nearly three years as commissioner, I had begun to feel comfortable having about 80 percent of my team in place. I had known them all for years, of course. Building my staff in Los Angeles would take considerably longer and be made more difficult by the fact that I started off not knowing any of them. To be successful as chief, you've got to have your people in the right spots, where they can do the things you want done and watch your back at the same time. Although most police chiefs don't have every staff position filled the way they would like, to be completely comfortable you should be able to go to bed at night knowing that the people in place are doing what you want because they know it's the right thing to do and, secondly, because they know it's what you want. Until you get to that point, it can be scary knowing that the best people for the job aren't always in place and yet, you're responsible for everything that goes on twenty-four hours a day, even in the midst of the worst crisis imaginable.

I let my LAPD staff know in clear language at that first meeting that I had no interest in Monday-morning quarterbacking—after all, everyone is blessed with twenty-twenty hindsight. Instead of hearing what the department should have done last month or last year, I wanted to focus discussions and decisions on what we should be doing today and tomorrow to fight crime and rebuild the public's trust in the Los Angeles Police Department.

"I want you to look on June twenty-eighth"—my first day on the job—"as the first day of the rest of our lives," I emphasized. "I don't care what went on before."

My staff looked as if they wanted to believe me. Even so, it took months for some of them to quit fretting about the past and begin to look to building the future.

"Everyone has a clean slate," I continued at that first meeting, "including me. What you write on that slate is up to you. I know your job involves making decisions, and sometimes mistakes will be made. But if you were doing the best you know how, you won't have a better friend. I ask you to work with me, listen and learn about me, and maybe I'll earn your respect and support before I leave this organization.

"From this day forward, we have to be a team. There are three and a half million people in this city depending on us, as well as seven thousand sworn personnel and two thousand civilian employees of this department."

A police department does not change just because the chief wants it to. And since change can only be done from the inside, I would have to plant seeds among the ranks of management— as Kevin Tucker had done in Philadelphia—to see who would step up with a desire to make changes in the LAPD. Those who did would become my "change agents," as I had been one of Tucker's. You can have commissions, committees, blue-ribbon panels, and other external groups, but you cannot force change from outside the department. That's why it's necessary to have the right people in place from the top down to accomplish major reform. The speed with which significant change can be made varies. If the department is very structured and civil service from bottom to top—like the LAPD—then it's going to be a slower process putting all of your "change agents" in the right power positions.

As I was harshly reminded a few hours after my first staff meeting, events in this bustling city weren't about to slow down so I could take six months to decide how to fill top staff positions and direct the department toward orderly change.

Police Officer Douglas J. Iversen, a fifteen-year LAPD veteran, and his partner were patrolling on their police motorcycles in South Central L.A. early in the evening on July 1. Iversen and his partner spotted an unregistered tow truck parked in a gas station at Florence and Crenshaw. Ignoring an emergency call to respond to an auto theft in progress elsewhere, Iversen pulled into the gas station to question the driver, John L. Daniels. (Unregistered tow trucks are subject to immediate impoundment.)

Iversen parked his bike and walked to the driver's side of the truck. The officer talked to the driver, who showed his license and registration. The driver got out of the truck. Further conversation led to an argument over the legality of the truck's papers. Eventually, the driver returned to his truck and attempted to leave the scene.

When the driver refused to stop, Iversen drew his weapon and fired at Daniels.

Witnesses heard Iversen's partner, Police Officer Patrick Bradshaw, ask him, "What did you do *that* for?"

The tow-truck driver was dead at the scene.

I received a call at home around 7 P.M. from my chief of staff informing me of the OIS—officer-involved shooting. I was informed that the shooting had been fatal, that the victim was a black male, that it had occurred a short distance from the intersection (Florence and Normandie) where the riots had begun, and that a crowd was already forming.

My heart sank.

This was just what we did *not* need.

I asked my chief of staff to call me back as he had more information, and also with updates as to how the crowd was behaving. I ordered that extra personnel be brought into the area—just in case.

The incident drew immediate attention from the community and the media because of the nature of the shooting and the racial overtones of a black citizen being killed by a white police officer in the wake of the riots. Everyone in the city, I think, felt a great sense of urgency. Nerves were so frayed already that the apprehension in the air was almost palpable. Could this be the one incident that would trigger another riot?

Due to early concerns about this shooting, I immediately

ordered Officer Iversen removed from street duty and assigned to a desk job, which was all I could do. Under the "Bill of Rights" for LAPD officers, an officer could not be fired or suspended until his or her case had gone through the entire administrative review process. (It had been easier for me to suspend or fire officers in Philadelphia, which I had done several times.)

Though the LAPD chief has the authority to reassign an officer, in the past, reassignment in OIS cases had been rare in Los Angeles. Traditionally, the officer took a couple of days off, visited the department psychologist, and then went back on the street to wait out results of the internal investigation. This manner of dealing with such cases could give the impression that they were being handled with a business-as-usual attitude.

I had such concern with the circumstances of this particular shooting that I took the quick action and made the reassignment even though I knew it would be unpopular with the rank and file. Though among themselves officers were already whispering that the death of the tow-truck driver was "not a good shooting," I knew their fear would be that I was prejudging Iversen guilty of an "out-of-policy" shooting before the investigation was concluded (which ended up taking several months).

We had an administrative system within the department as well as a judicial system—this case would run its full course and my action in taking this officer off the street would not change that.

I had enough information to recognize that the preponderance of preliminary evidence showed that Officer Iversen may have acted inappropriately in using deadly force. Someone was shot who shouldn't have been shot; someone was dead who should still be alive. I couldn't imagine allowing Iversen to climb back on his motorcycle the next night and patrol the same streets. It wasn't right. And what kind of signal would that have sent to the community at large?

Unlike other LAPD chiefs, I didn't consider myself simply the chief of the department. I had two important constituencies: the department, and the 3.5 million residents of the city.

Several months later, after the required disciplinary papers had been filed, Iversen was suspended from the department without pay. Some months after that, when the case landed back on my desk, I ruled that Iversen, whose conduct had led to three earlier suspensions without pay, had violated department policy on the use of deadly force when he shot and killed the tow-truck driver. The case next went to the Board of Police Commissioners, who also ruled the shooting "out of policy."

The Iversen case was to wend its way through various hearings and appeals and court cases for two and a half years—Iversen was charged with murder while on duty, but two trials resulted in mistrials. In the first trial, it was reported that all jurors were in agreement over guilt but split between second-degree murder and manslaughter. The second mistrial was split between guilty and not guilty.

Finally, on March 16, 1995, concurring with a unanimous recommendation from the LAPD Board of Rights (composed of three police captains), I was able to fire Iversen for violating department policy.

The next day, the Police Protective League—complaining that LAPD officers had not previously been fired for "out of policy" shootings—announced it would fund an appeal for Iversen through the courts.

I am not sure I ever had a honeymoon on my new job in Los Angeles. If I did, it lasted only one day—the day of my ceremonial swearing-in.

From the second day on—when the tow-truck driver was needlessly shot and killed by an LAPD motorcycle officer—I found myself playing serious catch-up.

CHAPTER THREE

THE LOS ANGELES POLICE DEPARTMENT'S four geographic bureaus—West, South, Valley, and Central—are subdivided into eighteen areas, called divisions, spread out over 450 square miles. In reality, each division is a separate command, with jurisdiction over widely diverse peoples and cultures.

During my first few weeks on the job, I attended at least one roll call in all eighteen divisions. In order to make roll call for the "days," "P.M.," and "morning" watches, I began my day before 6 A.M. and did not often get home before midnight. I visited Wilshire Division, Rampart, Harbor, Van Nuys, North Hollywood, Devonshire, Hollywood . . .

The entrance lobbies to police stations and precincts have the same look to them everywhere. Bulletin boards filled with notices and announcements, wooden benches, soda-pop machines, and always the pictures—framed portraits of officers from the station killed in the line of duty; some long ago, but none forgotten.

The Seventy-seventh Street Division's seventy-year-old station—the oldest in use by the department—stood in the heart of South Central L.A. I had visited here prior to becoming chief. On my second night after moving to L.A., I had shown up at the Seventy-seventh while riding through South Central L.A. with a unit from the LAPD's elite Metropolitan Division. (Based downtown, Metro includes Rapid Response, SWAT, and Crisis Negotiation teams.)

The Seventy-seventh's old brick building was in such disrepair that a few years back the second floor had to be condemned and removed from the structure for fear that it would collapse. With cramped quarters, bad lighting, and leaky roof, this ramshackle building should have been replaced long ago. The fact that officers had to work in such decaying quarters did not help morale in this otherwise proud division. "If you can work Seventy-seventh," officers of the division liked to boast, "you can work anywhere in the city." The Seventy-seventh Division policed 138,000 residents over fourteen square miles, a swath of inner-city Los Angeles where the annual murder count exceeds one hundred.

"I'm not here to announce any new or startling changes," I began my remarks at roll call. "I'm here to give you a peek at the new chief. Maybe you can learn a little about me and maybe I can learn something about you."

I hoped to begin to alleviate some of the anxiety and suspicion that I knew the rank and file must be experiencing at having an outside chief. I remembered what a traumatic experience that had been for us in the Philadelphia Police Department when my predecessor, Kevin Tucker, a U.S. Secret Service administrator, had been brought in to run the department.

The Secret Service is not exactly a community-based policing agency. The fact that someone from such a background ended up championing community policing and successfully reforming one of the country's largest municipal police departments proves, in my opinion, that thirty years of police skills aren't as important as management skills when it comes to running a major police department.

After the MOVE bombing report and all the public criticism leveled at the department, the low point had come when we were unable to protect a black family in southwest Philadelphia. Anonymous threats warned that the family, a target of racial attacks, would be "burned out." A patrol unit was assigned round-the-clock to sit in front of the house. Despite the police guard, the house was torched. Luckily, no one was hurt. In the next day's newspaper, an article about the arson attack began prophetically: "The next Police Commissioner does not currently reside in the Philadelphia Police Department . . ."

"I've been a police officer for twenty-eight years," I said by way of introducing myself at the Seventy-seventh Division roll call. "Uniform assignments about two-thirds of that time. My oldest son, Will, is a police officer in Philadelphia, and my wife has two uncles who are retired from the department. We are a police family.

"Although I am new here, I am not a new chief of police. I can tell you my style is going to be a little different from your former chief's. But I am not here to be used as a tool by any person or group that may have wanted Chief Gates out of office. I am not here to beat up on you. I am here to undertake and complete, with your help, a process of orderly change."

Not just change for change's sake, I emphasized, but change where it was needed and for the better.

"I know of your lack of faith and trust in senior management. I am also acutely aware of the need for materials and supplies and equipment. It is my job to address these problems right away and find solutions."

After attending a number of roll calls, my sense was that the men and women of the LAPD still had good self-esteem and self-worth. They seemed to value the work they did as police officers and felt up to the job that needed to be done. The problem, as I had feared, was morale.

Morale can be especially affected by outside forces and events over which management has little control, perhaps more so than by those issues that can be contained within the department. The public bashing that the Philadelphia Police Department took following MOVE caused morale to suffer. Although it did recover as the department took positive steps on the path to reform—ensuring that such a tragedy would never happen again—it took years.

Morale in the LAPD, a force deeply divided and unsure of what was going to happen next, was at rock-bottom. The Rodney

King incident had put the entire department on trial, and there was strong public sentiment that all 7,600 LAPD officers were like the four officers accused in the beating. Then came the riots. The LAPD had been criticized for what did and did not occur at the intersection of Florence and Normandie and for what took place during the riots. The department had suffered because of political infighting between the chief and the mayor. The department had endured a lack of cohesiveness among senior managers,* which reverberated to the rank and file. There was not one but two major independent investigations of the department. Its longtime chief, popular with the rank and file, was seemingly driven from office. Now comes a new chief from the East Coast.

The community was demanding that the new police chief make wholesale changes in the department. Management wants to take the department this way, but the rank and file thinks that management doesn't have a clue. Management and the rank and file were at opposite poles—neither was sure how to reach the other or even if they were being listened to. Officers were working without a labor contract, and negotiations were going nowhere. The city was saying it had no money even for relatively small cost-of-living adjustments and, to add insult to injury, was demanding some givebacks of current benefits. The greater Los Angeles community is divided into racial and ethnic camps, financial camps, political camps, you name it, and the police department feels the heat from every sector. Last but not least, virtually every major media outlet in the world was running around L.A. looking for another Rodney King or riot story.

*Testifying before the Christopher Commission, Assistant Chief Dave Dotson stated, "In the last thirteen years in the Los Angeles Police Department, with a couple of very notable exceptions, we have not had, at the top, very effective leadership. We do not have clarity of mission in our general operations. We don't have a clear understanding of where we're going and what our priorities are, let alone how we ought to get there." Another assistant chief, Jesse Brewer, also testified to a lack of top leadership and complained that no one was held accountable for the actions of subordinates.

With all this swirling around, no wonder morale at the LAPD was about three feet below ground level.

At each roll call, I fielded questions. At some stations there was reticence at first, but before long, the troops were peppering me pretty good.

Question: Not coming from Los Angeles, how did I intend to learn and run the department?

"With a lot of help. I'll listen and observe at first as much as I can, but I need your help."

Question: How was I going to find out how the rank and file really feels about things?

"By having sessions like this and instituting an open-door policy downtown." Every Tuesday, I would set aside half the day for "one-on-ones" with any member of the department—rank aside—who wanted to talk to me.

I promised to listen to a variety of opinions from the rank and file as well as from my command staff.

"We're going to talk with each other," I said. "We're going to have the right to disagree with each other and no one will be buried in the far corners of the city."

Aside from the questions, there was wholesale airing of grievances. "A lot of us are embarrassed by the department's response during the riots," one officer admitted. "The worst part is we know we could have done the job if someone had just let us. If someone had told us what needed to be done, Chief, we would have done it."

"I know you would have," I said sympathetically.

Someone speculated that had the contingent of officers ordered to "stand by" in a parking lot not far from the Florence and Normandie intersection known what was happening to Reginald Denny, they would have retaken the intersection and rescued the truck driver even if it had meant a potential loss of police officers' lives. Instead, they awaited further orders—and since there was no television in the parking lot, they didn't know what the rest of the country did.

"In the future," I said, "we will try to have better advance planning and leadership in the field. You will be given every opportunity to do your job."

I knew of no better way to start my tenure than going to roll calls and listening to the rank and file.

The majority of them wanted the department to get out of the limelight. They wanted to get back to doing the jobs that they did well every day, and they wanted credit for it. If this took a measure of reform to accomplish, then they would probably support at least some change. As to what percentage of the department would have endorsed the whole reform package, who could say? They had heard and read in the press that the entire department needed major surgery, when, in fact, some parts of the department were operating just fine. With an outsider being brought in to wield the scalpel, they were of course apprehensive. Who could blame them?

I firmly believe that low morale is curable. What I did not and could not know at the time was the immense challenges that the immediate future held for the Los Angeles Police Department.

It would eventually become clear that no police department in this country's history had ever had to endure such a string of high-profile incidents and public batterings for such a significant period, beginning in 1991 with the Rodney King beating and extending with little relief right into 1995 with the O. J. Simpson murder case.

With one thing coming after another, we would hardly have a chance to catch our collective breath.

I'm getting ahead of myself now, but at some point I did begin to wonder, *Won't the hardworking folks in our department ever catch a break?*

The Webster/Williams Report, coauthored by former FBI director William Webster and Hubert Williams of the Washington-based Police Foundation, turned out to be highly critical of Los Angeles city government and its leaders. The report, titled "The City in Crisis," resulted from a five-month investigation by a team of one hundred attorneys and other professionals, conducted after the riots at the behest of the Board of Police Commissioners.

The special panel spread the blame for the inadequate response to the riots around city government, but the brunt of its criticism was directed at Daryl Gates, who "failed to provide a real plan and meaningful training to control the disorder."

The initial response by police and city officials to the violence that followed the not-guilty verdicts in Simi Valley was "marked by uncertainty, some confusion and an almost total lack of coordination," the report stated.

I was relieved to see that the report made a point of stating that its criticism of the police should not be interpreted as reflecting badly on the "dedication and ability of the brave men and women" who served in the rank and file of the LAPD.

When the report was unveiled at a news conference, Webster added, "This city is plagued by hostility, rage, and resentment in many areas . . . where minorities and economically deprived citizens believe the LAPD did not treat them with respect or extend the same level of protection as elsewhere."

Side by side with the Christopher Commission Report, the Webster/Williams Report, in my view, served as part two for change. I saw it as a further blueprint to remake the department, embracing, as it did, community policing, while explicitly rejecting the paramilitary policing style of the past.

The report noted with disapproval that Mayor Bradley and Gates, apparently feuding, had not spoken to one another for fourteen months prior to the riots.

I found this unbelievable.

Tom Bradley had served his city with distinction: five consecutive terms as mayor and, formerly, as a member of the LAPD. Too, I had always respected Daryl Gates, whom I had known for years as a fellow law enforcement professional. (Had Gates retired before the Rodney King incident, he would have been viewed as the guru of U.S. police chiefs. The fact that that incident, the riots, and the LAPD's dreadful lack of planning all came on his watch meant, at the very least, that he had over-stayed.)

I couldn't understand how Bradley and Gates had been will-ing and able to avoid each other for so long. A mayor should never allow the chief of police not to communicate with him. And the police, as well as the general public, should not let the chief fail to communicate with the top executive in the city. Police managers must recognize that they are part of government and not apart from government and accept that they must work in the spirit of cooperation with other city leaders.

The LAPD receives its operating funds through the mayor's annual budget, which is approved by the city council. How could the chief effectively lobby the mayor for increased fund-ing or *anything* if the two weren't speaking to one another?

Gates was seen as a fighter of the system—a chief who refused to "play politics." This made him popular with many of the rank and file who think politics is a dirty word, but his fail-ure to work cooperatively within the system came at a great cost.

Fighting the system and not building bridges with the mayor and other political leaders is part of the reason why LAPD didn't get any new patrol cars for four years.

Fighting the system is why LAPD graduated just a couple of academy classes in two years, adding only about 100 new offi-cers to the department while in the same period it lost more than 600 veterans through retirement and other attrition, reducing the department from nearly 8,300 sworn officers to 7,800.

Fighting the system is why the department took no steps toward automation and computerization to replace its 1950s paper-driven system for processing by hand thousands of reports daily.

With a chief who often isolated the police department and fought against the city's political system, it was no wonder money had not been available for hiring, equipment, overtime, and a list of other vital needs.

Now, to some police officers, just having their chief deal with politicians is viewed as morally corrupt. They are outraged whenever the chief meets with the mayor—they view this as interference.

Some L.A. cops still believe that the department should be out there by itself, accountable to no one. These officers, many of them hired in the 1960s and 1970s with military backgrounds, still see themselves and the department in the 1990s as separate and apart from the community.

I had to get across to my new department that we were not an island unto ourselves. We were part of city government, not apart from it. I knew such talk would cost me acceptance among the rank and file in the short run—they were not accustomed to hearing this kind of talk from an LAPD chief. But it was the only way I knew how to manage this, or any, police department.

In the past, the LAPD had been so isolated that it had virtually pulled out of county and state law enforcement activities, even effectively withdrawing from mutual-aid agreements that provide support and assistance from other jurisdictions in declared emergencies. (The Webster/Williams Report had criticized the LAPD for not notifying county and state authorities in the early hours of the riot that outside help might be required. Such notification and assistance could have resulted in better coordination of forces and less opportunity for lawbreakers.)

I can't imagine anyone wanting to live in a city where the citizens do not have ultimate control of the police through their elected and appointed representatives. Personally, the last thing I want is a police force that could go out and do whatever it wanted to do, whenever it wanted to do it. This should not happen in America. It is against everything this country has stood for since 1776.

The job of chief of police is meant to be apolitical, of course. The chief should not get involved in political campaigns or make partisan endorsements. But that does not mean that the chief should isolate himself and the department from the political processes of city government—such as building public support for budget requests. As I see it, the chief must serve *all* the constituents of this city. The public elects their representatives and I work with them without considering political labels or philosophies. The chief has to be attentive to the needs and wants of the elected and appointed leadership of the city.

Reaching out beyond the department is a key component to community policing. Had I come in and just tried to be popular with the rank and file—you can do that by calling regular press conferences and shooting from the hip—I wouldn't have had external support when I got around to making hard choices and tough calls. By securing key support bases throughout the community, among political leaders, in corporate business circles, within the media, I would have a much better chance of making the major internal changes that needed to be made within the LAPD.

Upon my arrival, I had asked the people of Los Angeles to hold me "accountable to do things differently."

Daryl Gates was now an ex-chief and I wished him well in retirement. There was only one Los Angeles police chief, and now, I was it.

I reached out to the community as I had to members of the police department, attending public meetings and accepting some of the more than five hundred requests a week for appearances from neighborhood, civic, business, and law enforcement groups. Not just from within Los Angeles, but from other cities and even out of state.

Concentrating on visiting local churches, civic functions, schools, business luncheons, and homeowners and neighborhood meetings allowed me to take the pulse of the city. Not surprisingly, I found people frightened.

Even with so many varied audiences in different locations throughout the city, the most often asked questions were universal: "What are you going to do to keep this from happening again?" and "Are you going to make sure the police will be here next time we need them?"

I responded to an invitation to meet with a group of Catholic priests who represented 32 parishes and 250,000 Catholics located in riot-torn areas. A priest from South Central L.A. said, "Probably our biggest concern is that police do not seem to be a part of the community." I stressed my commitment to establishing community-based policing, describing it as a philosophy of management. "If it's appropriate and the community wants it, I plan to employ foot patrols and neighborhood police substations like we did in Philadelphia."

I did not mention that the first neighborhood substation we opened in Philadelphia, at the corner of Seventeenth and Wallace—one of the most notorious drug corners in the history of the city—had been damaged by a hand grenade shortly after it opened.

The idea of a substation—it can be just a room next to a 7-Eleven or any small storefront location—is to provide a place for foot-beat officers and community volunteers to work together to address neighborhood concerns. Officers spend 75 percent of their time walking beats in the area, while volunteers come in and answer the phones and provide nonemergency services to people who walk in to make a complaint or file a report. In this way, reports can be made to the police and/or passed on to other departments in city government without tying up 911 emergency service.

The two Philadelphia police officers assigned to our Seventeenth and Wallace substation spent the bulk of their time helping residents trying to reclaim their neighborhoods from two generations of drug dealers. It was one of those places where kids couldn't walk down to the corner without passing drug dealing, prostitution, and violence. Apparently, we were beginning to have an impact because one night, when the substation was closed, someone tossed a live grenade through the window.

The community responded as one, and within a few days the substation was reopened for business.

In a meeting with leaders of the L.A. Korean community, which probably suffered the largest loss in terms of burned-out businesses, there was the omnipresent fear, but also something else: a seething anger directed at the Los Angeles Police Department.

"We know better now!" hollered one irate businessman. "We'll take care of ourselves next time!"

I was asked by many residents what I was going to do about coordinating civic reparations. I was not surprised because I had already seen that the wants and fears of those who had gone through the nightmare were overlapping and interwoven. Law enforcement needs were blended with riot damage, housing, and other issues.

I found myself explaining, once again, that I wasn't hired to build buildings or bring jobs back. "My job is to make sure we have a well-functioning, hardworking police force that will be prepared and will respond to wherever the situation demands."

Time and again, I promised, "We will be there for you next time."

I couldn't tell how many people believed me.

I spoke at an NAACP Legal Defense and Education Fund awards luncheon a month after I took over, even though there were angry calls to my office from officers wanting to know why I was going to speak to "that group." As the NAACP was involved in a number of lawsuits against the department, it seemed that the chief was going into the enemy's camp. (When Jesse Jackson came to Parker Center to meet with me, some officers were similarly outraged. "Why is *he* coming into *our* building?" they demanded to know.)

One of my drivers, a twelve-year veteran who has worked on one of the most elite units in the department, said, "Chief, you don't know how different things are since you've arrived. The places and meetings I've taken you to—some guys in this department would be beside themselves if they knew the bridges you're trying to build. They'll never understand what you're trying to do."

In my mind, passing up the opportunity to address the NAACP or any community group would only foster the us-against-them mind-set that had ruled the LAPD for too long. Too, community support in all sectors would be necessary for us to have any chance to make the type of changes in the police department that were on the drawing board.

At the NAACP gathering, I began, "According to my inside sources, this is heresy. So, I may have to call on some of you to defend me sometime.

"As Los Angeles chief of police, I am reaching out to all elements of the community and going to neighborhood meetings and doing whatever it takes to improve the police department. In the coming months, we'll be getting officers, the media, and different segments of the community together in an attempt to customize our service to meet the needs of all parts of the city."

I was not willing to close the door on anyone. I believe a police chief must meet with any community group, whether he likes or dislikes what they stand for.

In Philadelphia, I had sat in my conference room across from the Grand Whoever of the Ku Klux Klan when they were planning a rally so we could discuss what we would and would not let them do on the streets. Some people couldn't believe it. And when I brought Nation of Islam members in for a meeting, before they hit my office on the third floor, people were asking, "What are the *bow-tie* guys doing in *this* building?" It was as if their presence stained the very essence of the Philadelphia Police Department. The Muslims came in to talk about setting up an antigang program in town similar to one they had set up in Washington, D.C. What kind of police commissioner would I have been had I refused, out of misplaced principles, to have this meeting?

I didn't deliver any different message at the NAACP from

what I did anywhere else. "Police departments and individual officers must get beyond the hear no evil, see no evil, and speak no evil attitude that is so pervasive. In the LAPD, there must be accountability."

Reiterating my promise to the people of Los Angeles to put more uniformed police in black-and-whites on the street, I told the NAACP that I was investigating whether the LAPD had too many people behind desks (we did), and why our fleet of vehicles had more unmarked than marked cars by a nearly seven-to-three ratio (I resolved to reverse these numbers and not designate any new cars for administrators until we did).

The city of Los Angeles could only be described in the aftermath of the riots as being unusually fragile—longtime political and civic leaders were stepping aside and leaving a huge vacuum at the top. The Los Angeles Times called it a "panicked exodus of the governing elite vanishing from public office."

There I stood, the new kid in town, untainted by all the things that had gone so wrong. Frankly, I became concerned that the expectations of what I—or any chief of police—could accomplish were way too high. When it comes to the flow chart for city government, the police chief is nowhere near the top. I wasn't the mayor or district attorney or county administrative officer or superintendent of schools—all of whom were on the long list of departing Los Angeles public servants. (I guess that's why I was getting all those speaking invitations.)

In truth, the city's leaders could provide only part of the solution. Ordinary citizens, so many of whom were still haunted by memories of their city on fire and their police department not in control of the streets, would have to help us set things right. For them, and for all of us, remembering what had happened in April 1992 was a painful but necessary part of moving forward.

We had to stop bickering among ourselves. We had to put aside political and racial divisions and work together to see that nothing like it ever happened again.

*   *   *

My mandates in the summer of 1992 were clear:

- Reform the department following the couple hundred recommendations of the two independent panels, and begin to do so without the promise of additional funding.
- Implement citywide community policing for the first time throughout the whole department. Although such an ambitious plan could certainly benefit from additional manpower and resources, this would also have to be accomplished without added revenues. I concurred that a chief should be held accountable for delivering the police services required by the city with the resources he's given. If he can't, he shouldn't be chief of police.
- Rebuild the emergency response operations of the department and, as chairman of the Emergency Operations Board, the city's entire emergency-operations process.
- Improve morale in the LAPD. Among other things that would help: resolving the labor dispute, and fighting to find the money to buy better equipment and pay officers for their overtime hours. The LAPD was the only major police department in the country that didn't routinely pay cash overtime—officers received mostly compensatory time off.
- Remove the LAPD from the negative spotlight that began with the Rodney King beating. To do this, we had to return the perception of professionalism to the department and, perhaps even more difficult, the perception of fairness.
- Restore the public's confidence—severely shattered during the riots—in the LAPD. Images such as the beating of Reginald Denny with no police present had burned long and deep and would not be easily forgotten.
- Rebuild the LAPD's management staff. Prior to Rodney King, the LAPD—to the chagrin of the mayor, council, and community—had been virtually an independent

agency, not financially but operationally. The attitude of some of the department's top management had long been that no one could tell them how to do their job better.

- Restore communications between the department and the mayor and council and, in doing so, stop the steady slide whereby the LAPD was losing money and manpower. First up on the agenda, lifting the 1991 hiring freeze imposed on the department (and the rest of the financially strapped city government) and finding the money to hire more officers. Though police departments universally clamor for more manpower, the LAPD could make a better case than most.

- Rebuild bridges with other law enforcement agencies, as well as with other city departments; most notably, the L.A. Fire Department. In the early hours of the riot, the fire department had requested police escorts for their emergency vehicles. But the LAPD was already so inundated that it was decided not to provide fire trucks with escorts. This decision had caused a great deal of friction, which still lingered between the two departments. While fighting fires during the riot, several firefighters were shot and critically wounded—the fire chief's son was among those wounded.

- Address, for the first time in many instances, social issues within the department, such as the need to hire more women and minorities, that had resulted in lawsuits against the LAPD. "Find out what's going on and deal with it," the Board of Police Commissioners told me.

My plate was full—much more than it had been when I had taken command in Philadelphia four years earlier. In fact, I couldn't think of a parallel in American policing where a chief had come in under such adverse conditions as those that existed in Los Angeles.

What was driven home to me as I went out into the community during those first weeks and months was that people desperately wanted their city returned to them. Someone or something had taken it away, and they wanted me to help them get it back. They wanted order and a sense of calm.

Not too much to ask for.

Yet I knew I couldn't do it alone.

CHAPTER FOUR

In EARLY JULY, I ordered the offices of LAPD's Organized Crime Intelligence Division (OCID) closed and sealed pending an investigation of allegations that the unit had for years spied on well-known politicians and celebrities.

Since accepting the LAPD job three months earlier, I had been receiving information from various sources about alleged improprieties in the unit within the past eight to ten years. More such claims were contained in a new book by a former OCID detective.

I directed that OCID's two offices at Central Division station and Los Angeles International Airport be padlocked and temporarily sealed to maintain the integrity of the unit's files and documents during the investigation.

As I had been on the job only ten days, the press called it my "first bold strike" as chief. I moved quickly because I had been unable to get any clear answers as to what types of files were being kept by the unit. By my action, I hoped to assure the public that I wasn't going to allow any such activities to take place on my watch. I also wanted to send a signal throughout the department that if this *had* taken place in the past, it wasn't going to happen under this chief.

I knew my decision would not be popular with members of OCID or the department's rank and file. Every police chief wants to be popular with his officers, but at times, you have to make a tough call regardless of what it may do to your popularity within the department.

The next day, I met with all forty-five officers assigned to the intelligence detail. Without a doubt, it was one of the most difficult meetings I'd ever had in all my years of law enforcement. "I'm not implying any wrongdoing on anybody's part in the unit," I stressed.

I could see the pained looks on their faces. *Here we go again,* they must have been thinking, *getting painted with a broad brush due to unfounded allegations.*

I went on to explain that the internal investigation was needed to clear up the rumors, once and for all. As for closing OCID offices, it was in the best interest of the department to preserve the files and other materials.

The following month, after personally reviewing findings of the investigation, I allowed OCID to reopen.

Later that year, as part of a reorganization plan to streamline the police department's operations, we combined three units—organized crime, antiterrorist, and vice—into one new Criminal Intelligence Group.

Today, important intelligence work is being conducted by the LAPD in investigating organized crime, and these efforts have proven to be very effective.

In early August 1992, federal prosecutors announced a two-count indictment against the four LAPD officers acquitted by a Simi Valley jury of assaulting Rodney King. (Interestingly, more LAPD personnel—nearly fifteen hundred employees—live in the Simi Valley area, a 120-mile round-trip commute, than in the city of Los Angeles or elsewhere.)

According to the first count of the federal indictment, Officers Laurence Powell, Timothy Wind, and Theodore Briseno "did willfully strike with batons, kick and stomp Rodney King . . . resulting in bodily injury." Sgt. Stacey Koon, the senior officer at the scene, was indicted on the second count of allowing the beating to take place. If convicted, each officer faced up to ten years in prison and as much as a $250,000 fine.

The announcement capped a federal investigation that began

immediately after the incident but was suspended when the state filed charges against the officers. It was reopened following the not-guilty verdicts and subsequent rioting.

The officers would stand trial again, this time in federal court for violating King's civil rights. This specter raised some questions, particularly in law enforcement circles, as to double jeopardy. Historically, federal civil rights laws had been used to charge officers who escaped vigorous local prosecution, most notably in the Deep South. The four officers in this case, however, had been prosecuted by local courts and subsequently acquitted after a lengthy trial.

I'll leave the finer points of this argument to legal scholars—the fact is that the federal government assumed jurisdiction of the case. Any personal feelings I had about whether the officers should or should not be retried or should be found guilty or not guilty were pushed aside. I knew I would receive their personnel packages for disciplinary review at some point as the department's internal administrative process continued. When that time came, I would sift through the facts and make my decision as to the law enforcement careers of these four officers.

My immediate mission was clear: get the department ready for not one but two potentially explosive new trials—the other was the trial of street-gang members accused of beating Reginald Denny. Both trials were expected to be held within the next six to nine months.

Since my inaugural, the one constant refrain I had heard no matter which section of the city I visited was, "Chief, I want to feel safe again in Los Angeles."

Somehow, we needed to find a way.

Most Angelenos didn't say "what if" there was another riot after the new trials. People were so sure that the city would erupt again that they spoke about *when* the next riot came. Even if the four police officers were convicted in the second trial, it was widely speculated that there would be "celebration" riots. If someone had polled members of the LAPD, I am sure the majority would have agreed with the doomsayers. Everyone was ready for World War III.

There was a run in Los Angeles on retail outlets that sold guns. In May (1992) alone, local gun dealers filed documents with the state for the sale of 14,125 handguns—a 64 percent increase over the previous May. (About 4,500 firearms—handguns, rifles, assault weapons, etc.—were seized during the week of the riots.) Even to law-abiding citizens, increased gun sales would inevitably lead to more tragic accidents, lethal domestic disputes, and thefts that ended up putting guns into the hands of criminals.

Gun sales continued to soar throughout the summer, reflecting a high level of fear. The public was arming itself in unprecedented numbers because they didn't have any faith that the police would be around to protect them when the next riot occurred.

The Los Angeles Police Department needed a new emergency-response plan in place, and soon. The old plan was the department's standard tactical manual, which of course did not discuss possible scenarios for what might happen after the Simi Valley trial. Heretofore, the LAPD had not been trained to respond as a single force, but, instead, as smaller isolated units without unified command.

I made the decision over the summer to retrain not just a few hundred officers in specialized units but essentially the *entire department*—a massive undertaking.

I did not make the assumption that there would be another riot. In fact, I took the position publicly as often as possible that just because there were going to be more trials did not mean there would be further civil unrest. First, I believed that, and second, I felt that the police chief absolutely had to tell the people so.

Still, I told my top commanders that none of us would be taking any vacations while these two cases were in trial. This department was not going to get caught like last time with a sizable segment of its command force out of town.

Determined to ensure that the department would be prepared for any eventuality, I worked with my senior commanders developing a sixteen-hour Unusual Occurrence training program to be taught at the police academy to every sworn member of the department. The curriculum was a mix of some new things we had learned the hard way—as a result of the riot—and reinforcing standard crowd-control procedures. We broke tradition by sending our trainers (members of our elite Metro Unit) outside the department for expertise. The LAPD, more insular than most departments, had never believed in sending people elsewhere for training. The prevailing attitude: "We don't send people outside of the department because we are the best at doing our business." In fact, when I assumed command, the LAPD had no funds whatsoever available for outside training, and our in-service training budget was nearly zero. Money was not spent to better train LAPD personnel. Traditionally, from the police academy to a thirty-year pin, a Los Angeles police officer received little formal additional training in supervision and management, and little new tactical training.

We developed a curriculum that included tactical leadership, field force concept, conventional crowd-control methods, use of chemical agents during crowd control, squad formations and tactics, arrest and control, use of the baton, civil-disorder tactics, mass-arrest procedures, citizen-rescue tactics, patrolling hostile areas, gang convoy stopping measures, shopping-center looting arrest situation, and hostile-crowd dispersal.

The fear that a riot could happen again and that we might fail the test a second time was widespread. The idea was to give the rank and file not only the tools to do the job right, but also the confidence that they could succeed in any situation.

"You may never use all this training," we told each class. "If you don't, that's okay. That'll be a real sign that we are doing some other things right."

I ordered that all ranks—sergeants, lieutenants, captains, etc.—be interspersed in the classroom with the rank and file.

For some of the department's bosses, this was a little disconcerting. The message that I wanted sent to the entire department was that everyone was learning the same lessons, so that if or when we had an "unusual occurrence," we would all be on the same page. I received the same training as did nearly five thousand LAPD officers between fall 1992 and spring 1993.

The retraining helped boost department morale. It instilled renewed confidence in everyone that the department could handle these types of emergencies.

At the same time, I enthusiastically supported use of new nonlethal tools. These included what we generically call "rubber bullets," which are designed to stun rather than kill. If aimed properly, they strike suspects in the shins and knees, scaring and disorienting them. Guns that fired rubber bullets and handheld launchers that fired small bean bags would, we planned, be available to special tactical units trained to deal with unruly or violent crowds.

We began testing a new chemical spray that temporarily disabled. The new spray—a chemical agent called oleoresin capsicum—was similar to tear gas, except that it didn't disperse through the air and irritate police and bystanders. Commonly called pepper spray, it disables only the person who is sprayed. When sprayed in the face, it causes—for up to one hour—tearing and burning of the eyes, coughing and minor bronchial spasms, and disorientation.

Pepper spray was given a field test by five hundred beat officers in the fall of 1992. It was found far superior to Mace, and an acceptable alternative to the baton in forty-five arrests that might otherwise have escalated into deadly force situations. It was particularly effective with suspects who were drunk, under the influence of drugs, or otherwise insensitive to pain. (The four officers accused in the Rodney King beating claimed that they would not have used their batons that night if they had some other use-of-force alternative, such as an effective chemical spray.)

86

The idea was to give us effective alternatives to Mace and the Taser, neither of which officers had confidence in, and the baton, which could cause serious injury and even death. With the new tools, the scenario of cracking heads and knees with flying batons would no longer be the first or only choice. Instead, an officer could maintain control using only the degree of less-than-lethal force that was required and no more.

In one incident, officers used pepper spray to disperse gang members who had physically attacked them. The supervisor at the scene believed that if pepper spray had not been used, there would have been numerous injuries to suspects and officers, who would have been forced to use their batons to subdue the youths. After being sprayed, they fled in panic. Officers recovered discarded firearms dropped by the fleeing gang members.

Eventually, we widened the field testing of pepper spray, making it available to nearly five thousand officers assigned to uniform patrol, vice, and narcotics units. Both the pepper spray and rubber bullets soon found wide acceptance among the department's rank and file.

Training at the academy went on twelve hours a day, seven days a week. The department had never been very open to the media and public before, but I wanted to publicize what we were doing as a way to spread the word to law-abiding citizens as well as to potential lawbreakers.

I was warned that we could be setting ourselves up to take heat from the leaders of various minority communities. "They'll say you're raising an army."

In a sense, we were training an army for war. We needed to enlist our citizens and, at the same time, be sensitive to their wants and needs.

I had a feeling that the minority neighborhoods could end up being big supporters of our effort. My reasoning was that the greatest victimization and destruction during the riots occurred in their communities. A lot of black, Hispanic, and Korean residents believed that the police had intentionally left their neighborhoods unprotected because they didn't care about them. Many of them were still angry at us and needed reassuring that the police would not let them down again.

In an appearance in South Central L.A., I told the two hundred residents who turned out, "You are our most important customer. Part of the process of doing things differently is involving you, the men and the women who live in the city, the men and the women who work in the city, the men and the women who pay taxes. I need your help and I need your assistance in making the Los Angeles Police Department work."

I explained that all LAPD officers were receiving additional training—"this includes riot training as well as sensitivity training"—and promised to change the force to better reflect the city's diversity.

Asked during a question-and-answer period what role the department might play in helping to reduce the number of liquor stores in the area, I answered, "It is not for the city or the police to tell you what you should have in your neighborhood. The community should determine what it wants in the future. The role of the police department is to create a safe environment that will encourage business to come back to your neighborhood and stay."

We also needed to address the very real concerns of the white community of greater Los Angeles. What they had seen on television had wrongly convinced many of them that black and Hispanic street gangs would invade white areas in the next riot. Rumors were spreading like wildfire that there was going to be a race war. The public's perception was that "they" would soon be coming over the hills to rape, rob, and pillage. (Most people didn't realize that at least as many Hispanics were locked up during the riots as blacks, and that 18 percent of those arrested for violence and looting were white.)

Such irrational fears were fanned by the media, particularly television. Whether those in the media agree or not, they do make the news in part by deciding what to report. The media can and does shape the public's views and values. In fact, it can steer the course of events themselves.

I am sure that no reporter or news producer or camera operator intended to provide a catalyst for further looting and chaos during the L.A. riots, but the live coverage revealing that the police were nowhere to be seen at Florence and Normandie and other locations throughout the city did just that. These televised reports were crucial in informing potential rioters that police were not responding to the melee. It sent out the signal, "You can go out and rob and loot and get away with it for a while." I don't think any of the TV crews in the helicopters thought that they were aiding and abetting the lawbreakers. They probably thought they were simply covering a news event as it was unfolding, but their coverage certainly did influence events.

I tried to make these points in a meeting L.A. County sheriff Sherman Block and I had with some one hundred managers from television, radio, and print outlets.

I filled them in on the department's new planning and training. Then, I implored them to be careful in how they interpreted incidents and events in the future, and to consider the consequences of their reportage.

That segment of the public that so willingly allows its opinions to be shaped by the media would do well to remember that members of the press aren't necessarily professionals in the field they report on. Whether the subject is politics, medicine, space, the law, or policing, oftentimes important points do get lost in translation.

News is a competitive business. And it *is* a business, driven largely by ratings and advertising revenue. But the media has a moral responsibility to consider what the potentially dangerous outcome may be of their coverage or slant. Some media people I know disagree vehemently and are quick to say, "No, we just show it. It's not our job to look at it and ask what it will mean."

"You can't always push the responsibility on to someone else," I told the media representatives. "You live in this city, too, and you have loved ones who live, work, and go to school here.

You have a responsibility like other citizens to do what you can to help keep our streets safe."

I get along with the media, by and large. We have our clashes, particularly when I believe that a reporter—usually more so than a network or station—flavors and interprets things in an overly sensational way so as to get his or her name and face on the six o'clock news for two minutes. In Philadelphia, I had seen the media report certain events in a manner totally at odds with the facts. News coverage, I found, too often reflects the strengths, weaknesses, and biases of the individual reporter.

For my part, I promised to make the LAPD more open to the media than ever before. Often in the past, local media outlets had no choice but to report one side of a story because the LAPD wouldn't talk to them.

"Your people can come in and ask questions and we will give them the facts as we know them, so long as it doesn't jeopardize an investigation," I explained. "You can interview our people and take 'ride-alongs.' The flip side is that I may ask you from time to time to hold off reporting a story for a while if we think it is in the best interest of public safety."

Too often, the good we do does not make for as powerful a story as when we make a mistake. Still, we have to keep trying. We took the media and groups of residents up to the academy regularly to let them see all our new tools in action. The department had never done anything like it before. Previously, no one ever dared discuss what type of training, tools, and weapons the department had at its disposal. I took a risk in inviting some of our harshest critics—even people who were suing the LAPD.

We explained that we were looking for alternatives to using force when something else might work. We let them fire the rubber bullets and see the effects.

"If you're uncomfortable with these tools or if you don't think we're doing the right thing," I said, "don't walk away but stay here and help us find something else. Work with us." This was community policing in action.

This was also the type of approach private business takes when making a major change in service or product. Successful businesses try to be sensitive and intuitive as to what their customers want. They go out, talk to their customers through focus groups, and test-market products to see how they go over. That's very much what we did with our new nonlethal weapons and training.

In the old days, police found it easier to talk to the citizens. When an officer walked the same beat day after day greeting merchants and residents by name and handing out sticks of gum to youngsters, there was no need for a fancy label like "community policing." That bond or partnership between police and residents, which went far in preventing crime and promoting public safety, happened naturally. But as the automobile became the most prevalent means of transportation, the foot-beat cop was replaced by the motorized officer. Police moved from a walk-and-talk mode of "community" policing to one whose goal was to respond to calls received at the police communications center, which dispatched squad cars. Nonemergency, routine personal contact between police and residents was lost to a system of reactive policing. We ended up not knowing our "customers" nearly as well as we had when we walked a beat.

When computers arrived, police departments were able to take even more calls at a time, and faster. I remember in my early days on the force in Philadelphia trying to respond to all of the calls that came in as fast as possible, often without regard to their importance. Out of necessity, prioritizing soon followed. On the surface, this seemed correct. We then found ourselves running from call to call, responding to the most serious one first. Life-and-death calls are obvious; they will always be first in anyone's book. However, this was the ominous beginning of police agencies making decisions unilaterally about what was and wasn't important without consulting with their constituents, the residents of our neighborhoods. The attitude of many police departments was, "Leave policing to us, the professionals."

Take illegal drug activity, for example. Police have traditionally placed a priority on the type of lengthy and exhaustive
investigation necessary to stop the big-time "French Connection" dealer—after all, every cop likes a big bust. However,
almost universally, the folks in the neighborhood will tell you
that ridding the corner of junkies and small-time pushers is
more important to them. Those are the corners their children
walk past to go to school.

By the early 1980s, many police administrators began to realize that their efforts were not having a positive impact on crime,
and the residents were not happy. Crime was still rising in many
cities, fear was not decreasing, and community dissatisfaction
with the police was high and still growing. Police were not meeting the needs of their communities. From these concerns came a
belief that police must go back to the neighborhoods and pose
such questions as: What type of service do the residents want?
How do they want it delivered? How much are they willing to
commit of their time to accomplish these goals? And *listen* to
what the residents tell us. In going back to our roots, community
policing was born. Or, some would say, reborn.

In the late 1980s in Philadelphia, as an example, a community discussion with residents about crime revealed their primary concerns: abandoned vehicles, deserted homes, sanitation
problems, and loud music. As a result of this and other community meetings, a new specialty was born in the Philadelphia
Police Department: sanitation–abandoned-vehicle officers, who
were given the time to work with these neighborhood-service
issues.

Through such contacts with the residents, as opposed to riding around in patrol cars waiting for the next call, we found that
we really started solving problems. As a result, our patrol units
didn't keep getting called back, day after day, week after week,
to the same problems that had little to do with traditional police
work. It freed them to respond quicker to real emergencies.

This approach employed officers not solely as crime busters

but also as agents of social change to improve neighborhoods while deterring crime. While the community was quick to embrace this change in department philosophy, some members of the Philadelphia Police Department were less inclined. When I was police commissioner, some of my senior commanders came to me complaining because they had to go out and meet community leaders. Unbelievably, they didn't think it was their job to talk to residents and actually listen to what they said.

By the mid-1980s, we had developed an entire cadre of specialists, who were aided by civilian volunteers. Crime-prevention officers worked with local residents in trying to stop crime before it happened. Victim-witness officers worked with residents and other specialists to keep the victims of crime and the witnesses from continuing to be victimized as their cases moved through the criminal justice system.

Previously, when it came to the LAPD adding new weapons to its arsenal, I have no doubt that the department would have done it much differently from the way we did in the summer and fall of 1992. The chief would have okayed use of the pepper spray, for instance. The department would have obtained approval from the police commission, then briefed personnel on its use and put it on the street.

Instead, by following a basic tenet of community policing, we consulted with our "customers," showing them our new products and asking them what they thought. We wanted the residents to help determine whether these new tools were acceptable. After they saw how they worked and understood what we were trying to accomplish, they signed on in a big way. Having them with us, not against us, from the beginning could mean the difference between success and failure down the road.

The Los Angeles media, responding to our new open-door policy, was a great help this time. The extensive coverage we received reached millions of law-abiding citizens as well as the tens of thousands who had taken part in the riots, all of whom had witnessed the disarray in law and order for a few days one April.

I wanted everyone to know that this police department would not let the community down. I wanted the residents reassured that we would be there to protect them. To members of the department, I said our new vision should include that "never again will anyone have to worry about whether the LAPD can do what's expected of it." And I wanted everyone on the street to know that from the moment the juries returned their verdicts in the new trials, any opportunity to rob, steal, and loot would be nonexistent.

We would always have to deal with a group of hard-core habitual criminals. But every time I had a chance, I targeted my comments to those individuals I called "the opportunists": "If you rob or steal in L.A., you will go to jail and we will lock you up. No ifs, ands, or buts."

Making that kind of harsh statement is not my usual style, but I felt that was what the public needed to hear. I was dead serious in my warnings, too. I wanted the community to know that the police were back in control and that there would *not* be anarchy in the streets.

I also wanted to send a strong message to my officers that I was in control and willing to do what needed to be done to reverse the loss of faith in the leadership of the department. I wanted to get across to the rank and file that we were doing things differently.

By the time we finished retraining, everyone in the department knew our plan. We became adept at moving various groups of our personnel—from ten to a thousand—quickly as coordinated units. We could take people from different divisions in any one of our four geographic operations bureaus, put them together, and have them operate as one cadre because they knew the standing orders and knew what positions to fill. We were interchangeable parts, now. No longer did we have to count on Central Bureau and West Bureau plans meshing with the Valley Bureau plan without conflicting with the South Bureau plan.

We now had an LAPD plan.

*   *   *

Tackling social and cultural issues within a police department is never easy, and the LAPD was—and is—no exception.

Police, by nature and regardless of their ethnicity, tend to be conservative. Issues such as sexual harassment, discrimination, and bias inside the organization don't often get talked about, let alone resolved, even when changes in attitude are long overdue.

The Christopher Commission found that racism and bias within the LAPD had aggravated the problem of excessive force and other "unacceptable behavior" on the street. This correlation should have come as no surprise to anyone.

Before I had even assumed my duties in Los Angeles, a group of women LAPD officers, anxious to lobby the incoming chief, had taken Evelina and me to lunch. Over soup and salad, the officers eloquently made clear the importance they placed on my addressing employee issues within the department such as sexual harassment and gender bias, which took in promoting women to more senior ranks.

Like most modern police departments, the LAPD had prohibited, by policy, all forms of discrimination for some time. But the commission found that a "tension remains between official policy and actual practice."

In 1987, for example, an LAPD study found that female officers were subjected to a double standard and subtle harassment by their fellow officers and were not accepted as part of the working culture of the department. Four years later, the Christopher Commission concluded that this problem had not abated: "Although female LAPD officers are in fact performing effectively, they are having a difficult time being accepted on a full and equal basis."

I remember the day women were first assigned to patrol duty in Philadelphia. It really wasn't so long ago—1976, as I recall. It is remarkable, in fact, when one thinks of the enormous impact women have made in the law enforcement field in a relatively short time. Today, the public is not surprised at all when a woman police officer pulls up in a patrol car to answer a 911 call. That certainly wasn't always the case.

The Philadelphia Police Department and the city went through a terrible discrimination lawsuit prior to women being allowed to work patrol and other street duties. After a settlement was finally reached, a federal court order cleared the way for women. Even then, there was a concerted effort by many top managers within the department for women not to succeed. The leadership simply didn't think women belonged in police work—a harsh opinion shared at the time by leaders of most police agencies in the country.

In a lot of areas of the city, new foot beats were created for women down by the docks and the wharfs and along warehouse districts. Every time a woman stubbed her toe, a disciplinary action was brought up against her.

At the time, I was a lieutenant. My captain and I had been academy classmates back in 1964, and we thought a lot alike. He said, "Give the women the same jobs and opportunity that you would the male recruits." Which is what I did. Mind you, this sentiment was not widespread throughout the department. Had I found myself working in an adjacent police district, I might well have had to fight the captain in charge for not keeping my foot on the necks of the female patrol officers. We made the decision there would be no special foot beats, nothing special at all. It was difficult for many men in the department—it took them a while to understand that a woman could drive a squad car and pull out a gun and make an arrest as well as a man.

The first four women who showed up for patrol work in my platoon arrived with four male recruits from the same academy class. Two of the women turned out to be very good officers and two average. Of the men, two turned out real good, one average, and the fourth didn't belong in police work. From then until now, I've found no disparity in the success rate of men and women in policing.

We soon began teaming women together as partners, which

some cities were reluctant to do at the time. One night, two women partners on patrol—one later became a sergeant—radioed from the field for a sergeant. That usually meant something was up. I happened to be in the area, so I drove to their location.

When I arrived on the scene, the women officers had several beefy guys prone on the ground and one handcuffed in their patrol wagon. They had been called to the corner where we had been having a lot of purse snatchings after residents complained about loiterers. When the officers decided to clear the corner, the guys refused to budge and started giving them guff. At that point, the women officers ordered everyone to face the side of the building in a prone position. When a few objected, a brief scuffle ensued. The loudest guy was handcuffed and order was quickly established.

One of the women came up to me later at the station. "Lieutenant, did we use too much force tonight?"

"No," I said. "You did what was appropriate and nobody got hurt."

One thing we soon discovered about women in police work is their innate ability to resolve disputes and family-disturbance situations verbally and with body language. Female officers tend to police in a style that minimizes the use of excessive force—their rate of excessive-force complaints is substantially less than their male counterparts. This seems to be a natural skill for them, while male officers have more of a tendency to move up to the next step quicker, whether it's to grab somebody to arrest them or push them back or get into some type of physical contact. People have said it's because men have shorter fuses or because women don't want to fight. But I think it's just a matter of men and women being different. The aptitude for solving situations other than physically is simply one skill that women have over men.

When women officers were first assigned to patrol, some male officers weren't shy about voicing their opinion that women would end up shooting more people. Their reasoning was that if a woman officer couldn't subdue a bigger suspect when necessary, she would be quicker to reach for her gun and shoot. In fact, quite the opposite happened. We began to see right away— and continue to see today—fewer officer-involved shootings with women police officers than we do with their male counterparts.

It is a benefit to have police partners with varying attributes and skills, whether they be language or culture or gender differences. If you have two partners who are carbon copies of each other, they can miss finding a better way to handle a situation. Merging the distinct skills of partners usually results in their doing a better job as a team—one reason why diversity on a police force is so vital.

The LAPD had made some progress in hiring women and minorities since a 1981 court consent decree settling a civil rights lawsuit against the department. By 1992, blacks made up 14 percent and Hispanics 23 percent of LAPD's sworn officers, with women increasing from 2 percent in 1981 to 13 percent.

Still, more than 80 percent of all minority officers in the department were concentrated in the three lowest entry-level ranks. Women represented only 3 percent of officers with the rank of sergeant or above in the 7,800-member department. Although more minorities and women were now being hired than in the past, it would take time for the promotional "pool" to expand.

White dominance of LAPD managerial positions was cited by the Christopher Commission as one reason for the department's continued tolerance of discrimination and bias in the workplace and on the streets. The commission implored the department to continue its efforts at diversity, including recruiting other minorities, such as Asians, not covered by the consent decree.

In September 1992, the L.A. city council passed a package of sweeping measures that I fully supported:

- Making the police chief personally responsible for eliminating gender discrimination, gender bias, and sexual harassment in the department.

- Calling on the police department to make attitudes toward women an additional criterion in making hiring and promotional decisions.
- Increasing the ranks of women in the LAPD to 44 percent—equal to the percentage of women in the city's general workforce. No time limit was set to reach this figure, but I agreed with council members that we should have goals of increased female representation in every academy class. "We want to have [more] women police officers because they have a new style of policing: open communications, less use of force, and de-escalation of violence," said one council member. "I cannot recall one case of a female officer being involved in an excessive-force lawsuit," said another council member, who noted that the city annually pays tens of millions of dollars in settlements and court judgments in such cases. (The Christopher Commission had noted that none of the 120 LAPD officers most frequently charged with excessive use of force were women.)

A 1991 Police Foundation study found that police officers in Los Angeles kill or wound proportionately more civilians than police in any of the nation's other five largest cities. Many of us were hopeful that by having more women officers we could prevent some of these violent showdowns.

At my recommendation, the police commission had, two months earlier, lifted LAPD's ban on recruits over thirty-five years of age. A department study showed that older officers prompted fewer personnel complaints and were involved in fewer cases of excessive force and took fewer sick days.

Also at my urging, the department dropped inquiries during job interviews pertaining to sexual preference. Questions, as well as sections of the background checks, that had blocked gays and lesbians from consideration for police employment were eliminated. Asked by the media about this change in policy at a time when the U.S. government's dealing with gays in

99

the military had become so controversial, I said, "I could care less" about the sexual orientation of my officers. My view is that sexual orientation is neither a help nor a hindrance to becoming a police officer. What counts is performance on the job. I should add that my view on gays in policing has not won me universal support among the ranks of the Los Angeles Police Department.

All these discriminatory practices *had* to stop. I intended to see that our new officers, who would be serving well into the twenty-first century, would be black, brown, white, yellow, men, women, young, older, short, tall, straight, gay, you name it—a healthy diverse mix, just like the community we served. The makeup of the Los Angeles Police Department had to begin to reflect the ethnicity of the city it served. Some of my more conservative officers undoubtedly did not like me bringing this up, but if I didn't put it on the table and discuss it, who would?

In dealing with discrimination and bias within a police department, the leadership had to set the tone. From the chief on down, managers had to be clear in their message to subordinates as to what type of behavior would no longer be tolerated.

Numerous complaints of sexual harassment and gender bias within the department were being investigated when I assumed command of the LAPD. (Two of every five women responding to a survey of the L.A. city government's female workforce reported that they were subject to sexual harassment in their jobs within the past year.) In one case I vividly recall, an LAPD Board of Rights ended up ruling that a male officer who had allegedly pulled a woman officer's face into his crotch was not guilty of harassment because he had reportedly not derived gratification. This male officer was later suspended for different allegations involving the same woman officer.

Obviously, the problem was upon us as in the corporate world, yet the department had no formal training program in place to deal with it.

I assigned the training coordinator in our Behavioral Science unit the task of coming up with a full-day sexual-harassment training program that could be institutionalized by us. In other words, I didn't want it to be a onetime workshop put on by outside consultants who then departed. I wanted us to know how to put on such a program. By the end of 1993, we had a program that utilized experts from inside and outside the department.

Deciding we should start at the top, I sat in on the first class with my senior staff. Because there were no women in senior management positions in the LAPD, this group was all male. Even at this executive level, where everyone had to understand why we were there, a few individuals greeted rather lightly some of the anecdotal examples presented. The bad jokes only reinforced, in my mind, the absolute need for this type of training.

Undeniably, strong gender bias against women still exists in law enforcement today. There are police forces run by men today who have been very slow to admit that women can do the job. There are men in the ranks who still believe that women don't belong on the job, period. "They shouldn't be here because they are taking a job away from a man," says an insidious voice that may not be heard at roll call but is heard in the locker room. Then you have men who feel that if women do have the temerity to join the department, they have to become one of the boys and put up with cursing and off-color language and sexual innuendos. In comments both publicly and privately, I made it clear where I stood: "There's no place in this police department for males who feel they have to harass women."

Subsequent training sessions were conducted for ranks down to lieutenant and their civilian counterparts in the department. I led off many sessions with a personal message on the importance of this training. Everyone soon knew were I stood on the issue, but I couldn't be everyplace at all times. For such a policy to be effective, it had to have muscle behind it. The laws of the State of California and the force of the Office of the Chief of Police had to be behind the policy in the event violations took place.

When I told my captains, "You will be held accountable for

your actions and for the actions of your subordinates" in the workplace, I meant it. Not only did I need to get their attention and support, but they had to be prepared to follow through and give similarly clear messages to their personnel. Everyone had been put on notice through training and clear instructions from the top that they could no longer encourage or ignore such situations or claim they had no idea what to do about them when they did occur. From now on, supervisors who failed to deal with complaints and incidents of sexual harassment in the workplace would be disciplined.

No more would a manager be able to say dismissively, "Okay, I'll get back to you," and hope a difficult situation would just go away. Sexual harassment, we learned, seldom goes away on its own like the common cold. A victimized employee is left hoping that something is being done when nothing is being done. Eventually, the victim comes to feel that management is taking the offender's side. If the offender knows that the victim went to management, the fact that nothing happened sends the message that the offensive behavior can continue unchecked.

"It won't be just a case of being suspended or not being suspended. Such a situation on your watch may well impact your ability to be promoted," I warned my commanders. "It's going to impact on the types of future assignments you receive."

Sexual harassment training is now part of the curriculum for every recruit class at the LAPD academy. Whether addressing sexual harassment, gender bias, or other discrimination issues in the workplace, simply declaring a new policy isn't enough. It means changing all the procedures that blatantly or subtly supported or allowed these situations to exist. It means changing the department's reward system, personnel evaluation system, and testing system. The entire support structure has to be changed to send a signal that if you're involved in any such activity in the department, either directly or indirectly, it is not going to be condoned or winked at.

Each time I hear the old arguments about why women shouldn't be assigned to a certain detail, I am taken back to 1976, when some top law enforcement leaders firmly believed that women could not handle patrol work. You can laugh at the silliness of these assertions today, given the vast numbers of women who are handling patrol and other stressful duties in virtually every city in the country, yet those pioneering women officers back then were faced with much narrow-mindedness.

In fact, they faced worse. In Philadelphia, for example, the system that was set up to evaluate women on patrol as a result of the court case was doomed to fail. We were first told that we had to keep women recruits separate from male recruits, and that we had to keep all the recruits separate from the veterans. Supposedly, in this way we could measure the productivity and activity of male and female recruits separately. The problem—and it was a major one—was that rookie officers are not trained in isolation. They are best put with veteran training officers for a time to learn the ropes on the street.

Most of us knew that regardless of the outcome of this ridiculous study, women in police work were here to stay. Frankly, I don't know what happened to the study. Being only a lieutenant at the time, word didn't get down to me. But I do know that in short order we started integrating women into regular assignments in our district and eventually throughout the city, allowing them—as well as the male rookies—to work with trained officers.

When I joined the police department, a recruit had to be at least five foot eight and weigh 160 pounds. Size, brute strength, and physical deterrents were the signals that police departments sent out. But as big as an officer might be, there are always going to be bad guys bigger and stronger. What we came to realize through the years is that you don't need to be a combat Marine to be a successful police officer. Granted, there will always be a place on the force for ex-Marine types, because there will always be those types of jobs to do. But day in and day out, we want police officers on the streets who bring something else to the job, such as good social skills and the ability to communicate and use personal interaction to defuse potentially serious situations.

As chief, I want officers in my department who are more interested in serving the public than in jumping over buildings in a single leap. With community policing as our call to arms, we need officers who understand that 85 percent of their job involves delivering services to the public. Twenty-five years ago we didn't recruit officers to help community people to sandblast graffiti, to investigate abandoned vehicles in the neighborhood, to help teach kids in grammar school and junior high how to remain drug-free, to work with our Jeopardy program trying to keep youths out of street gangs, or to assist concerned families trying to get their kids out of gangs. These are some of the things we are doing today. They are a major part of the job when it comes to being a police officer in America—big cities and small cities alike.

Training is key. A lot of what police officers do every day is using skills that can be taught, such as dexterity, leverage, and knowing how to maintain a tactical edge. We don't get in all the knock-down-drag-out fights that the public, from watching TV police shows, thinks we do. We do have our scuffles, however, and we do find ourselves having to "convince" people to walk calmly along. How we usually accomplish this is by our demeanor and bearing, determining factors in achieving compliance without having to use physical force. Through the years, we have found ways to teach all this to our smaller employees; eventually, height and weight requirements were dropped by all police departments due to persistent legal challenges.

In teaching our people how to compensate for their size, we have given them effective nonlethal weapons to use when appropriate. We have also instilled in them that lack of size and fear of getting beat up are not acceptable excuses for whipping out their service revolver and firing away.

In 1971, then-LAPD-chief Ed Davis was reported to have

told a stunned audience of one hundred women officers that they didn't belong in patrol cars and couldn't be trusted with guns during "that time of the month." The LAPD, at the time, prohibited women officers from working patrol, limiting them to handling juvenile offenders or working in women's jails. It wasn't until a year later (1972) that the LAPD was forced by federal legislation to assign women officers to patrol.

Today, there is no job in a police department that a woman cannot do. Throughout the country, we have women chiefs and sheriffs, women working homicides, women in bomb squads, SWAT, and canine units, women divers, helicopter pilots, you name it.

Yet I fought for two years to get women into SWAT, our elite Special Weapons and Tactics unit. The LAPD was the originator of SWAT more than twenty years ago, but not a single woman had ever served in the unit. Yes, SWAT members need to run fast and shoot proficiently and have nerves of steel when facing down armed suspects. I knew all that, and certainly, there were many women in the LAPD so qualified. A few women had applied to SWAT previously, to no avail. Finally, I was able to order a qualified woman officer into SWAT to settle a work grievance she had filed. I'm sure she would have done a good job in SWAT had she not left the department prior to starting that assignment. I'm looking forward to more women seeking entry into this most elite unit in the Los Angeles Police Department.

I must admit to my own double standard. If my daughter, Lisa, expressed an interest in law enforcement as a career, I'm afraid I would feel required to tell her some things I did not need to tell my son Will before he joined the Philadelphia Police Department. I'd let Lisa know that she was considering a field where, because of her gender, she would not, in some quarters, receive 100 percent immediate acceptance or respect.

I'd tell her there were still mountains to climb.

On the afternoon of December 14, 1992, at the very intersection where the riots had started seven months earlier, a demonstration in support of the four gang members accused in the Reginald Denny beating turned ugly.

The small demonstration at Florence and Normandie had started out peacefully enough, with members of the defendants' families and some friends handing out leaflets and being careful not to block traffic. Then, a large group of observers—including known gang members—who had been drinking and who were not part of the demonstrations, began occupying the four corners of the intersection. They taunted police, who were monitoring the demonstration, and began throwing rocks and bottles at passing vehicles. A passenger in a pickup truck was injured when an object smashed through the vehicle's rear window and struck him in the head.

Shortly after 3 P.M., a crowd of about one hundred blocked traffic at the intersection and continued pelting police and passersby with rocks and bottles.

The crowd dispersed under police pressure only to regroup two or three times. Reports came in that a roving band was battering a service station at the intersection. The windows in the station's office were broken, and the crowd looted the place before withdrawing in front of approaching police. There was also a report of a city fire department ambulance being pelted with rocks and stones a short distance away.

A swift and massive show of force was necessary to let the individuals involved, as well as the city at large, know that we would not tolerate civil disorder. We called a citywide tactical alert, a state of readiness in which officers handle only high-priority calls and need permission to leave at the end of their shifts. Officers arriving for later shifts are deployed as needed throughout the city. This enabled us to flood the affected area with more than 350 officers, with another 200 remaining nearby on alert.

I stayed in close contact with the commander on the scene, Deputy Chief Matthew Hunt. The agitators were not showing any signs of calming down. Quite the contrary, they seemed intent on trying to touch off another riot.

106

"Chief, it's getting out of control," Hunt reported. "We're now in two blocks."

I knew we couldn't afford to wait and see if things cooled down on their own. Not here, not anywhere on the streets of Los Angeles. Not now, not at any time.

The previous spring, the department had ordered officers to retreat from this same intersection and did not make a timely show of force, which may have cost the department the chance to confine the disorder to a relatively limited area. A tactical alert was not declared at the first sign of trouble and was delayed for hours. We would do things differently this time around.

"Matt, shut the area down," I ordered.

Within minutes, with police helicopters lighting the way, police units had cordoned off the streets around the intersection. Vans loaded with officers from our elite Metropolitan Division emptied out, and Metro personnel undertook a street-by-street sweep, arresting lawbreakers and dispersing the crowd as they went.

In facing down the unruly crowd, Metro used our newest option in crowd dispersal: the rubber bullets. Five rounds—cylindrical projectiles about an inch and a half long that resemble chunks of sausage—are contained in each cartridge fired from a .37-millimeter gas gun. Officers aim the weapon at the ground and allow the rounds, nicknamed knee knockers, to ricochet into the crowd. I am told it feels like being belted by a hard-hit squash ball. Typically, one or two officers in a squad of ten carries one of the weapons as they approach a crowd. The other officers carry batons, handguns, and other traditional firearms.

I went to the South Bureau emergency command center around nightfall. In addition to coordinating our overall response and maintaining contact with my field commanders, I was also briefing city officials on the incident.

Though the situation remained volatile for several hours more, I was satisfied that we had plenty of personnel and resources in the area to do the job. The crowd had been dispersed, arrests were made, and we had control of the situation—all accomplished without having to use more firepower than rubber bullets.

At a makeshift press conference, I described our response as swift, efficient, and professional. To a question as to whether I thought the department may have "overreacted," I pointedly suggested that our performance this day be compared with what took place during the riots.

"This time," I added, "it worked the way it is supposed to."

I was pleased that the media were generally restrained in their reporting of the disturbance, with television focusing primarily on the show of police force.

We made fifty-five arrests and there were no serious injuries on either side.

The Los Angeles Police Department was back.

CHAPTER FIVE

Tens of thousands of Angelenos discovered during the riots that if they called 911, they might not get through. The city also learned the hard way that Los Angeles police officers, in need of quick backup, couldn't depend on the field communication system to link them to their stations or to ask for help from neighboring law enforcement agencies like the sheriff's department.

The 911 and police communications networks were in crisis—not just during unusual occurrences but day in and day out. Every day, we were losing hundreds of emergency calls. Everyone's worst nightmare had arrived for some: Dial 911 in a crisis—a fire, a flood, a heart attack, an intruder—and get put on hold for ten minutes, if you can get through at all.

The LAPD's 911 and dispatch system was housed in a fourth-level subbasement in city hall, which could easily become inaccessible in the event of a major earthquake or other natural disaster. It was equipped with only twelve dedicated telephone lines for 911 calls, connected to a computer system that had operated beyond capacity for the entire eight years of its existence. Callers frequently were put on hold or got a busy signal not just during riots or earthquakes but virtually every evening. In a disaster or another civil disturbance, we feared that the 911 system and the entire police radio network would break down.

The Webster Commission, investigating the police response to the riots, verified that the failure of police and emergency communications contributed directly to the loss of life and destruction of property that occurred. At crucial moments, the LAPD could not talk to itself, and the public could not reach the police.

In a city as spread out as Los Angeles, with a police force that was acknowledged to be too small for the area and population it served, a failure to communicate meant that the limited officers who were available could not be deployed to the highest-priority trouble spots.

While Los Angeles is the nation's second-largest city, its police department is one of the smallest in the ratio of officers to population, making it the most underpoliced major city in America. With a force of 7,800, the LAPD had 2.2 officers for every 1,000 people (1992). At the same time, New York City had more than 27,000 officers, or 3.8 officers per 1,000 people. Chicago had more than 12,400 officers, or 4.1 per 1,000. Philadelphia, 3.9 per 1,000.

In high-density Philadelphia, patrol officers complained if they had to cover more than fifteen or twenty blocks during their shift. They would not fathom the distance that one LAPD squad car is responsible for covering—in some cases, eight or ten *miles*. This is why all LAPD patrol cars have two officers— emergency backup could be many miles and five or ten minutes away. In contrast, cruisers in Philadelphia are all solo cars, with backup no more than seconds or, at the most, a few minutes away.

There are sections of Los Angeles that a police car may not patrol for twenty-four to forty-eight hours. If there isn't a call to a neighborhood, three or four shifts might not have the chance to cruise through it because they are being pulled by calls some-place else.

The LAPD, always undermanned, had never been allowed to grow to its optimum size, which should be between 12,000 and 14,000 officers. And realistically, this was not going to happen anytime soon. Yet we had to increase just as soon as possible to between 10,000 and 10,500—no ifs, ands, or buts about it. That would allow us to do some basic policing in our sprawling, thinly policed city with a few extras, such as moving forward effec-tively with our community-policing program.

Two propositions went on the November (1992) ballot—one to

finance a new 911 and police communications system, and the other to raise property taxes to provide for as many as one thousand new police officers. I campaigned for both propositions.

The measure to create a dedicated trust fund to hire, train, and equip one thousand new uniformed officers was to be paid for with about an $85-per-year increase in the property tax for the typical homeowner. Combined with other reorganization and redeployment steps I was taking, this influx of new personnel would result in an 18 percent increase in the number of uniformed officers available for patrol.

"We are going to move ahead with community-based policing in Los Angeles to improve our ability to deter and fight crime," I promised the citizens. "One thousand more officers will make this approach more effective, increasing the visibility and responsiveness of our police where it really counts."

I was careful not to tie community policing too tightly to economics. In good or bad financial times in any city, you can have successful community policing if you know what the people in various neighborhoods want and if you make the nonmonetary adjustments you can to meet those needs. Community policing is not a luxury. In fact, in a very real sense it is getting more bang for your buck.

Granted, you cannot be as successful with community policing if you don't have some of the necessary resources—particularly in an organization whose strength in numbers, physical equipment, and technological resources have been allowed to decline, as they had in the LAPD. But in my view, you cannot use a lack of financial backing as an excuse for not doing certain things. Whenever I hear, "We don't have the money for community policing," it tells me that the leadership is simply unwilling to try.

The measure to add the new officers received well over 50 percent of the vote, but fell just short of the two-thirds required for passage. If we were going to put new uniformed officers on the street, we would have to pay for them in some way other than by raising taxes. In other words, we would have to get very creative.

The good news was that the 911 proposition was approved. The resulting $180 million bond would enable us to build new police communications dispatch and 911 centers in the San Fernando Valley and on the west side. We would turn the old city hall center into a backup with upgraded equipment during the five to eight years it would take to complete this major overhaul of police communications.

Not only was gaining an influx of new officers out of the question at the time, the department, still stuck under the hiring freeze, was *losing* personnel at the alarming rate of approximately four hundred a year to retirement and normal attrition. (A portion of the latter went to work for suburban police departments that offered higher pay and better working conditions.) In other words, the already undersized LAPD was *shrinking* at the rate of about 5 percent a year.

For months, I lobbied the mayor and city council for the hiring freeze to be lifted from the department. In spite of the public's fear of rising crime and the demonstrated desire of a clear majority of residents to have a greater police presence on the streets even at the cost of increased taxes—as well as the city's own goals to hire more women and minorities to better reflect the city's diversity— the hiring freeze remained in place. As we continued to lose officers through retirement and attrition, by January 1993, the number of sworn personnel was down to 7,550.

Granted a minor concession, I had been given authority to hire, in September 1992, exactly thirty-one recruit cadets—a single academy class, funded with existing dollars from savings found in the department's budget.

My sixth month on the job I returned about ninety officers to patrol. In a department the size of the LAPD, this is an insignificant number—yet it was a start. With the public clamoring for increased police visibility, I transferred forty officers from nonuniform assignments and fifty from specialized functions. The hue and cry could be heard throughout the department and even in parts of the community. To everyone who protested, I asked the same question: "Don't we want more uniformed police officers on the streets?" Yes, most agreed, then added, "But why me?" or "Find them somewhere else." But with the department unable to hire, additional patrol officers had to come from *some* place.

One officer complained, "Now I'm back answering radio calls. I was doing a better job in my other unit."

"No one said you weren't working over there," I answered.

Although the headlines reported "Williams to Put Desk Jockeys Back on the Street," these weren't desk jockeys. They all had been doing the job they were told to do. Yet some tough decisions had to be made.

As it was now, all we could do was bare-bones, no-frills policing. Without the manpower to do the job, we were like one of those cut-rate stores where you have to bring paper sacks and bag your own groceries.

A further complication was that contract talks between the city and the police labor union were stalled. As far as I could tell, in the six months since the police contract had expired, there had been no serious attempt by the city to settle the dispute. The city claimed it had no money to offer in the way of raises to *any* city workers. The city wanted police officers to forgo a pay increase and, in some instances, even pushed for givebacks of benefits won by labor in previous contracts.

As I had feared, the labor standoff was eroding department morale. To the men and women of the LAPD, working without a contract and not having their employer make any serious attempts to negotiate told them that the city didn't care much about them. Nothing anyone said changed their minds. As for the new chief who spent so much time in the community, many in the rank and file complained, Why wasn't *he* helping us get a contract?

They wanted me to come out swinging, blast the mayor and the city council, and win a pay raise for them. Unfortunately, city labor negotiations aren't that simple. I did tell anyone and everyone who would listen that my officers deserved a substantial pay raise, but beyond that there was little I could do. The LAPD chief—whether it is me or Daryl Gates or Bill Parker—has no authority to negotiate over salary or other money issues. The same is true in every major city in the country.

All city appropriations in Los Angeles are decided by the fifteen-member city council, to whom the mayor must submit his annual budget every spring. The police department's budget and the operating budgets for other city departments are included in the mayor's budget. In fact, I am authorized to spend no more than $2,000 on any item not provided for in my department budget. I cannot order the purchase of ten bullet-proof vests at $300 each for the Wilshire Division unless they're in my budget.

Though the men and women of the department couldn't help but be disillusioned and even angered by the lack of progress in the labor talks, neither they nor I could do much other than continue to do our jobs and hope for an equitable settlement in the not-too-distant future.

Also undercutting morale was that promotions inside the department had been halted with the city's hiring freeze. After hounding the mayor and council, I was finally granted authority to fill key management positions from within the department and to promote more than three hundred officers who had been awaiting advancement, some more than a year.

The new year found the LAPD committed to improving police services and to preparing a nerve-shattered city for the new trials that many thought would result in more rioting, all while our hard-pressed officers worked without a labor contract and an under-manned department strained at the bit under a hiring freeze.

Welcome to big-city policing.

Fear can be as contagious as the plague.

By the spring of 1993, public fear had reached epidemic proportions in the city of Los Angeles.

The second trial of the four police officers accused in the Rodney King beating had begun in early February at the federal courthouse two blocks from Parker Center. As April came and the civil rights trial sped to its conclusion, everyone knew that the decision would soon be in the hands of another jury. With the damage done to people and property in the last riot still vividly etched in everyone's memory, that expectation translated into increased tension and pessimism citywide.

Residents of the South Central L.A. neighborhoods that had suffered the worst a year ago were afraid of losing what was left—the businesses burned to the ground in the last riot had not been rebuilt; the only thing left to burn was residential property. In areas that had been spared last time, people lived in fear of its being their turn.

The high level of anxiety gripping the city was compounded by the media. On the ten o'clock news one night, three Korean merchants with semiautomatic weapons were interviewed in their stores. Another story showed a number of white women practicing at a downtown L.A. gun range. The racial implications of these stark images were obvious.

The next day, I called the TV station. "Don't you understand this is fear compounding fear?"

"But it's a fact," the news producer said.

"What is the message you're sending people?"

"That they might want to buy a gun to arm and protect themselves," he answered righteously.

"You're helping to create fear and mass hysteria that a riot or race war is going to break out and that people will have to protect themselves."

In anticipation of the "next riot," the press had descended on Los Angeles like hungry locusts. Five hundred to a thousand worldwide media representatives were in town, practically tripping over one another as they canvassed the city for stories. As the last riot had been unexpected, the media had been caught off guard. This time, every major news outlet was determined to be staffed and in position to cover the story that they were certain would unfold: L.A. on fire again. In the meantime, every TV reporter wanted to do a "stand-up" in front of Parker Center or the federal courthouse or a burned-out building. Or better yet, get an on-the-street exclusive with some idiot gang member who would brag, "Yeah, man, we're gonna do it again." Such sensational images were broadcast around the world.

Los Angeles, according to the national press, was "a city in a race with time," "wracked with anxiety," and "braced for trouble." *Time* warned of the "armies of idle and restless men" who might again set the city afire if the new verdicts were "not to their liking."

Everyone, it seemed, was preparing for the *next* riot. Friends told one another of elaborate preparations for protecting themselves or for fleeing the city at the first hint of new violence. People were continuing to buy guns by the thousands every week. Walls and barricades were being built around homes and places of business. People were making open airline reservations to visit family or relatives around the time they thought the trial would end. Out-of-towners were canceling trips to L.A. as the time for the verdict approached.

Attendance at community meetings at which I was scheduled to speak months in advance would normally be expected to draw between fifty to a hundred people. Now the crowds ballooned to five hundred to a thousand, with the frightened and concerned residents packed in so tightly that latecomers could hardly squeeze inside.

At one meeting in Porter Ranch—located in our Devonshire Division in the far northwest corner of the city—I faced fifteen hundred local residents who wanted my assurance that the LAPD was ready and prepared for any eventuality.

Before a standing-room-only crowd of five hundred in Sherman Oaks, my message was one of reassurance—"this department will never, ever again perform in such a way that you lose faith in it"—coupled with stern warnings that down the road the city needed to find ways to fund the hiring and training of more police officers in order to provide adequate law enforcement. I told of the extra training and field exercises that had been conducted to prepare the LAPD in case there was trouble after the new verdicts were announced. "I want to assure you that this department has heard your awakening call."

At a packed luncheon in the San Fernando Valley I was asked the question that seemed to be on the minds of a lot of residents in predominantly white neighborhoods: "Are the black street gangs planning to come into the Valley and finish what they started last time?"

"You're asking if they're going to come across the hills and through the dales as in the nursery rhyme?" I asked rhetorically.

There were a few chuckles.

"No, the gangs aren't planning to come over here. In fact, they seldom leave their own neighborhoods, where most of their real victims live. But I suppose some people would advocate that we should build the Berlin Wall along the crest of the Santa Monica Mountains so that distant street gangs can't get into the Valley. Let's see, we could blockade the San Diego and Hollywood Freeways. You could make your last line of defense Ventura Boulevard."

Of course it was absurd, and by then, most everyone was sharing in the laugh, though many nervously.

I also went to South Central L.A., where I found the greatest fear yet. Significantly, the fear I found so prevalent here had not been widely reported by the media. It was on these streets where the worst of the anarchy had taken place, yet the vast majority of residents were law-abiding citizens trying to raise families. They feared for their lives and the lives of their loved ones in the event of new riots, and also for the few possessions they owned.

Most of the property destroyed in the last riot had been businesses and commercial properties not owned by the local residents. Yet these stores had been the source of jobs, food, clothing, shoe repairs, and many other products and services that a neighborhood takes for granted until they are gone. The majority of these homes and the personal property inside them were not covered by insurance, as the commercial properties had been. If these folks were burned out, where would they live and how would they replace their belongings?

The city as a whole sensed grave danger ahead.

We had worked out elaborate plans with the fire department to provide motorcycle escorts for its emergency vehicles responding to fires or other calls. In the event of a riot, firefighters would receive police protection—unlike last time—while working to save lives and property.

At a city hall news conference called by Mayor Bradley the first week of April, I provided a highly unusual public briefing on the LAPD's plan for quelling any civil disturbances that might break out at the close of the second trial of the four police officers. I had a dual purpose: to calm rising tensions among residents, and to deter any individuals who were contemplating violence.

I revealed there would be a massive deployment of most of our 6,500 officers assigned to around-the-clock street duty across the city as soon as jury deliberations began instead of waiting for the verdicts to be announced.

"If an officer is shot at," I warned, "we will return fire." In cases where deadly force was not called for, I explained how we had equipped officers with less-than-lethal tools and equipment—including pepper spray and rubber bullets—to disperse unruly crowds where we didn't want to use guns or wade in with batons flying.

I reiterated how nearly every officer had undergone sixteen hours of unusual-occurrence training in which they learned special tactics for dealing with mobs, looting, fires, and other riot-related problems.

For the umpteenth time, I told the public not to expect the worst, as we did not anticipate a rerun of last year's riots. "Take it easy, we're here," I said. "We're not going to fail you this time."

The message that this chief of police and the LAPD were

delivering to the residents of Los Angeles about the possibility for renewed rioting was very clear: "Not in L.A., not this time."

On April 9, the civil rights case went to the jury. The next day, I ordered a heightened state of readiness for the department, canceling days off and redeploying staff to bolster police presence by putting about one-third more officers on the streets citywide.

As the days passed while the jury deliberated, things did not come to a standstill. I telephoned the mayor's office and asked for help in calling a meeting of ministers, explaining, "I'd like to meet with the ministers before this weekend to get the word out about what we're doing."

The mayor's aide promised to bring together about thirty or forty black ministers.

"No, no," I protested, "not just black ministers. I need the rabbis, the priests, the monks, the leaders from the mosques. *Everybody.*"

When a community is trying to pull together, it helps if there are natural leaders already in place. One of the big differences between the two cities where I had managed the police department was that in Philadelphia there was a cadre of black, white, and Hispanic community leaders who were quick to come forward in a crisis at any time of the day or night and who could, if necessary, mobilize tens of thousands of residents from all walks of life: ministers, doctors, lawyers, street people, you name it. I didn't see as many leaders in Los Angeles who were as close to the pulse of the city. Here, with everything so spread out and many residents enjoying a more laid-back lifestyle, events and people seem more disconnected.

In the beginning, I had wondered why the people of Los Angeles were looking to the police chief to address so many of their concerns that had little to do with policing. *Hey, wait a minute,* I had thought with some irritation. *This isn't the chief's job.* Since then, I had come to accept my stand-in role in the sizable vacuum that existed. Anyone who could do anything to help keep Los Angeles calm in the spring of 1993 had to try.

A day or two later, I met with a hundred religious leaders at the West Angeles Church of God and Christ.

I addressed directly the fears and rumors.

"The people in South Central L.A. and East L.A. are as scared to death of another riot as the folks in San Fernando Valley and West L.A.," I said. "We are in this together, and together we will get through it."

I assured them that the LAPD was not favoring any one section of the city with increased patrols, but that we were prepared to uphold law and order citywide. I told them of all the specialized training the department had conducted in the past months and of the extensive plans we had begun to carry out as soon as the jury received the case.

"Nobody told us this before," said one minister.

I nodded. "That's why I'm here."

I asked the ministers of every faith to spread the word to their flocks over the weekend—to plead with their followers to help in any way they could to keep their neighborhoods calm and peaceful while rejecting the anger and divisiveness that had ripped L.A. apart a year earlier.

We had an elaborate system set up with officers observing quite a few potential "hot spots" to see that things stayed calm. Ironically, one corner we didn't have to worry much about was Florence and Normandie. With about five dozen TV-camera trucks parked at the corner, it was probably about the most observed and photographed intersection in the United States about then. Anyone who stepped foot in the intersection to commit a crime would be on live national television.

With all the increased police presence on the streets, it was a very bad week to commit a crime in Los Angeles. There was one liquor store that had been robbed four or five times. And when three or four guys went in and robbed it again, they ran headlong into eight or ten uniformed police officers who happened to be in the area.

Statistics showed that street violence citywide dropped dramatically during the first five days of jury deliberations. Homicides were down 20 percent, and assaults and robberies each fell 10 percent. The message was obvious. If you hire more officers and put them in uniform on the streets—in cars, on foot beats, on bicycles, wherever they were needed—you *can* make a community safer. You *can* reduce crime.

We had worked out an unprecedented arrangement with the federal court to receive advance notice of the verdicts. The department would not be told whether the police officers were guilty or not guilty, only that an announcement was imminent. This time, we would have a chance to move to the highest degree of readiness and position our forces throughout the city.

Just before 4 P.M. on Friday, April 16, a member of the federal judge's staff called Parker Center and spoke to one of my top commanders. I received the word minutes later: An announcement would be made by the court the following morning at 7 A.M.

An "announcement" did not necessarily mean there were going to be verdicts in the case, but we were not going to quibble at this point. We would be ready.

I immediately called a citywide tactical alert. All police officers at work would be kept on duty so that when the next shift reported to work, we could increase our uniformed presence on the streets that evening.

At 8 P.M., Mayor Bradley made a televised address from city hall, asking the residents of Los Angeles to accept the verdicts with calmness and reason.

In the previous months, the mayor, who had already announced that he would not run for reelection in June 1993, had personally kicked off a "neighbor-to-neighbor" program, with thousands of residents going door-to-door organizing neighborhoods. The idea was to ensure that all over the city people would be on their porches and sidewalks when the trial ended, declaring ownership of their neighborhoods and helping to keep the peace—not as vigilantes, but as concerned residents working in partnership, when necessary, with police.

Cement barricades were pushed into position by tractors in front of Parker Center. Barricades also went up in front of the Foothill Division, where the four defendants in the civil rights trial had been assigned the night of the Rodney King beating.

As night fell, patrol units in all parts of the city reported the streets calm, but everyone was tense.

Did a gathering of youths at a corner in South Central portend anything ominous? It turned out to be nothing. When a police car was fired on from a housing project, we held our collective breath. It was an isolated event, however, and the officer wasn't hurt.

By nine o'clock, it was clear that everything was going to be all right that night. It was as if the city had gone on autopilot. But what would happen tomorrow morning?

Too keyed up to go home, I had my driver, Officer Kerry Anderson, cruise through Rampart Division. Situated on the edge of downtown Los Angeles, Rampart encompasses only eight square miles but is home to half a million residents, many of them first-generation immigrants from Central and South America.

Monitoring the police communications channel, we heard a domestic-disturbance call involving a man with a gun. We pulled up to the location shortly after two uniformed officers had entered the residence. I think it startled them when they turned around and saw the chief walk in the door. For a moment, I was afraid my presence would take their minds off what they were there to do.

Staying in the background, I watched as they deftly took control of the situation. The quarreling couple were separated, each taken to a different part of the house. A backup unit arrived. An officer who spoke Spanish obtained enough information to locate the handgun in the bedroom. The husband was eventually taken into custody.

I stuck around after the call was cleared and chatted with five or six officers at curbside—all of them had gone through our special riot training. Knowing that they were to remain on duty after their shift ended, they were a little nervous and tense about what tomorrow would bring.

"I think everything is going to be all right tomorrow," I offered. "If there's a problem, we're ready."

These officers had in the trunks of their vehicles ballistic helmets and flak jackets—just in case. They let me know how glad they were to have the extra protective gear, which had been handed out just days earlier.

For years, the department had used standard police-issue riot helmets made of hard plastic, which were adequate for stopping rocks and bottles but not bullets. During the riots, the rank and file had little confidence in their lightweight helmets. The SWAT unit had Army-like ballistic helmets, which could stop a bullet. I made the decision, not long after I arrived at LAPD, that the rest of the force needed them, too. We put together a team of rank-and-file officers to study the marketplace and decide for themselves which helmet would best meet our needs. With the help of our technical and research people, they tested the helmets by firing various-caliber bullets at them. They ended up picking not the cheapest helmet, but the second or third most expensive. The company that manufactured them was partially foreign-owned, and the competing companies started raising Cain, holding up the contract. When it became clear that we were not going to have the helmets in time for the second King trial (it ended up taking fifteen months to acquire them), we had gone to the California National Guard and borrowed five thousand ballistic helmets.

Having them told the men and women of the LAPD that somebody did care about them. Knowing they had the right equipment would also give them more confidence in their ability to perform their job under the most difficult circumstances.

But I wanted to make a point to the Rampart officers. "You know, the best day is when we don't have to use any of our extra training or equipment," I said. "No matter what the verdict is tomorrow, if you don't have to put on that helmet and flak jacket, it will be a good day."

The officers nodded. Most of them were young. The veteran among them probably had eight or nine years on the job. I told them they had done well this evening, and that I knew they would do just as well tomorrow.

As my driver and I left, I had to chuckle, knowing that no sooner would we turn the corner than an excited call would go out to the sergeant to let him know that "Staff One," or whatever pet name they had for me, was nosing around.

We drove west for a while, showing up at the Wilshire District station, where they had already set up an emergency field command post in the parking lot. I spoke to the commander there, and some of the supervisors who were busily checking out the emergency communications gear.

Then, we headed into the Seventy-seventh Division, fourteen square miles of South Central L.A., which had seen most of the violence and damage during the 1992 riots. When we arrived at the station, it was a typically busy Friday night. Four or five prisoners were handcuffed to a hallway bench awaiting processing. Whenever prisoners recognize the chief of police, they almost always start yelling about why they shouldn't be there. This group was no different.

I attended the morning-watch roll call, which, unfortunately, represented only eight or nine officers. Scenes like this illustrated for me how terribly undermanned the LAPD was.

These officers, I could see, were on edge, too. They also knew they would not be going home until after whatever was going to happen tomorrow happened.

"We're ready this time," I said in my brief comments. "By tomorrow morning, we'll have everyone on the street. No one in this department from the chief on down has a day off. Everyone is working. In the event we need mutual aid, the sheriff's department is ready and so is the National Guard."

After roll call, I rode around some more, answering a few more routine calls. In truth, the chief was as much on edge as his police force. Driving around, answering radio calls, attending roll calls, talking to my officers and supervisors—it was the best therapy possible for me.

I finally got home after midnight. I didn't get much sleep, as I set my alarm clock for 3:30 A.M. By 5:15 A.M., I was back in the car heading for my office.

On the way, I spoke by phone to Assistant Chief Frank Piersol, who had spent the night at our downtown emergency command center. All was quiet, Piersol reported.

When I got to the office, I made sure the coffeepot was turned on, then went to my desk and busied myself with paperwork as I listened to my favorite jazz station.

At 6:50 A.M., ten minutes before the court was to make its announcement, my senior staff gathered around the television in my office to hear the news with me.

All over the city, residents were in front of TVs and radios waiting to hear the verdicts.

In churches, they prayed.

On the streets and in staging areas throughout the city, thousands of police had been mobilized in the largest show of police force in the city's history.

In front of the courthouse, hundreds of reporters and photographers waited for the big story.

No morning, it was reported in the *Los Angeles Times*, had carried more dread—"no other moment in the long, fractured history of Los Angeles had arrived so pregnant with the fear of war on the streets."

Then, live from the courtroom: "We the jury in the above entitled cause find the defendant, Stacey Koon, guilty . . . the defendant, Laurence Powell, guilty . . ."

The other two officers were acquitted.

Some in the community would call it justice, or at least partial justice, while others would decry it as no justice at all. Those judgments didn't concern me.

I was told later that my only visible reaction to the verdicts, as I jotted them down on a notepad, was that I arched an eyebrow briefly. The only thing that interested me now: How would the city respond?

All those guns—the thousands stolen during the riots and the many thousands sold since—were still out there. The anger, the rumors, the racial tension, it all went into the same simmering pot.

How would the city respond?

A few minutes later, looking out my sixth-floor window, I saw a number of helicopters circling tightly above the courthouse, which was surrounded by forty-five television broadcast vans. At one point, it looked as if there would be a midair collision, so anxious were the news crews to get pictures of the crowd—mostly more reporters and photographers—on the courthouse steps.

Despite nonstop requests from the media for an interview, I decided not to make any statement until events that day became more clear. So far, things remained quiet.

At 9:40 A.M., I went across the street to city hall for an emergency meeting of the Emergency Operations Board, which I chaired. Normally, I would have walked, but today I drove to avoid the horde of reporters.

At the board meeting, representatives from each city department reported that everything was okay. The only question came from the department in charge of parking tickets: "At what point do you think it's going to be proper for us to start writing parking tickets again?"

With the overflow of media covering the trial, downtown parking had been a mess for months. To accommodate all the official visitors, we had put a moratorium on parking tickets and vehicle towings in certain areas.

"Probably sometime Monday would be fine," I suggested.

Everyone laughed, which seemed to let off some of the pressure in the room. After all, if the city's Emergency Operations Board was dealing with parking tickets on the day verdicts in the second Rodney King trial were announced, how bad could things be?

Shortly before 11 A.M., I joined Mayor Bradley for a televised press conference.

"Chief, what would you suggest to the people of Los Angeles on how they should spend the rest of their weekend?" one reporter asked. "Should they stay home?"

"I think the men and women of Los Angeles should go about their daily lives," I responded. "Go to the movies, go shopping, go to the beach, have a barbecue. They should do whatever they were planning and enjoy themselves on what looks like a nice day."

I next took a ride through Koreatown. People were out and about, filling up their cars at the corner gas station, going to Pizza Hut—a normal Saturday afternoon.

I got out of the car and walked, stopping at a few businesses to say hello. Everyone seemed pleased that the chief of police had taken the time to come here, where so many residents and business owners had felt badly betrayed by the LAPD during the riots. I hoped that my presence here today would be a strong symbol that the people of this community were not going to be forgotten.

At one mom-and-pop dry cleaners, a boy of seven or eight looked up at me and said something to his mother in their native language.

"He wants to know if you are Dr. Martin Luther King," she said, smiling.

"No," I said, introducing myself and hoping that I didn't let the boy down too much. "I remember Dr. King when I was a young boy about your age. He was a great man who believed in nonviolence."

Midafternoon, I began visiting police stations.

The day Los Angeles had dreaded for months had turned out to be unusually calm. The rank and file were as relieved as I that things were quiet. Pressing the flesh and taking turns posing for pictures with the troops felt good. I had spent all my adult life as a police officer, and being here at the station house was where I felt most at home. I had never asked an officer to do something that I hadn't done myself or hadn't been willing to do. When they succeeded, it was my success as well, just as when they failed, it was my failure. Today had been a good day—we could all pat each other on the back and take snapshots as if we were at commencement ceremonies.

In a sense, we had graduated.

A police department can never really prevent a riot from happening. It can limit the loss of lives and property, however, by responding quickly and effectively.

No riot had broken out this day. But had one started, the LAPD would have been ready. The message that we were ready had gotten out to the community at large.

The press encamped throughout Los Angeles ended up giving thorough coverage to a disaster that didn't happen. They had no choice, really, although some media outlets were more willing than others to accept the responsibility to show good news as well as bad. (Ted Koppel, who in my opinion is one of the two best interviewers on television—the other being Bryant Gumbel—headlined his April 23, 1993, *Nightline* show from Los Angeles "What Went Right.")

On the streets of Los Angeles, people were downright giddy. On the way home around 7 P.M., I pulled over on Crenshaw Boulevard to speak to a city councilman I had noticed was out of his car. My standing on the sidewalk in full view of the oncoming traffic practically caused a major standstill.

Car horns blasted; people waved, whistled, and hollered as if celebrating a citywide sports victory.

"Good job, Chief!"

"Way to go, LAPD!"

For some reason, I recalled at that moment the comments of a longtime police commander in Philadelphia at his retirement dinner: "I've had a front-row seat for the greatest show on earth during my thirty years in law enforcement." He was right. There was nothing like it.

This day was my first anniversary of sorts, as it had been

announced that I would become the new Los Angeles police chief exactly one year ago. The intervening 365 days had made up the busiest year of my life.

I knew I could go home, lay my head down, and sleep well tonight, feeling good about the community and feeling great about the Los Angeles Police Department.

The best day is when we don't have to use any of our extra training or equipment. If you don't have to put on that helmet and flak jacket, it will be a good day.

The verdicts in the beating of truck driver Reginald Denny were handed down six months later.

There was not the same intense buildup and media circus that had preceded the end of the second Rodney King trial. Notwithstanding the earlier demonstration that had been taken over by gang members, it was clear that, whatever the verdicts in the Denny trial, we weren't going to have any widespread problems.

Nevertheless, the LAPD was again ready, with another heavy presence of uniformed police officers on the street and a well-rehearsed strategic plan that covered all eventualities.

When the verdicts were announced—some convictions of gang members on reduced counts, and some acquittals—there wasn't a blip on the screen anywhere. The reading on the Richter scale was a flat-line zero.

Residents and city officials alike had displayed growing confidence as the end of the trial approached because we had managed to get through the second King trial problem-free. Also, there was little empathy anywhere in the city for the young men who had so savagely beaten the truck driver. People realized that the attackers were wrong.

Unlike Rodney King, the gang-bangers who beat Reginald Denny were not viewed as victims. They had nearly killed an innocent man in the intersection that day for all the world to see, and most people agreed that they had brought disfavor on their race and their community.

*   *   *

Not until early 1994 did I receive for final review the personnel files of the officers involved in the Rodney King beating—this following the department's lengthy administrative-hearing process. All four officers had been on unpaid leave since 1991.

Since a felon cannot be a police officer in California, the two officers convicted of violating Rodney King's civil rights—Stacey Koon, who as the senior officer on the scene could have stopped the beating but did not, and Laurence Powell, who had delivered many of the baton blows and kicks while Rodney King lay prone on the ground—were dismissed from the department after a police board of rights hearing that was a formality. The board had simply accepted evidence of their felony convictions, then dismissed them. The federal court sentenced Koon and Powell to thirty months in federal prison. I am free now to say that I believe the federal jury's decision in convicting Koon and Powell was correct.

The LAPD careers of the two officers acquitted of criminal charges in the beating were in my hands, as the chief of police is the final arbiter of discipline in the department. I could either accept or modify the recommendations of the police hearing boards that heard their cases individually.

Regarding Officer Timothy Wind, a probationary officer still in training that night who had taken part in the baton beating, the LAPD hearing board recommended a six-month suspension—retroactive to 1991—meaning Wind would have received back pay and returned to work immediately. Instead, I decided to dismiss him.

The board recommended the dismissal of Officer Theodore J. Briseno, who had also taken part in the beating using his baton. I upheld the board's recommendation.

When making a decision regarding the firing, suspension, or reinstatement of an officer, a chief must not be ruled by public opinion or debate, no matter how strong. I tried my best to be fair and unbiased to each man, and to make my decision accordingly.

Based on the facts in the case, I believe that none of the four officers involved in the beating of Rodney King should have continued as members of the Los Angeles Police Department. I am very comfortable with the disciplinary decisions I made—my hand wasn't shaking when I signed the dismissal papers.

To deny that the Rodney King case seriously divided the Los Angeles Police Department would be untrue. There are still members of the department who think that all four of those officers acted properly and should be working as police officers today. There are others in the department who believe just as strongly that those four officers were dead wrong.

When our use-of-force experts from the academy were called by the prosecution to testify in court against the accused officers, they received vulgar and threatening letters both at work and home. We ended up having to place security on them at times.

One of the deeply rooted cultural rules that some police officers still live and work by is to not "rat out" fellow cops who have done something morally or ethically wrong. In my judgment, such a "code of silence"—which was known to be stronger in some departments, such as the LAPD, than others— cannot be tolerated at any time.

Coming up through the ranks in the Philadelphia Police Department, I had never seen brutality, although I believed it existed. Had I ever seen it, I would have first tried to stop it, then promptly reported it to my superiors. A police officer can do no less.

A police officer must always do what is right in the name of decency and justice, even if it means turning in another officer. Clearly, police officers should not be immune from society's laws.

Our academy instructors and experts took a tremendous amount of flak for simply being professional and standing up to say, "These officers were wrong . . . there were other and better ways to subdue the suspect."

The LAPD had lived with the Rodney King case and its tragic consequences for three long years. When I signed the dismissals, it was officially and finally over.

For the Los Angeles Police Department, the videotaped Rodney King beating was the shot heard around the world. It forever changed how the residents of Los Angeles and the public outside the city viewed and questioned the department.

Prior to the incident, the LAPD had practiced a great deal of autonomy in implementing its policies and operations—often, to the chagrin of the mayor's office, members of the city council, and the public at large. After Rodney King, this independence—really a self-imposed isolation from the city the LAPD served—was lost forever. The department found itself under a broad mandate for accountability to the people of Los Angeles and their elected leaders—the same type of mandate that every police department in the United States should operate under.

The Rodney King incident, however, also inflicted a great deal of damage on the LAPD's public image as well as the morale of its hardworking men and women. It was the kind of damage that would linger for a long time. The incident reinforced negative views about the LAPD and its officers from the chief on down to the newest rookie, views that would continue long after constructive changes were made in our use-of-force training and long after we added new and improved tools to our arsenal to provide officers with other effective ways to subdue suspects who resist arrest.

I can't say that we've guaranteed there will never be another Rodney King incident, but I can say that we've greatly reduced the odds of its happening again.

CHAPTER SIX

THE U.S. GOVERNMENT'S battle with religious cult leader David Koresh and his followers began on February 28, 1993, when a team of agents from the Treasury Department's Bureau of Alcohol, Tobacco and Firearms (ATF) attempted to serve search warrants on the Branch Davidian compound near Waco, Texas. Ambushed by heavy gunfire, four agents died and twenty others were injured, some seriously.

A siege ensued.

Fifty-one days later, Koresh and most of his followers were immolated within their compound in a fiery blaze that his believers reportedly set after FBI agents ordered Army tanks to punch holes in the walls so they could teargas the structure to end the standoff.

Only nine of the eighty-five people inside escaped the inferno; nineteen children died. Seventeen victims died of gunshot wounds, many believed to be self-inflicted (including Koresh's head wound). Coroners found victims, including children, shot by fellow Davidians, presumably to prevent them from escaping.

Ten days later, responding to public and media pressure, President Clinton ordered the Treasury and Justice Departments to conduct their own investigations of the incident. Justice's investigation would examine the FBI's role in the siege and the destructive fire that ended it, while Treasury's would center on the actions of ATF.

I was asked by Ronald Noble, assistant secretary of the treasury for enforcement, who oversees Treasury's law enforcement agencies (including ATF), to serve as one of three independent reviewers of Treasury's investigation. I agreed when I was assured it would not entail many extended trips outside Los Angeles. The other reviewers were former Watergate special prosecutor Henry S. Ruth Jr. and University of Southern California professor Edwin O. Guthman, a former aide to Robert F. Kennedy

Our review panel held two or three meetings in Washington, D.C., and several in Los Angeles, during which we met with the senior investigators on the case, as well as field agents. We received background briefings on what had happened, asked a lot of questions, reviewed interview statements, and were kept abreast of all crucial findings.

In a real sense, our review would be an investigation of Treasury's inquiry. We were to oversee the work of close to one hundred veterans from other law enforcement agencies within Treasury, making sure that they were not inhibited in their search for the truth and, in the end, that nothing would be censored from the final report. We had carte blanche to go directly to anyone involved, ask any questions, and see any reports, transcripts, or other pieces of paper. If we felt there was any hint of a cover-up attempt from the upper echelons of the Treasury Department, we would pull out and call a press conference.

It was clear to me from the beginning that this investigation was not going to be a whitewash. Senior people in Treasury were intent on having a fair, honest, and open inquiry. The investigators pulled no punches; they were willing to look critically at any office or rank and go wherever the trail led them.

Although some ATF middle- and upper-level managers attempted to resist—going so far, in some instances, as to provide incorrect or misleading information about what had happened—our investigators found ATF's line agents cooperative and committed to finding the truth.

The insights we received into this horrific incident would serve as an eye-opener as to how law enforcement should—and should not—deal with the very real threat posed today by radical fringe elements that arm themselves to the teeth in the heartland of America, while espousing revolution and divisiveness.

In my signed comments, which became part of Treasury's five-hundred-page report, I concluded that the ATF's initial investigation of Koresh and his group was appropriate. Based on intelligence it had received, the ATF had ample probable cause to investigate purchases of huge amounts of weapons parts, firearms, and ammunition.

The evidence that the ATF subsequently accumulated during an eight-month investigation was more than sufficient by early 1993 to justify seeking either arrest warrants or search warrants.

Information was developed that Koresh had received M16 parts that could be used to illegally convert AR-15 semi-automatic rifles into fully automatic weapons similar to M16 machine guns. When ATF agents determined that an arms dealer had lied to them in an attempt to hide the purchase of illegal weapons parts by Koresh, this further strengthened the evidence that Koresh was unlawfully possessing and manufacturing machine guns.

Once stocked with these parts, Koresh needed only a metal lathe and milling machine to make more than one hundred machine guns. Reliable sources made it clear that Koresh possessed both machines at the compound and that he had experienced operators. (In fact, after the April 19 fire, agents found a milling machine at the compound with a gun barrel mounted on it. In the same room, they found trigger assemblies and other weapons parts.)

Investigators also gathered evidence that Koresh had in his possession gunpowder and other ignition items that, when coupled with the shells he had purchased, gave him ingredients to illegally manufacture grenades.

The ATF agents consulted with the U.S. attorney's office during the investigation and properly secured a search warrant for the Branch Davidian compound from a U.S. magistrate judge.

The trouble started with ATF's plan for the tactical operation of February 28. There were major gaps in planning, gathering, and analyzing the necessary intelligence to carry it off, as well as operational issues, command and control from Washington, D.C., and at the scene, and a disturbing tendency to make underestimates and overestimates to justify the tactical plan.

The operation made several key assumptions that in totality seemed to ensure success. The most critical factors were the surprise arrival of the ATF at the compound and the presumed inability of Koresh and his people to react, pass out weapons, and take up positions to repel entry. Other key assumptions included ATF agents finding most of the men outside and working in a pit area north of the compound, even though no more than a dozen had ever been seen in the work party; quickly and successfully gaining entry to the main structure; and seizing an upstairs armory by surprise entry from a second-floor window while the residents were detained by other agents on the first floor of the compound.

Faulty intelligence led the ATF to believe the Branch Davidians kept their guns under lock and key in the arms room, and that it would take time to distribute them. In fact, semiautomatic and automatic weapons and plenty of ammunition were widely distributed to men and women throughout the compound and were close at hand.

As two pickup trucks, each pulling a long cattle trailer containing about thirty-five ATF agents, came up the driveway, there was no sign of activity in or around the compound.

At least two approaching field agents sensed that the absence of activity was a bad omen. "There's no one outside," one agent noted over the radio.

"That's not good," responded a second agent.

Nevertheless, the operation that counted so much on the element of surprise was not aborted by supervisors.

The trucks stopped in front of the main building as planned. Agents with fire extinguishers for holding the compound's dogs at bay were the first to exit the lead trailer. One agent opened the gate in front of the compound, and another discharged a fire extinguisher at the dogs. Simultaneously, other agents exited the lead trailer.

Koresh, who believed he was the Messiah and that the world was out to persecute him and his flock, appeared at the front door. "What's going on?" he shouted.

The agents identified themselves, stated they had a search warrant, and yelled "Freeze!" and "Get down!"

Koresh slammed the door before the agents could reach it. Gunfire from inside the compound burst through the door, its force so great that the door bowed outward.

Gunfire then erupted from every window in the front of the compound. Agents approaching from the front took the brunt of the initial barrage and scrambled for cover.

Meanwhile, another team of ATF agents had exited the second trailer and approached the compound from the side. While one agent provided cover from the ground, seven others had climbed to the roof. Four of them were to enter Koresh's bedroom on the opposite pitch of the roof, while the other three were to enter a nearby window that, according to an ATF undercover agent who had recently been inside the compound, led to the arms room.

The agents on the roof came under immediate attack. Those who were to secure the armory came under intense fire from the room and the hallway, as well as from the first floor, where Davidians fired blindly through the ceiling. The agents retreated back to ground level under blistering fire—some were actually knocked off the roof by gunfire—taking serious casualties.

Caught in a vicious firefight in the face of unrelenting automatic and semiautomatic weapons fire from virtually every area of the compound, the agents had no choice but to remain in whatever covered positions they could find. The open terrain made retreat impossible. (One of the two trucks that had brought them to the scene was disabled by gunfire.) They returned fire whenever possible, but tried their best to conserve their ammunition. They also fired only when they saw someone engaged in a hostile action, such as pointing or firing a weapon. Neither of these constraints applied to the armed individuals inside the Branch Davidian compound. Well stocked with several hundred thousand rounds of ammunition, they were free to fire at will, and did.

An hour and a half later, a cease-fire was negotiated over the telephone between the ATF and the Davidians, allowing ATF to remove its dead and wounded.

Four agents had died, and three Branch Davidians were killed by return fire from agents. (Two other cult members, possibly caught in the crossfire, were killed by fellow cult members, and a third was an apparent suicide.)

The FBI arrived on the scene and assumed jurisdiction within forty-eight hours, replacing the ATF for the long siege that followed.

Neither our review panel nor Treasury's investigative report indicted the individual men and women of the ATF teams that attempted to serve the warrant.

"When faced with overwhelming gunfire," I wrote, "ATF agents demonstrated extraordinary discipline and courage. They still made every attempt to meet and complete their objectives. Several acts of bravery saved lives and prevented further serious injuries to agents."

Such as: Special Agent Tim Gabourie, a medic from ATF's Dallas office, who repeatedly exposed himself to gunfire to treat several wounded agents. Braving gunfire for nearly two hours, he had one of his medical bags shot out of his hand by .50-caliber gunfire. Or Special Agent Bernadette Griffin, who, when she found another agent severely wounded in the arm, elevated his arm and compressed the wound with her hand for ninety minutes until help arrived.

In retrospect, these federal officers attempting to serve the search warrant had a difficult task to accomplish even if everything had worked as designed. But the plan began to unravel almost immediately, and the raiding party was ambushed and assaulted with the type of firepower that no municipal or federal law enforcement agency had ever before experienced.

Our careful look at the operation found that the ATF supervisors who planned it well in advance kept it only in their heads and never put it on paper so that other personnel involved would have an opportunity to review the tactics and question the assumptions. Thus, agents in the warrant-service teams had no clear understanding of what was expected of them and others, with many being kept in the dark throughout the operation.

Not having a clear written plan listing the critical elements for success almost guaranteed that when these factors were lacking—such as the element of surprise—no one would grasp the significance of the unfolding events.

The tactical plan itself was not well thought out. There were no provisions for contingencies in the event things started to go wrong. Command and control of the ATF teams were inadequate. Intelligence gathering was spotty at best, and analysis of information gathered proved faulty. Oversight from senior ATF management was inadequate. Insufficient reserve personnel were available in the event the first-strike teams ran into trouble. Not enough first-aid personnel were on-site, and there was no medical evacuation plan—it took one hour and forty minutes to medevac the wounded agents from the scene.

The flawed raid plan was based entirely on the element of surprise. Shockingly, despite knowing at the very beginning that the element of surprise was lost, the raid commanders decided to go forward. This mistake was brutally exploited by David Koresh and his followers, resulting in an unconscionable loss of life.

After I reviewed interviews conducted with ATF personnel who planned the raid, it was clear to me that the planners never anticipated a partial or full collapse of the operation. This, in my opinion, was one of the greatest failures of ATF management in this disaster. How could you send men and women out on an operation against such entrenched, well-armed foes without considering the possibility that some things could go wrong?

Unbelievably, at the time there was no requirement for ATF field personnel to notify anyone in the Treasury Department that ATF was about to implement a raid as large as the one executed at the Branch Davidian compound on February 28. (Such notification is now required.) Had such oversight taken place, many questions that needed to be asked would doubtless have come up. Review and intervention by experienced managers at ATF headquarters, or at Treasury, might have led planners to reevaluate the faulty assumptions upon which they relied so heavily.

For example, perhaps ATF leadership would have looked at the apparent size of the cult's arsenal, the members' resolve to use the weapons, and the presence of a large number of children on the grounds, then suggested an attempt to negotiate entry instead of trying such a brazen frontal assault.

Planners of the raid had chosen a direct assault, they told us, because they believed that Koresh never left the compound, and that he could not be isolated from his followers. But the evidence would show that Koresh had left the compound several times in 1992, and again just weeks before the assault took place. ATF never knew this until Treasury's investigation.

ATF's surveillance of the compound before the assault was hit-and-miss. Inexplicably, only eleven days before the raid, the ATF ended all surveillance. Several of the raid planners claimed they were unaware of this gap until our investigators told them. (ATF planners were told by their surveillance team that the compound had no sentries. It did.)

In our investigation, we determined that the ATF had contacted a local newspaper before the raid in an effort to work cooperatively with the media. Such a breach of security was especially alarming given the importance placed on the element of surprise. Indeed, there was evidence that Koresh and his people were alerted by someone from the news media shortly before the raid.

Two days before Treasury's report was made public in September 1993—it challenged the existing leadership of ATF to make a commitment to "positive change and reform"—Stephen Higgins, ATF director for ten years, resigned.

A lot of people were shocked by the level of criticism the review meted out. A number of ATF supervisors who botched the Waco operation and later lied about why it had failed were named. The weight of the evidence showed that supervisors declined to call off the raid even though Koresh and his heavily armed cult members were expecting the agents. Six supervisors involved in the planning and execution of the raid were suspended.

The Justice Department's report, on the other hand, absolved the FBI of responsibility for the fiery ending to the fifty-one-day standoff between authorities and Koresh's followers. Branch Davidian cult members killed some of their own children, according to the report issued in October 1993, and set the blazes that consumed their compound.

Eleven surviving cult members were tried in federal court for conspiracy, aiding and abetting the death of federal officials, and gun-law violations. Several were convicted of one or more counts and are serving terms up to twenty years in federal penitentiaries.

"I know well that no inquiry can bring back any of the lives that were lost near Waco," Treasury secretary Lloyd Bentsen wrote to President Clinton in an open letter attached to the report. "It is my fervent hope, however, that this review and the changes it will precipitate will prevent the recurrence of such a tragedy in the future."

In the summer of 1995, nearly two years after our investigation was completed, Congress conducted hearings and called witnesses to review the actions of the ATF and FBI at Waco. Reportedly, congressional interest was reignited by the April 1995 bombing of the Oklahoma City federal building—an act allegedly committed by armed right-wing zealots out to avenge Waco.

I am not sure what the congressional hearings accomplished. Some groups and individuals may have hoped to weaken, vilify, or even eliminate the Bureau of Alcohol, Tobacco and Firearms—a longtime foe of the pro-gun lobby. ATF's job, regulating three popular if potentially destructive products in our society, is a difficult one. It is even prohibited by Congress from keeping computerized gun records, thereby making its search for illegal weapons and their owners more difficult. Others may have hoped the hearings would erode public support for federal firearms laws and the assault-weapons ban. In the end, Congress found no government cover-up in the investigations by Treasury or Justice, only plenty of bad decisions at Waco.

Gun-lobby groups would have us believe that the ATF and other federal law enforcement agencies are a threat to our individual freedoms and constitutional rights. Nothing could be further from the truth.

Federal officers did make mistakes in Waco on February 28, 1993, but they were acting at all times to enforce laws in the hope of saving lives, not ending them. The bad guys at Waco were not the federal agents. The day the agents arrived with a warrant to search the Branch Davidian compound, the weight of evidence showed Koresh and his cult members to be lawbreakers. Before the morning ended, they were murderers.

The truth is that David Koresh, like Jim Jones, who annihilated nine hundred of his followers in the Guyanese jungle two decades earlier, was a mass murderer. Koresh gave the order to open fire when federal agents showed up to execute a lawful court order. Before that day ended, ten people had died. Then, fifty-one days later, Koresh ordered the incineration of his followers—according to evidence obtained by arson investigators—and seventy-nine more people died.

Certainly, the ATF made bad decisions and tactical errors in conducting their operation in Waco. Heads rolled and policies changed—as they should have.

The four ATF agents who died that day were doing the job they had been trained to do. Conway C. LeBleu, thirty-one; Todd W. McKeehan, twenty-nine; Robert J. Williams, twenty-seven;

and Steven D. Willis, thirty-three, were no different from any other professional law enforcement officer who goes to work in the morning with the hope of returning home that night.

When they do not, when they fall in the line of duty enforcing our laws, it is a sad day for us all.

The facts in the Waco case speak volumes about the need for effective gun control in this country. Who could be heartened that much of the Branch Davidian's ample weaponry—including semiautomatic AR-15s and AK-47s—which gave them more firepower than the teams of ATF agents, were legally purchased under our existing laws?

There are almost as many guns as people in these United States. We are a country of *220 million guns,* practically one for every man, woman, and child. About half of all American homes have at least one gun.

For the first time in 1994, guns surpassed vehicle-related accidents as the leading cause of fatal traumas in this country. In one year alone (1993), more than 40,000 Americans were killed by firearms in all categories—homicides, suicides, and accidents—with additional injuries totaling as many as 250,000. Nearly as many Americans are killed with guns *each year* as we lost in a decade of fighting a war in Vietnam.

It should come as no surprise that the United States is the most violent country in the Western world. Handguns were used in the murders of more than 13,000 people in the United States in 1992. Comparing our violent death toll to countries that strictly regulate the sale and possession of firearms, 33 people in Great Britain were killed by handguns that same year, 13 in Australia, 36 in Sweden, 60 in Japan, and 128 in Canada.

I am a strong proponent of gun control, or what I call "gun management." While I'm not against legitimate hunting, I believe we need policies that prohibit the domestic manufacturing of most semiautomatic and automatic rifles, as well as the importation of these weapons.

For example, take the Chinese infantry rifle, the semiautomatic SKS, once a standard weapon among Eastern bloc forces and used against U.S. ground troops in Vietnam. In 1994 alone, according to the ATF, U.S. importers brought in almost 1 million SKSs—more rifles than *all* the U.S. manufacturers made that year. The SKS falls outside the strict definition of weapons covered in the assault-weapons ban passed by Congress in 1994. Yet it was designed and built to do only one thing: kill people. The SKS has become popular among neo-Nazi groups, white supremacists, and street gangs. What makes this semiautomatic rifle so attractive is its power and range, low price (under $60), and the fact that it skirts most firearm regulations in this country. Flooding our neighborhoods with such cheap imported weapons is certainly not making our streets safer.

I've never been hunting in my life, but I know that high-powered weapons such as the SKS and AK-47 aren't used for shooting rabbits, birds, or deer. These are strictly weapons of war to be used for hunting human beings. We do not need them. The easy availability of these and other powerful semiautomatic weapons can be blamed for much of today's high level of random violence, such as the mentally disturbed man who, twenty years ago, might have gotten on a New York commuter train and yelled obscenities at passengers, today boards with a semiautomatic weapon in his hand and starts shooting. Or the Los Angeles city technician who, following two poor job-performance reviews, shoots and kills four supervisors with a semiautomatic pistol in the hallways of their workplace.

We also have to restrict the ridiculously easy access to standard firearms. I do not believe there's any reason why everyone in America should be able to go out and buy a gun on demand. We license people to drive motor vehicles. We certainly ought to license them to possess firearms.

I have heard it said that America would be safer if more law-abiding residents carried a gun. That is ludicrous. Arming every adult over twenty-five years of age would not stop crime. It would only mean more guns on the street, more shootings, and more deaths. Who wants to return to the time of Dodge City, where anyone at the slightest grievance pulled out a gun and took aim? Boot Hill contains the remains of many individuals who thought they could protect themselves with guns. Arming our communities more than they already are is not going to put an end to crime. And is an armed, divided, and frightened America really the legacy we wish to pass on to our children and grandchildren?

In Texas, the state legislature last year passed a bill to allow citizens to carry concealed weapons. Twenty-two other states, including Pennsylvania and Florida, already allow nonfelons to carry a concealed weapon with a permit that can be obtained without showing any reason or need to be armed. (Sixteen states, including California and New York, allow concealed weapons with a permit issued by police—the applicant must show a true need, such as regularly carrying large sums of money. Concealed weapons are outlawed in ten states. In Vermont, anyone can carry a concealed gun without a license.)

Enabling residents to carry concealed guns is intended to send a loud message to robbers and rapists that their next victim may be armed. However, police officers everywhere have become very concerned that anyone and everyone walking down the street may be armed. What happens if an individual is reaching for identification and the officer sees the gun? The officer will feel threatened, naturally, and probably draw his or her service revolver. A tragic shooting could result. What happens when armed residents have arguments? Instead of yelling or blowing their car horn, they may pull out a gun.

When our Founding Fathers wrote the Bill of Rights more than two hundred years ago providing for the right to keep and bear arms—let's not forget they were talking about *muskets*—we were still a very new nation not far removed from a revolution we had fought with a citizen army on our soil against a foreign occupying force. The context in which our forefathers protected this right, although vital, is often overlooked. I quote the Second

145

Amendment verbatim: "A well-regular militia being necessary to the security of a free State, the right of the people to keep and bear arms shall not be infringed." They did not intend for every individual in this country to have a right to carry a gun whenever he or she wanted. Rather, they intended for us to have the right to "keep and bear arms" *in defense of our country.*

In a civilized society, there must be checks and balances. For example, requiring background checks before firearms can be legally purchased and instituting waiting periods to purchase a gun. Banning armor-piercing bullets and assault guns. Improving gun-safety devices and providing mandatory gun-safety education. Yet these and other sane efforts to manage gun ownership—including a 1965 bill to end the mail-order marketing of guns that was spurred by the purchase of a rifle through the mails by Lee Harvey Oswald—have been bitterly contested, usually successfully, by the National Rifle Association and other powerful pro-gun forces.

I do not advocate disarming all Americans or banning all guns. But in an effort to stop the outrageous carnage in our cities and streets, I am convinced we must halt the proliferation of semiautomatic and automatic weapons and control existing weapons by making handgun purchases difficult. These are not popular views in some quarters, but 85 percent of U.S. law enforcement officials agree.

Not so long ago, most law enforcement officers were on the exact opposite side of the gun control issue. Instead of advocating gun control, they staunchly defended the public's right to bear arms. Many chiefs, sheriffs, and rank-and-file officers were card-carrying NRA members and recreational hunters themselves.

Law enforcement's big turnaround on gun control came in the last decade as we experienced the unchecked proliferation of guns in our streets—when we saw the significant possession and use of weapons by young people and by gangs; when we saw the significant increase in violent death and injury, attributed to guns in the home, during domestic disputes and accidents; when we came to realize that most law-abiding people who buy guns never use them for self-defense, and that fully half of the guns legally bought in this country are lost, stolen, misplaced, or given away; when we began facing on the street criminals armed not with just .22 pistols and .38-caliber revolvers, but with .45-caliber or 9-mm semiautomatic and automatic weapons, most of them stolen during home burglaries.

Law enforcement finally came to gun control largely because we were on the front lines. We were the first to respond to the carnage at the scene and in hospital trauma wards. We had to notify a mother that her teenage son was shot dead as he walked home from school. We had to break the news to a man waiting to have dinner with his wife that she wouldn't be coming home because she had been shot and killed in a grocery-store parking lot during a carjacking attempt.

One by one, these cases nicked away at us until our views began to change about easy access to guns. It was an extremely difficult shift for many in law enforcement. Some police chiefs went willingly, others were dragged along by the will of the people and political leaders of their communities. Today, most law enforcement officials are on record as proponents of strong gun control.

Realistically, however, I don't think we are going to see any more tightening of gun regulations in the next few years. In fact, I fear we are going the wrong way. While 1994 was a big year for federal gun control, with passage of the Brady law and the assault-weapons ban, in 1996 the political climate threatens to result in rollbacks of these sensible, life-saving laws.

The disturbing trend has already begun. Last summer, the U.S. Supreme Court, in a 5–4 vote, struck down a federal ban on guns within a thousand feet of a school on the grounds that the problem was "too local." This law was one of the ways that helped us keep the immediate zone around a school safe for our children. Under this law, we had tried to create a safe island where kids could go that was almost like a neutral zone. The high court's action reversed that.

Whether we were conducting narcotics or other types of investigations in the vicinity of schools, this federal law had given us one additional tool. Having the law overturned sent the signal to parents that their children aren't important enough for the federal government to be concerned about, and that the school zones are no longer a special place to be protected by the laws of the land. The last thing we need in this country is for a walk to school to be more dangerous.

I recognize that large numbers of firearms will be a part of our lives in this country for years to come. Even if we banned the domestic manufacture and importation of semiautomatic and automatic weapons this day, we wouldn't notice a significant difference for about ten or fifteen years. The price of guns would go up, and it would become more difficult to find spare parts. There are, however, plenty of guns on America's streets and in the pipeline to keep everyone who wants a gun well supplied for many years.

In Los Angeles over the last couple of years, we have recovered twenty thousand stolen guns—a dent in the huge number of guns reported stolen during the same period. The fact is that guns are seldom used for the intended purpose: self-protection. Instead, they are far more likely to be stolen and used in the commission of a crime or to kill a young child by accident in the home.

A ban on the weapons themselves, however, would be more effective than trying to restrict the manufacture of certain types of ammunition. While I have endorsed a local L.A. measure requiring ammunition buyers to present identification at the time of their purchase—this in an effort to keep the implements of violence out of the wrong hands—I do not think we could easily keep ammunition for illegal weapons out of the country altogether. With our open borders, ammunition of all types could find its way into the U.S. despite our best efforts. Smuggling restricted ammo would not prove any more difficult than getting illicit drugs across the border.

Federal gun laws such as the Brady law—which requires a waiting period and background check for any handgun purchase (some states, including California, already had such gun laws)—and the assault-weapons ban are not cure-alls but small steps in the right direction. They are not unlike mandatory seat-belt laws a decade ago and today's ever-tougher drunk-driving laws.

The vast majority of Americans support gun control, according to poll after poll. Many people favor banning them entirely except for hunting. Yet they feel helpless when it comes to doing anything about the proliferation of guns in our daily lives. I know exactly how they feel.

We live in a democracy. As such, our elected leaders hear from us on a regular basis. Unfortunately, they also hear from the NRA and other pro-gun groups on a regular basis, too. But if the majority of Americans in every city and every region decide that they want to get serious about stopping the spread of guns and keeping the implements of violence out of the hands of those who would use them against us, they would be a force to reckon with.

People can make a difference, for starters, by electing leaders who will stand up to the mighty gun lobby. We need courageous legislative leadership. Look at how strong government action resulted over the past decades in increasing car safety and decreasing automobile fatalities. In our lifetimes we have seen a comprehensive and effective campaign that changed the way we drive in this country. Manufacturers have been required to build safer cars, and strict laws have been enacted that require us to ride with seat belts and provide safety restraints for young children. And why is it illegal to drive drunk? Because drunk drivers kill, and we as a society wanted to do something about it.

Guns kill, too. It is clear that the communities in which we live are under attack by a type and extent of violence that previous generations have not experienced.

With the will of the people, government can and should

launch a similar campaign to reduce the opportunity for firearms to kill and injury innocent people.

Ordinary citizens can start by writing letters and bringing pressure on Congress to retain the 1994 federal ban on a list of assault weapons—combining this with a campaign to add more weapons of war to the list.

Americans everywhere can and should:

- Push for local and state ordinances making handgun ownership more difficult.
- Campaign for tougher laws regarding gun sales and possession.
- Require local regulation of all gun sales.
- Oppose concealed weapons of any kind.
- Restrict the sale of high-powered ammunition.
- Allow expanded rights for police to search people on the street for guns if they are suspected of having one illegally.

None of this will be easy. There will be organized and well-financed opposition. It will take perseverance and diligence, but we can do it.

In fact, we must.

If we are to retake our streets, we cannot sit idly by while gun sales and deaths by firearms soar.

CHAPTER SEVEN

AFTER SEVEN MONTHS of grueling classroom academics, extensive firearms and self-defense instruction, as well as exhaustive physical training, LAPD's first academy class in nearly two years—and my first as Los Angeles chief of police—graduated on April 16, 1993.

Twenty-seven recruit cadets out of the original class of thirty-one hired the previous September had made the grade; a third were women. Statistically, this single academy class accounted for little: For one month we gained almost as many new officers as we lost veterans through retirement and attrition. Yet as I looked at the graduates standing at attention on the parade grounds, I couldn't help but feel optimistic about the department's future. Police recruits, exuding so much hope and pride from fresh-scrubbed faces, have a way of doing that to me. For them, it was the end of one passage and the beginning of another.

"Each of you is beginning a career full of new and exciting challenges," I told the recruit graduates from the podium that day. "You do so at the same time that our police department continues to move forward and prepare itself for the twenty-first century."

I had greeted these same cadets much less formally—in a classroom setting at the academy—during their first week of training. I told them about my background in law enforcement and answered their questions about the training and what a police career might hold for them. I always made a point of greeting each class early on to help the recruits feel like part of the department.

There were changes taking place at the academy, too. In place of having every subject taught independently by a different instructor, we had instituted team teaching. A core of eight instructors stayed with a class from day one until graduation, delivering 90 percent of the course material and, in the process, tying everything together. (Firearms and self-defense were still taught by qualified specialists.) We were already seeing a higher retention rate among the cadets. As we had hoped, they seemed to be learning more and remembering it longer, with less need for remedial work to get through the difficult course work.

Behind the recruits now, in folding chairs on the closely cropped grass of the marching field, were proud families and friends—probably two hundred visitors in all.

I detailed some of the challenges the new officers could expect to face on the street: "Preventing crime from occurring. Reducing the fear of crime in our neighborhoods. Serving an ever-needy population that includes the aged, sick, homeless, and even the unborn child who will enter this world addicted to crack at birth. Over the coming months and years, your new assignments will be as varied as the neighborhoods of Los Angeles. Many of you will work in our inner cities, where the need is so great. Others in our bustling center city area. . . .

"Community policing is not a program, but an outlook on how we provide service to our community. We need to adapt to the ever-changing needs of our city. The bond between police and the community must remain forever strong. 'Protect and serve' is not just a slogan."

As I had watched our newest police officers perform flawlessly in close-order drill to open the ceremonies, I had found myself wondering whether any of these officers would one day make the ultimate sacrifice.

My thoughts drifted that morning to my own graduation, and how much law enforcement had changed in the passing years. The streets are so much more violent today, police work so much more dangerous, and the stakes so much higher in our never-ending war against crime.

I also thought of my son Will's graduation four years earlier from the Philadelphia Police Department academy. He had been in the very first academy class to graduate after I became police commissioner. I had worn two very different hats that day when I spoke to my son's class: commissioner and father. Recognizing the journey my son and all the sons and daughters of his class were about to embark on and knowing full well the life-and-death chances they would inevitably be required to take, I had directed my remarks to the families, too. It is something I still do to this day, many graduation speeches later.

Looking into the sea of relatives behind the tight formation of blue-uniformed LAPD recruit cadets, I greeted the families. "Welcome, for you, too, have joined the Los Angeles Police Department."

I don't stand before families at graduation strictly as the chief with four stars on my shoulder boards and three decades in law enforcement. I let them know I am also the father of a young police officer. I let them know that I know what it is like to worry about my son's safety on the job—much more, I confess, than I ever worried about my own.

To be successful in law enforcement, officers need to have the support of their families. It takes someone special to be married to a police officer and put up with the irregular hours, work on holidays when other families are together, and all the fear and worry.

Being a police officer is not a normal nine-to-five job that can easily be left at the office. We deal with citizens who have been victimized, and with bad guys. We are responding to crises and resolving disputes. We live with violent crime, abuse, neglect, and disrespect daily. As the pressures build, an officer can easily take them home.

Every graduation I speak at I ask the families to give their sons or daughters or husbands or wives on the force a little extra room when they come home from work. "If they don't want to talk about their day right away, that's okay," I went on. "Under-

153

stand the difficulties they face, and be patient. Support them when they're home, and support them when they're working overtime and have to miss a special family function."

Policing is a family unto itself. We teach our officers to bond with their partners for security and safety, and to operate as a team. Even more so than in the military, a strange symbiotic relationship can develop between partners, with each finding it easier to be closer to the other than to "civilians" such as wives or husbands or nonpolice friends. Some officers make a habit of shutting out their loved ones, not telling them about what went on at work. It's as if they live in two worlds. Others want to tell family members everything, but that doesn't always work because often spouses don't want to hear and absorb all the details. It is too much. Only police buddies understand first-hand what they're going through every day. Colleagues are often the only friends that have the same odd days off—the only buddies who can go fishing on Monday morning or bowling on Wednesday afternoon. An officer's life can soon revolve around other police officers both on and off the job. Sometimes these dynamics become unhealthy and work to the detriment of an officer's personal life and can cause a great deal of stress at home. Not surprisingly, the divorce rate among police is higher than the national average.

"Remember that there's life after your eight- or ten-hour shift," I reminded the recruits. "Talk about your job when you are ready. Remember that your wife or husband and children and parents are part of your life. Try to become involved in activities outside and away from policing. Don't let this organization be your whole life."

I never listened to people who said police officers shouldn't take their work home. I have always taken some of mine home. I think it's fine to share what you can, but it's a two-way street. You then have to be prepared to put away police work for a while and listen to what the rest of the family have to say about their day. That's stress relief for everyone.

"Enjoy your graduation parties, then remember, be early to roll call. Good luck."

I presented a diploma to each new officer, shaking hands twenty-seven times. Then, the class heaved their caps in the air and let out a big cheer. Some of them would report for duty at midnight. Others, at 8 A.M. or 4 P.M. the next day. Their police careers were about to begin.

Will had surprised his mother and me when he took the test for police officer. I had never encouraged him to join the department. In fact, I wanted him to finish college before he made any career decision. But when he passed the test, he took the appointment to the academy. However, not before promising to return one day to finish school.

As it happened, the son of Jim Clark, my close friend and first deputy commissioner, was in Will's academy class. Jim and I stood there side by side as our sons, longtime neighbors and childhood friends, graduated together.

Besides everything that any new officer goes through, I knew Will would face hurdles that he couldn't imagine. Would his peers trust him and be willing to work with him? Would his supervisors treat him differently? Would they be afraid to say anything around him for fear of its getting back to his dad? I wouldn't have wanted *my* father to be commissioner of the department when I was a young officer.

Will had still been living at home when he graduated from the academy and received his first duty assignment. He had been on the job only a few months when he came home one day with his uniform shirt bloodied. When I arrived home later that evening, Evelina said sternly, "Just go upstairs and talk to your son."

"What's wrong?" I asked.

"Go look at his shirt down soaking in the washtub in the laundry room. He's all right, but go talk to him, Willie."

When I found Will, he told me excitedly about chasing a theft suspect through a downtown mall, and how just as he reached the man, they crashed through a large plate-glass display window. "The guy got cut up a little, but I made the arrest," he explained.

I congratulated him. "About your shirt . . ."

"That's not *my* blood, Dad."

"I'm glad it's not," I said, smiling. "But, son, listen to me. Even though you're full grown and a police officer now, you're still your mother's baby. Take my advice: Keep a change of clothes in your locker at the station and don't ever come home with a bloody shirt."

When, a few years later, Will passed his first sergeant's test, I told him, "You did better than Dad."

I had failed my first sergeant's exam.

It turned out that Will had joined the study group that had so helped me and other young officers get ahead in the department. Our group, which had been mostly black but is now well integrated, was helping a second and even a third generation of young officers prepare for advancement.

A police officer never forgets his first big arrest.

I was working nights with another officer, Fred Jerado. It was pouring rain when we received a call of an armed robbery not far away and a description of the suspect, who had fled on foot. We started looking for the guy right away, figuring he would be easy to spot. He was described as a black male with "processed red hair."

A block or two away, here came this black guy walking down the street, no raincoat, no hat, soaked to the bone. We pulled up behind him and got out. After placing him against a wall, Jerado shined a light up to a full head of straight red hair. I patted the guy down, found the gun in one pocket, and a wad of money in the other.

It was my first robbery arrest and I was pumped. As a young officer, getting the bad guy is what it is all about. At the end of the week you got a paycheck, which was nice, too, but you weren't doing this just for the money.

You need that kind of enthusiasm in young police officers everywhere. If you stop and think about the dangers involved in the job, the civil liabilities that you might incur if you make a mistake, and the relatively modest pay you will receive, not too many people would sign up for the job. For a starting salary that can be as low as $18,000 a year in some cities and that might top at $45,000 annually, the average person would probably ask, "Why would I want to take those chances for that kind of money?"

I think that's why there's a certain cut of individual for all different types of jobs. I would never be a firefighter. I just can't imagine going into a burning structure filled with smoke. I am thankful there are people willing to fight fires, but personally, I'd rather go up against somebody with a knife or a gun whom I had a chance of dealing with one-on-one.

At some point as you settle into a daily routine, the sky-high enthusiasm you had for the job as a rookie naturally begins to wane. It takes a lot of special moments and events throughout your career to keep the fire burning, especially for the majority of officers (me included) who are not John Wayne types.

A good friend of the family's told me later that he had been shocked when he heard that I had become a police officer. "I just couldn't imagine the Willie I knew in uniform arresting people."

When I informed my father that I had joined the police department, he said, "They're gonna give *you* a gun?"

According to every recent public opinion poll, the number one concern of Americans is not the budget deficit or nuclear proliferation or national health care. It is crime. Los Angeles is no exception.

In June 1993, Los Angeles elected a new mayor, Richard Riordan, a wealthy businessman who promised to make the city safer by expanding the police department. Vowing to make government more efficient by running it like a business, Riordan pledged to reprioritize the city budget to add some three thousand officers to the force in four years without raising taxes.

Since my arrival in 1992, I had heard a constant refrain from every corner of the city, resonating as clearly from the Hispanic and black communities of East and South Central L.A. as from predominantly white neighborhoods in West L.A. and San Fernando Valley. Everyone, it seemed, wanted more uniformed police officers on the streets in order to feel safe from crime.

Increasing police visibility to deal with both the reality and the fear of crime had been a paramount concern since my first day. To that end, I had moved as many personnel as possible back into patrol. I also sought to elevate patrol work from being the stepchild of the department to an assignment coveted by our best and brightest officers. Incentives were needed for officers to work patrol. We eventually came up with a financial bonus package, developed better work schedules, and bought new cars, radios, and other equipment—all for patrol.

Cops on the beat are society's first line of defense. They are also something tangible that hard-pressed taxpayers can actually see. Increased deployment sends residents the message that city leaders are listening and that somebody actually cares about their wants and needs.

Shortly after Mayor Riordan was elected, he asked me to begin developing a new public safety plan for the city—one that would enable him to keep his campaign promise. "Don't worry about how it will be financed, Chief," Riordan said. "I'll take care of that."

It wasn't just a matter of putting out a hiring call the next day for three thousand new officers. For every recruit who enters the academy, nineteen applicants do not make the cut. To hire three thousand officers we would have to process some sixty thousand applicants. Also, our existing academy had the facilities to train only about five hundred recruits a year. Where would we put all the new hires? Our training and teaching staff would need to double or triple in size to handle the wave of new recruit classes we would soon start hiring. How could our already overcrowded and outdated station houses around the city handle a 30 percent increase in personnel? We would need more cars, more radios, more coffeepots, more everything.

After being stretched far too thin for much too long policing the largest city in the nation's largest state, the LAPD was about to undergo its most massive buildup in decades. Never before had I been given the go-ahead to undertake such an expansion of a police department. Typically, the fiscal edicts coming from city hall had been the exact opposite: cut expenses, reduce pay-roll, do more with less. The window of opportunity that had been opened in Los Angeles to improve and revamp the police department was now thrown wide-open.

Even with such strong political and financial backing, I knew there could be a danger in reacting to an emotionally motivated campaign for adding large numbers of officers without properly providing for their selection and training, and without a commitment to long-term planning.

The cost to hire and train one recruit cadet in the LAPD's seven-month academy is $100,000. This means that the cost of a single class of forty recruits is $4 million. (On average, there is a 10 percent washout rate.) After graduation, new officers receive a year of on-the-job field training with experienced training officers. The new officers are probationary until they satisfactorily complete their field training.

As much as I believed that expanding the department would help fight crime, I was strongly opposed to any plan to take shortcuts in officer training to achieve some lofty hiring goal. I would not condone lowering the screening requirements for police candidates or rushing academy training or increasing the size of training classes beyond what we could handle. Dumping on the streets partially trained officers—new hires who had gone through hurry-up training and were ill-equipped and unprepared—would not solve anything. Poorly trained officers would be a greater risk to themselves and to the community and could prove to be a big step backward for Los Angeles. We couldn't let the call to put more cops on the street or a call to "get back to basics" become a rallying cry that would okay once again a move toward the style of policing that abridges human as well as civil rights. We could not afford a replay of the Rodney King incident or anything like it.

I was prepared to champion the effort that would be necessary to expand the LAPD in line with the new mayor's campaign promise, but at the same time I wanted to be sure that we stayed on track to implement the Christopher Commission's long list of vital reforms, many of which came with sizable price tags of their own.

Growth of the LAPD—or *any* police department in the United States today—had to be based on a commitment to quality, and the implementation of community policing. To do otherwise in today's world would be shortsighted and irresponsible, and the public ought not to stand for it.

In July 1993, U.S. Attorney General Janet Reno, a former local prosecutor in Florida, came to Los Angeles for a two-day visit. I found her to be very direct, with an unusual blend of toughness and compassion. A strong advocate of community policing, she expressed the belief that the concept should be taken further with preventive programs headed by teams of police, public nurses, and social workers.

For several months I worked on the new public safety plan with my staff. We ended up with a twenty-one-page blueprint for expanding, modernizing, and increasing the efficiency of the Los Angeles Police Department. Together, the mayor and I went out to the public to sell the plan, which offered a concrete program to hire 2,855 new officers within four years and suggested ways to reduce attrition. (The average length of service of the forty-eight officers who resigned prior to retirement the first half of 1993 was 4.2 years. Thirty hired on with other police agencies, usually at a higher rate of pay—the LAPD's salary struc-

At the start of my career: a rookie Philadelphia police officer, 1964.

Former Philadelphia police commissioner Kevin Tucker, back to camera, and retired captain Francis Walker, right, my first mentor, minutes after I was sworn in as commissioner, 1988.

Evelina pinning on my new commissioner stars, 1988. In any police department, the fourth star weighs the heaviest.

My mother, Helen Williams, brought the family Bible with her all the way from Texas. I was sworn in by Philadelphia City Managing Director James Stanley White, 1988.

As commissioner, I had the honor of swearing in my son Willie L. Williams 3rd as a Philadelphia police officer, 1988.

With my mother at my retirement dinner in Philadelphia,
as I was now Los Angeles–bound, 1992.

My swearing-in as Los Angeles chief of police at the LAPD Police Academy, 1992.
Evelina, center, and my mother, at right. Note that the family Bible made another trip.

After the L.A. swearing-in ceremony, with my sisters, left to right,
Catherine Walker and Christine Bivins, and Los Angeles mayor Tom Bradley, 1992.

As a rookie in another league, with Dodger manager Tommy Lasorda, Dodger Stadium, 1992. I threw out the first ball, and they even let me keep the jacket.

With President George Bush, Philadelphia, 1992. We are visiting the mini-station at
Seventeenth and Wallace, which was rebuilt after being damaged by a hand grenade shortly
after it was opened. Some street hoods obviously didn't like the idea of a police station
in their midst. The mini-station is still serving the neighborhood and helping
to reduce street crime in the area.

On February 18, 1994, I presented the Tina Kerbrat Award, named after the first female LAPD officer slain in the line of duty, to rookie police officer Christy Hamilton on the occasion of her graduation from the academy. She had been voted by her fellow classmates as the "most inspirational" cadet for having accomplished, at forty-five years of age, her lifelong dream of becoming a police officer. Three nights later, responding to a "shots fired" call with her training-officer partner, she was tragically shot and killed.

ture ranked only twenty-fifth out of one hundred law enforcement agencies in southern California that hired from the same
pool of candidates. Through such attrition, other police agencies
received the true benefits of these individuals' having gone
through our academy and extensive field training. Increasing
salary and benefits is critical to reducing attrition in the LAPD,
but as with so many things it comes down to the same question:
Where will the money come from?)

I made sure the plan pulled no punches in publicizing the
fact that the LAPD's support equipment was in poor condition
and in dire need of replacement. Years of shrinking budgets had
eroded the department's infrastructure to unacceptable levels,
negatively impacting morale as well as the department's overall
effectiveness. Inoperable police radios, inadequate automated
systems, and poorly maintained facilities had become the norm
rather than the exception.

The plan also called for the civilianization of 640 positions.
Civilian employees, who did not require the same type of lengthy,
specialized training as police officers, could be hired to do work
that had traditionally been performed by sworn personnel,
thereby freeing 640 officers for street and investigative duty.

Because the public safety plan was bold and new, there were
naysayers waiting to see if we failed. If we failed, it would never
happen again. But if we succeeded with this well-planned
growth of policing and public safety in Los Angeles, it would
spread in spirit to other cities that were facing some of the same
crime-related problems.

In the fall of 1993, the L.A. city council, responding to strong
public sentiment, voted unanimously to lift the hiring freeze that
the department had strained under for two years. By then, public confidence in the LAPD had returned—from the low of 35
percent after the riots to around 65 percent, according to a *Los
Angeles Times* poll. It had been an amazing recovery. The public
had seen us get through the second King trial and the Denny
trial without difficulties. We had weathered a number of inci-

dents that could have turned out much differently. The city had budgeted more money for cash overtime, meaning we could put additional officers on the street, thereby increasing uniform visibility. We were on the road to reforming and reorganizing the department following the recommendations of the Christopher Commission.

However, department morale lagged, largely due to the unresolved labor dispute with the city. LAPD officers, still working without a new union contract, had chafed when the city had given Department of Water and Power employees a sizable raise while maintaining it had no money for police pay increases. Before the new contract was resolved in 1995—giving officers a 5 percent pay raise—there were short bouts of "blue flu," and all-around hard feelings on the part of the rank and file.

Entering 1994, the LAPD was the only city department completely free to hire and promote. As a second step to beginning the expansion of the department, the city council gave me the authority to immediately hire three hundred new officers. This first complement of new personnel would be added to black-and-whites, neighborhood substations, and foot patrols, I promised, and not assigned to desk jobs.

Mayor Riordan kept his promise to reprioritize the city budget. His first full-year budget (fiscal year 1994–95), which was subsequently approved by the city council, provided for 60 million in new dollars to the LAPD to help finance the new public-safety plan.

Unlike the federal government, the city of Los Angeles is required by law to have a balanced budget (most cities are in the same position). The police department cannot overrun its budget; this can be tricky because it is difficult to budget unanticipated expenditures like overtime for an earthquake. But there is simply no money to make up a budget shortfall, and I don't want the city coming to me for a personal check.

Since there were no new taxes, virtually every other city department took cuts in their funding to finance the buildup of the LAPD. The other department heads couldn't have been pleased with their diminishing budgets, but I am certain they understood that if there was increased public safety in Los Angeles, we would have a city with a much brighter future.

If there's a perception of anarchy on the streets and too few uniformed police officers to protect residents, the dollars spent on neighborhood parks and other city services won't mean much because fewer people will use those services. Existing businesses are going to relocate, new businesses won't come to town, and tourists are going to spend their vacations elsewhere. As a result, the tax base will shrink and every city department will lose out.

But if the police are able to regain and maintain control of the streets with the help of the residents—resulting in a safer city—many more people are going to feel like going out to the movies and to restaurants at night. New businesses will open. People will feel better about working late downtown. They're going to ride the new subway. They'll use the parks, recreational areas, and playgrounds. Tourism will help boost a healthy economy.

The same day the L.A. city council lifted the hiring freeze from the department, a new recruit class entered the academy. It was the first of eight new classes that would begin training by the end of the year—more recruit academy classes than the LAPD had graduated in the last four years combined.

Throughout the remainder of 1993, we continued to gear up for the hiring wave. Eventually, we would need to open a second training facility to handle the influx of new personnel. Recruiting the right individuals to fill our expanding ranks became as vital as any of the LAPD's missions.

Historically, the LAPD had been viewed as an organization where "the rubber meets the road." Without nearly as many officers per square mile as other departments, the LAPD went out and just locked up bad guys. Past LAPD chiefs had taken great pride in operating the department lean and mean.

Following an era of police corruption in the 1930s and 1940s, a new style of policing emerged, one that kept officers from getting too close to residents. When they received a radio call, they were to drive to the location, handle the situation, jump back into their cruiser, and get the heck out of there without being corrupted. It isn't any real mystery how and why the LAPD became so isolated from the community it was entrusted to "protect and serve." Somewhere along the line, law enforcement forgot that a large part of its job is not chasing bad guys down the street in a blazing gun battle, but dealing with people one-on-one and possessing effective communications skills.

As the ethnic makeup of the city changed dramatically from the 1950s to the 1980s, the makeup of the LAPD failed to change with it. In no longer reflecting the face of the city it served, the department further lost touch with the community. Certain neighborhoods—even those that suffered from high crime and desperately needed increased policing—were reluctant to seek a stronger police presence. Instead, they seemed to tolerate crime on their streets, all the while nursing a sizable grudge against a police force that they concluded wasn't there for them.

Now there was a major mandate for cultural change within the LAPD. It was a mandate from the public, the Christopher Commission, elected leaders, and even from inside the department. That is not to say that every member of the department approved—they didn't have to. These changes were going to take place whether some of the rank and file liked it or not. I made this clear to everyone.

As the first African-American to head the police departments in Philadelphia and Los Angeles, I was expected to address minority issues inside the departments as well as in our various communities. I had done that in Philadelphia, and I was now doing so in Los Angeles.

Communities have a right to be policed by a department that reflects their ethnic makeup. A majority (51 percent) of those polled by *Newsweek* in March 1995 agreed that local police forces should give minorities preference in hiring so that the police have the same racial makeup as the community.

In Los Angeles, where 62 percent of our residents are minority (42 percent Hispanic) with 44 percent of our police force minority, we had a ways to go. Los Angeles has established a system for ensuring that African-American, Hispanic, Asian, female, and gay police candidates would compete in an environment of fairness. In an effort to diversify our sources of applicants, the department ended its tradition of concentrating on military bases. Recruiters began using more television and newspaper advertisements and holding more recruitment expos in various parts of the city as well as making visits to colleges in an effort to recruit more minorities and women. The new personnel joining our ranks would be both genders, various ages and sizes, since long-time age and height requirements had been eliminated, and many colors of the rainbow, just like the community.

Just because a community is 62 percent minority doesn't mean that 62 percent of the applicants for police officers will be minority. It doesn't work that way. The largest "pool" for police work has traditionally been Caucasian. A smaller portion of African-Americans and Hispanics, in whose neighborhoods police are viewed much differently than in white communities, were interested in law enforcement as a career. The same can be said for Asian-Americans—many of their parents and grandparents simply didn't consider police work to be a worthy profession. That is changing now, but it takes time.

We have seen some progress. In 1994 and 1995, the ethnic makeup of our academy classes began to more accurately reflect the community at large. For example, in Class 4-94—which began in April and graduated in October (1994)—60 percent of the recruits were minority (Hispanic, African-American, and Asian-American). The department has a mandated goal that each academy class has at least 15 percent African-Americans and 23 percent Hispanic. (We have a voluntary goal of 6 percent Asian-American.) I have to say, though, that these goals are seen as a major threat to some white males who don't get hired for one reason or another. There's not much that I, as chief and as an African-American, can say to these individuals for them to see the situation any differently. I can't tell them that I've walked in their shoes, because I haven't. And they haven't walked in mine.

Affirmative action has become a hot-button issue. A major campaign is under way in California for voters to dismantle affirmative action via the ballot box this November (1996), and presidential candidates have raised the discussion several notches on the emotional scale.

In truth, affirmative action has not achieved anything close to what its detractors claim. It has not changed the color of the American workplace in local, state, and federal government or in the private sector. Management remains predominantly white male, and the "glass ceiling" that has kept most women and minorities out of the executive suite remains unshattered. It also keeps them out of the pipeline jobs that lead to management positions. Affirmative action has not done much to change the face of law enforcement in this country, either. The majority of American police officers across the country are white males, even in cities that are predominantly minority and have had hiring goals. The majority of chiefs of police and sheriffs are white. Out of four thousand or five thousand police chiefs in this country, there are probably not more than seventy-five black chiefs and only a handful of women chiefs.

One of the most common complaints about affirmative action is that it results in lower-caliber people being hired by police departments. Whenever I hear that gripe, I say as firmly and strongly as I can, "Let's get rid of that fallacy right now. Affirmative action does not mean lower qualifications."

I can truthfully say that I have seen no evidence in my professional career of a lowering of standards in police work as a result of affirmative action. From having managed police departments in two cities that have affirmative-action guidelines and court-ordered racial goals, I can attest that no lower-caliber personnel have been hired or promoted in Philadelphia or L.A. as a result of this policy meant to level the playing field.

If we lowered our standards in terms of hiring or graduating rookie police officers, we would only end up shooting ourselves in the foot. Pinning a badge on less-than-qualified individuals would come back to haunt us. I have no intention of hearing complaints—fifteen years from now when I'm retired—about the caliber of personnel we hired in the mid-1990s. What we are doing is deciding whom to hire from lists of *fully qualified* individuals who have taken the same tests and run the same course.

The entry-level test for law enforcement is a basic literacy test. Once we determine that candidates can read and write, they are given a battery of medical and psychological tests. Passing means they have met the minimum skills that are needed to be hired. They have not been tested on any law enforcement knowledge or abilities because they haven't received any training yet. Scoring at this point is simply used to come up with the order in which we will call the names. It doesn't mean that a person with a score of 100 will end up being a better police officer than someone with a score of 95 or 90. In fact, the person who got 100 may do poorly and flunk out of the academy, and the person who got a 90 may excel in training.

When the Los Angeles city council passed the goal of 43 percent women in the police department and we set out to increase the number of women in each academy class, there was a loud outcry from men, of course, that we had "lowered the standards." Suddenly, women were the threat under affirmative action—and the majority of the women being hired were white, not minority.

As a result, we reviewed the entire hiring process. We found that not one standard had been lowered or eliminated for women. What the personnel department did was decide that some tests should not be preselectors to get hired, but should be part of the training. For example: climbing over a six-foot wall. Previously, everyone had had to climb over the wall to get into the academy. Style didn't count—you could pull yourself over, run and jump, anything but use a ladder. Since men have more upper-body strength, this requirement discriminated against women candidates. It was changed to something that was taught in the academy. Once women were taught effective techniques for scaling a wall, they did fine. And today, everyone still has to get over the wall to be a member of the LAPD.

When the Philadelphia Police Department went to a semiautomatic service revolver with a fifteen-round clip for added firepower, we found that the shooting scores for women at the academy range dropped so low that a number of them washed out. The same thing was happening in Los Angeles. Some misguided male officers were quick to crow, "They can't stand up to our standards." It just didn't make any sense to me—women, since the days of Annie Oakley, had been able to shoot as straight as men. What was going on? Finally, we realized that the handgrip on the gun was too big for most women, whose hands are smaller on average than men's. They couldn't get a good grip on the weapon. I had to practically break some necks in both cities to switch to smaller handgrips or a different style of semiautomatic revolver for women (and some men) who needed one. This didn't change the firepower at all, yet there was an awful lot of bellyaching about "lowering standards." In no time, the shooting scores for women came right up.

Just how well are women succeeding in the academy when given an equal chance to compete? In the spring of 1994, a woman recruit finished first in her class in physical fitness, which includes self-defense. She was about five foot one and weighed probably 110 pounds soaking wet. In the past eighteen months, we've had several other women who have finished number one overall in their academy classes.

While I would rather that we not judge anyone by his or her race or gender, there were good reasons thirty years ago why affirmative action was adopted. We understood then that it was reverse discrimination to a degree. We also knew that affirmative action was going to be used intentionally to right a wrong. It was up to government, most of us believed, to eliminate discrimination historically suffered by many and to provide a mechanism for relief. Affirmative action was meant to heal the wounds of prolonged injustice.

Today, thanks to affirmative action, LAPD academy classes better reflect the makeup of the city of Los Angeles than ever before. Diversity in our ranks *does* help us in our relations with minority communities. In some cases, it may even have averted some Rodney King–type incidents. Scuttling affirmative action in law enforcement would be a major step backward.

If we leave affirmative action in place, we will begin to see significant changes in opening all sectors and levels of employment to minorities and women by 2010 or 2015. If we slow it down, we won't see positive change in our lifetime.

At the same time, I do not believe in promoting someone simply to achieve racial and gender balance. I think this is unnecessary. With hiring opened up, minorities and women will receive training, gain experience, study for promotional exams, and when they are qualified, advance in rank.

It is true that currently white males account for 85 percent of LAPD management, but this is changing. Almost 40 percent of those who have been promoted to detective in the last couple of years have been women, even though overall the department is still only 14 percent women. These women who made the grade have been with the department for ten to fifteen years and are rising in rank, in order, off promotional lists. Eventually, the department's high command will be fully integrated, too. It won't happen overnight, but it will happen.

I made sure to send a strong signal at every opportunity to the men and women of the LAPD as well as the residents of our various communities that I would be sensitive to discrimination issues and see to it that more minorities and women were hired and promoted. I wanted to throw open the door to officers who had long felt excluded from promotions and power in the department. Once again, I knew that such a policy would not be popular with some in the ranks and some members of the Police Protective League, which, to date, has never had a black director on its governing board.

Although I have always considered quality the key thing— "Everyone *must* be qualified," I have said over and over—I arrived at the LAPD committed to seeking out minority candidates on the department's lists of officers who had passed their examinations and were eligible for promotion. While I would set no racial formula for positions, I intended to place women and minorities in decision-making roles.

A qualified woman will one day be appointed LAPD chief. She will arrive with another set of expectations: She will be expected to address whatever issues involving women police officers are still unresolved at that time.

And when will that day come? The climate will exist soon, I believe, for a woman police chief in Los Angeles. I'd like to think that the system would allow for the appointment of a qualified woman to the position today. But right now the hiring "pool" is limited, with only a few women heading major police agencies. There's Jackie Barrett, the elected sheriff of Fulton County (Georgia). She is the first woman and the first minority to be elected sheriff in a major metropolitan area. There's also Elizabeth Watson, who was police chief in Houston for several years and is now chief in Austin, Texas. And there's Beverly Harvard, the chief of police in Atlanta, who gained her position after more than two decades of rising through the ranks of the Atlanta PD. That's about it for women in major jurisdictions. Realistically, I'd say that the candidate pool would be stocked with plenty of viable female contenders for the LAPD job by the year 2010.

The three highest women in the LAPD are currently captains. Last year, I appointed to head the Internal Affairs Division the most senior of them, Capt. Margaret York, who had been one-half of the LAPD's first female detective team (which I am told was the inspiration for the popular TV series *Cagney and Lacey*). We have also promoted a number of women lieutenants. Some in this group of captains and lieutenants will surely advance to commander and deputy chief. Eventually, several could be strong candidates for the chief's job in Los Angeles or elsewhere.

On February 18, 1994, I spoke to a police academy graduation ceremony honoring two recruit classes.

One of the classes—designated 7-93 because it had started in July 1993—had graduated the previous month. Their ceremony, however, had been delayed due to the powerful Northridge earthquake. The rookie officers from that class had been pressed into immediate street duty.

Instead of having a police graduation ceremony that month, we had a police funeral. LAPD motorcycle officer Clarence Wayne Dean, hurrying to report for work after the first jolt, was killed instantly when he drove off a collapsed freeway overpass in the dark.

The big earthquake that killed more than thirty people and damaged hundreds of structures proved to be a worthy test for our new emergency-operations plan. In my view, the department passed with flying colors—our officers were there when the residents needed them.

My family, like millions of others, had literally been tossed out of bed at 4:17 A.M. on January 17, 1994. The loud rumbling of the earth and the sound of the house shaking on its foundation reminded me of a speeding elevated train passing directly by the bedroom window—only a hundred times worse. Then, it was as if the train derailed and ran through the house, strewing furniture everywhere. Lights and water went off, and frequent aftershocks came one after the other in the dark.

Having been born and raised where earthquakes were only something to read about in the newspaper, I hoped that they didn't get any bigger than this one: 6.6 on the Richter scale.

"Never was there a finer example of meeting our mission than the magnificent response our department displayed after the earthquake," I told the rookie officers at their delayed graduation. "You were part of that response.

"Tomorrow, go forth and serve your community with pride, honor, and integrity."

After the diplomas were handed out, Officer Christy Lynne Hamilton, one of the ten women recruit cadets of Class 7-93, marched crisply forward to receive a special honor. I handed her a commemorative plaque, the Tina Kerbrat Award, named after the first female LAPD officer slain in the line of duty. Officer Kerbrat had been shot and killed in 1991, only three months after her graduation from the academy, when she and her partner stopped to question two men drinking beer on a sidewalk.

The members of Class 7-93 had voted to bestow the "most inspirational" award on Hamilton—the oldest by far in her class at forty-five years of age—in recognition of her efforts during her seven months at the academy.

Hamilton, the mother of two grown children ages twenty-four and twenty, was joined by her father, Kenneth Brondell, a retired thirty-year veteran of the LAPD, for a picture. Father and daughter beamed with pride.

That was Friday morning.

Three nights later, Hamilton, working the morning shift at Devonshire Division in the Valley, responded to a 911 "shots fired" call with her training-officer partner. Unbeknownst to them, a seventeen-year-old boy had already shot and killed his father inside the family home and had told others in the house that he was going to kill any police officers who showed up to arrest him.

When several police cars pulled up at the same time, two terrified women ran from the house. While some officers met them across the street to find out what was going on, other officers took cover and watched the house.

Without warning, the young gunman, hiding in a concealed position next to the house, open fire with a semiautomatic weapon. Using a powerful AR-15, the civilian version of the military's standard M16 rifle, he shattered windows in two police cars and left a dozen holes in the vehicles before retreating back into the house, where he eventually shot himself to death.

If another example is needed for tighter gun controls, the AR-15 packs considerably more power than any weapon carried by the officers on the scene that night. Some versions of the military-appearing AR-15 semiautomatic rifle used by the teenage killer are outlawed by state and federal laws, but not others.

One high-velocity round struck Officer Hamilton as she crouched behind the open door of her squad car. She was wearing her protective vest, but after puncturing the door the bullet went through an arm opening in the vest and lodged in her chest.

I received the call at home shortly after 1 A.M. that an officer had been shot and taken away by ambulance in very serious condition. Not waiting for my driver to pick me up, I headed for the hospital. En route, I was informed that the officer had died. I arrived about fifteen minutes later and learned that the dead officer was the rookie I had given the award to just days earlier.

Five minutes after my arrival at the hospital, Officer Hamilton's father arrived. He had already been informed of his daughter's death, but I was the first command officer to speak to him that night.

Just three days earlier we had been posing for the camera with a proud Christy between us, and now we were seated in a small hospital room and she lay dead not far away.

I told Ken Brondell what an accomplishment Christy's graduation and award had been, and how honored I had been to share those moments with her and her family.

"Christy would have been a good cop," he said.

I told him he was absolutely right.

Christy Hamilton was the fifth LAPD officer killed in the line of duty in the twenty months I had been chief. Each and every one of them was a profound loss to the family, the department, and the community.

Going to funerals for peers killed on the job is not something most people have to experience on a regular basis. I remember my first.

August 29, 1970, is a date I won't ever forget. A minute or two one way or the other and I could also have died that night, as could have any number of other officers.

Although we usually drove solo cars in Philadelphia—LAPD patrol cars always have two officers due to the great area they have to cover and how far away the nearest backup may be—that night I was doubled with another officer with whom I often worked.

We had stopped at tiny Cobbs Creek police station, where Sgt. Frank Von Collins was working alone, manning the front desk. After gassing up our vehicle, we chatted with the sergeant. Von Collins was going to be getting off soon. He talked about stopping on the way home and picking up pizza for the family.

When we left, we passed a patrol wagon heading toward the station. Inside were Officers Henry Kenner and James Harrington. We got about twenty blocks away when an out-of-breath Kenner came on the radio with a frantic "assist officer" call from the driveway a short distance up the hill from the station. Someone had walked up to the patrol wagon and shot Harrington in the face. Kenner rolled out of the vehicle, returning fire from underneath and behind the police wagon.

We raced back to the scene. The seriously injured Harrington was taken to the hospital, where he eventually recovered.

About twenty minutes later, as we combed the area and detectives conducted their interviews, a captain on the scene went down the hill to the station house to use the phone. He found Sergeant Von Collins dead behind his desk.

A group of a dozen radical "separatists," as they called themselves, had launched a well-planned attack that night to kill as many police officers as possible. They had wanted to attack a large police station, but decided that the smaller and somewhat isolated Cobbs Creek station was an easier target. The plan was to kill whoever was inside, ring it with grenades that had been stolen from Fort Dix, New Jersey, and then call for assistance. When police responded, the radicals would set off the grenades.

It turned out that they had been getting in place as my partner and I left the station. Had we stayed another minute or two talking to the sergeant . . .

By the time Kenner and Harrington pulled up, several radicals were already inside the station, killing Sergeant Von Collins. The lookouts engaged Kenner and Harrington outside, at the top of the driveway to the station yard, before they knew what had hit them.

The unexpected gunfight had obviously foiled the planned ambush. A bag of grenades was found about a block and a half from the station. Unbelievably, the next night, not far from the Cobbs Creek station, two more officers were critically wounded by suspects who turned out not to be related to this radical group. Both officers had to leave the department for medical reasons.

In the end, we caught all the suspects involved in the Cobbs Creek ambush, except one—a couple were sentenced to death but have never been executed. All the others are spending life in prison.

For my partner and me, the night hadn't ended at Cobbs Creek. About six hours later, we ran into a gang fight, locked up several people, and confiscated a half dozen guns. I remember walking into the house early the next morning thinking, "Thank God I made it home from this shift."

The next day, my partner and I were called in and told by a relief lieutenant from the old school that we were not to work together again for "socialization" reasons. Translation: We had violated the unwritten rule against two black officers riding together. The other officer and I looked at each other but didn't say anything. When our regular lieutenant returned, we asked to work together next time we "doubled up" and he agreed. But you don't forget that. Nor did I forget the days when black officers couldn't get the choice assignments. More than anything else, having experienced discrimination myself is why I became committed as I moved up the ranks to giving everyone an equal shot regardless of color or gender.

At Von Collins's funeral, there were hundreds and hundreds of police cars from departments up and down the East Coast. It was quite a sight. I was particularly moved at the sight of Frank's son, trying to look so brave. The boy later became a police officer.

The funerals get no easier when you are chief, even if you don't personally know the deceased officer. In fact, nothing is more demanding for a chief than having to deal with the death of one of your people. Had you done everything you could for him or her? Had they died because of a lack of training? Did they have the equipment they needed? The questions are endless, and the guilt can be crushing.

In Philadelphia, six officers were killed in the line of duty during my four years as commissioner. That count doesn't include two women officers I knew who were killed by male friends while off duty—one by an ex-boyfriend who didn't like the idea that she had joined the police department and was moving on in life without him.

More than three thousand police and friends gathered at the funeral for Christy Hamilton, which turned into a celebration of her as someone who had refused to let go of her dream and, in so doing, had inspired us all.

There was something intangible about the death of this middle-aged female rookie who had worked so hard to get through the academy. Her particular nemesis was the six-foot wall that every rookie must scale prior to graduation, and she worked at getting over that barrier long hours before finally conquering it. Her desire, perseverance, and ultimate success in the academy had touched her classmates, and the rest of us who came to learn of her determination. Wife, mother of two, daughter of a detective, recipient of the special award named after another woman officer tragically killed so soon after her own graduation, she had represented so much to so many.

Christy Hamilton's loss was felt as far away as Washington, D.C., where President Clinton eulogized her as a "policewoman who could have made a difference to people on her beat." At the same time, the president urged a ban against semiautomatic weapons like the AR-15, "which have no justification for sporting or hunting purposes."

To me, Christy Hamilton symbolized much of what diversity in community policing is all about. Middle-aged and female, she represented segments of society that had traditionally been discriminated against in law enforcement hiring. She broke the mold. She had long wanted to be a police officer and had finally acted on her dream after raising her children. She brought to the job an empathy that is needed on the LAPD, and on every police force in the country. In her short time on the job, she once spent a few hours with two toddlers left homeless after she had arrested their parents on drug charges. She possessed unique skills that promised she would become an exceptional officer. The fact that that promise was cut short was a tragedy we all had to bear.

There was something else insidious about her premature death. Officer Hamilton had been wearing her vest. She had taken cover in the dark, as directed, until the situation could be assessed. She had, in fact, done everything right. Yet she was killed.

It is a very real risk that every police officer in every city in America lives with each day he or she pins on the badge and straps on the gun belt. Their families must also live with it.

We train and equip our police forces as best we can in the hope that they will have some kind of advantage when they need it. Even though we are trained to keep a tactical edge, it is not always possible. You can't walk up to every car with a drawn gun because there are four or five people inside. You can't enter every room with your gun drawn because it's dark inside.

LAPD officer Charles Heim was knocking on a door of a seedy Hollywood motel in October 1994, following up a routine traffic stop, when he met a hail of gunfire from a suspect gang member inside the room. Heim, thirty-three, was killed. He left a young widow who was six months pregnant with their first child.

We can't go up to every door on a routine matter with guns drawn and order John and Mary Q. Public to lie down on the floor and slowly crawl out. We can take some precautions, but we cannot assume that everyone is out to kill a cop. Americans would not want that kind of policing.

Law enforcement officers put their lives on the line every single day. At the end of their shifts, they want to go home like everyone else. I'm afraid that a lot of people don't consider or appreciate the very real possibility for serious injury or death that police officers face daily. Most civilians probably take no more than one or two such risks in their entire lives.

This is what we get paid to do, I know. But I confess to wondering at times how many of our harshest critics would be willing to trade places with a street cop for a week, or even a single shift.

CHAPTER EIGHT

CHILDREN IN VIRTUALLY every community have a precarious challenge today just growing up healthy and living to become responsible adults in our society.

Childhood these days is much more dangerous than when I was a boy. Back then, the main threats we faced were getting into a fistfight at school and having our nose bloodied or being caught by the principal behind the school sneaking a smoke. The really bad kids were the ones who drank a beer in an alley and lived to tell about it.

How times have changed.

Too many kids in the nineties have to worry about the streets between home and school. They have to be concerned—as do we as caring parents—about their becoming innocent victims of assaults, robberies, and shootings.

If there is gang activity in the area, children have to find a way to get down the streets safely. Do they wear a certain color to walk through one neighborhood? But what happens when they enter another gang's turf showing the wrong color? Youngsters have ended up joining street gangs thinking that's safer than not being a member.

Even home often isn't safe. Shockingly, half of the children who get involved in drugs are introduced to them by someone in their home: parents, brothers, sisters, uncles, aunts, and other relatives. Too many are subjected to being around adults at home who are heavily involved in crime—robberies, burglaries, drug dealing, you name it. Some children are sexually assaulted by members of their own families and others whom they know.

Guns are on the street and even at school in such numbers that I've heard kids say, "It's not a big thing." That children are so accustomed to living with guns speaks for itself.

Drugs are everywhere. We had an incident in Los Angeles where an exclusive private school asked our narcotics unit to put an undercover officer on campus because there was so much drug activity. Years ago, this would never have happened—at least, not in this school. But drugs are a way of life today, from crack cocaine in elementary schools in some areas to marijuana and pricey designer drugs in high schools in more advantaged sections of town.

Raising a child to survive outside the home is one of the most difficult things facing parents of our time. Parents in the fifties and sixties could primarily concern themselves with raising a child to be safe in the home. They were most fearful of accidents and could feel comfortable when their children went off to school. We have no such comfort zone today. We have to concern ourselves with not only getting our children to and from school but also with their personal safety once they arrive there.

My parents were strict with us seven kids. I remember thinking that I would be easier on my children when I grew up. In fact, I was probably twice as hard because of the threats my children's generation faced—gangs and drugs and all the violence, none of which I grew up with in middle-class West Philadelphia in the forties and fifties. All of my childhood friends worked after school, and none were involved in drugs.

What can parents do today to protect their children? To start with, we have to talk to them candidly about personal safety issues. We need to do so with the intention of imparting valuable information without scaring them. This is an important distinction.

Conscientious parents know about teaching their toddlers not to touch a hot stove and to avoid playing with electrical outlets. And when children start playing outside, parents warn them about talking to strangers and not letting anyone touch certain parts of their bodies.

As children begin to venture farther away from home, the admonitions must be extended to the neighborhood. If children are playing outside and will be leaving the immediate area, they should always have someone they know with them. A parent, guardian, or baby-sitter needs to know where they are headed and when they will return. If they are walking to school, they should not do so alone.

Whether or not there is a visible crime problem in their neighborhood, parents should sit their children down and discuss with them the pressures and temptations they will inevitably face in the schoolyard and on the street, and how to best avoid trouble.

If people are coercing them to become involved in gang activity or drugs, they have to know it's appropriate for them to tell their teachers and their parents. They need to know that reporting their peers for illegal or immoral activities doesn't make them "rats" or "finks." We should try hard to instill in them the confidence to be leaders, not followers.

We also have to reassure them that we are going to find a way for them to go to school, to play safely with their friends and have normal childhoods. These are a child's inalienable rights. It is our job as parents to help provide for their safety and well-being, and it has never been more difficult to do so than it is today.

How many of us as children were left in the family car alone while a parent dashed into the grocery store? I recall its being a common practice in the forties and fifties. Today, no responsible parent would dream of leaving children unattended in the car in a parking lot, even briefly. We are afraid for our children, and rightly so. We keep our children with us as closely as possible, preferring to drive them to school and soccer practice instead of letting them walk or ride their bikes as we did.

Sadly, some parents have to teach their children to drop to the ground or duck for cover if they hear gunfire or any loud "firecracker" pops. They have to teach them to look up and down the street to watch for approaching cars and to walk either next to the buildings or next to the parked cars, depending on which would provide more shelter if needed. They have to remind them not to walk into a blind alley or anywhere they could get blocked off with no other way out, and to keep an eye open for any individual or group that may cause a problem.

By nature, it can be difficult for parents to teach their children such modern urban-survival techniques. They may be fearful of scaring their children unnecessarily and perhaps making them overly withdrawn or otherwise negatively affecting their personality. But we have to be more realistic and forthcoming with our children today than parents were forty or fifty years ago. We have to prepare them to walk out the front door and take care of themselves because mom and dad can't be with them all the time in what has become a much more hazardous world.

A parent's worst nightmare is having the paramedics or the police knock on the door to report that something tragic has happened. We don't want our children to walk blindly into a dangerous situation we may have been able to prevent if we'd just spent more time talking to them and providing them with valuable information.

We must teach kids as early as possible to understand that if they cross the line and get involved in illegal drugs or other criminal activities, they are going to be held responsible. This process is best started by holding them responsible for smaller things when they are younger so they will grasp the concept.

I am not a psychologist, but I believe that all children want and need limits. Teenagers may gripe about having to be home by nine or ten o'clock at night, but they want to know how far they can go. Without limits, they can feel unloved—no one cares enough about them to set a curfew, for example. They may try to stretch the limits occasionally, but they are doing so with a boundary that's already been established.

It's a mistake not to give children boundaries, and not to be consistent in applying sanctions for such transgressions as coming home late or not completing their homework or not doing their chores. In the old days, we had to sit in a corner or visit the woodshed. Today, it might be losing television or the VCR or Nintendo or their Rollerblades or being grounded for a time— whatever it is, to be effective it must be an enforced sanction that will get their attention.

If there are no sanctions and few limits, a youngster will keep reaching out and going as far as he or she can until someday someone says "Stop!" It may be the police or the courts or a judge who finally says enough is enough. And by then, it may be too late.

Children who grow up having assumed no personal responsibility and who receive little or no guidance from absent or apathetic parents and who never had limits or boundaries set may well succumb to the pressures of our society, joining the next set of crime statistics.

Ending up unfortunate victims who didn't make it.

Fifty to 60 percent of all violent crime in America is juvenile crime. Juvenile offenders are the driving force behind this country's alarming increase in violent crime. Juvenile arrests for murder, robbery, rape, and aggravated assault are all up sharply.

Although large urban centers where crack cocaine and weapons are more easily available have the most juvenile crime, violence by and among teenagers takes place in cities large and small, with no region immune to this exploding epidemic.

For decades, violent crime in this country was driven by adult offenders. Historically, children were involved mostly in property crimes such as vandalism. But during the past decade, as guns and drugs became more available in our communities, juveniles became increasingly involved in violent offenses until we had a complete turnaround.

I'd estimate that violent juvenile crime has escalated 500 percent since I entered law enforcement. Thirty years ago, we didn't have the epidemic of illegal drugs that we have today. We didn't have as easy access to firearms. We didn't have as many violent gangs. There wasn't the breakdown of the family structure that is so common today and that often leads to neglect and abuse. People—and criminals—didn't have the mobility we enjoy today. All these factors together are responsible, I believe, for our skyrocketing juvenile crime.

The statistics are sobering.

In 1993, 16 percent of all people arrested for murder in California were juveniles—according to the National Center for Juvenile Justice—an increase of nearly 50 percent from four years earlier. Nationally, the number of juvenile homicide offenders doubled between 1984 and 1991. In a nine-year period from 1985 to 1994, the death rate among fifteen- to nineteen-year-olds was up 150 percent. The arrest rate was up 125 percent.

In a national survey—by Roper Starch Worldwide—of high school and middle school students between the ages of twelve and seventeen, some 70 percent of teenagers reported that violence is a major part of the lives of young people. Forty-five percent felt that their schools have become more dangerous over the past five years. And about 50 percent of the teenagers surveyed in the West said they know someone who is involved in a gang, 45 percent in the Midwest, 41 percent in the South, and 32 percent in the Northeast.

Our courts and penal system are not designed to handle the flood of juvenile offenders who now represent the majority of our violent and hard-core criminals.

A 1995 Justice Department study, which took more than three years to complete, reported that juvenile arrests for major violent crimes grew from 83,400 in 1983 to 129,600 in 1992. New York had the highest violent juvenile crime rate, followed by Florida, New Jersey, Maryland, and California.

If the present trend continues and the juvenile population grows as expected—up 20 percent during the next decade to 40 million—the Justice report projects a staggering 261,000 arrests of youth offenders for violent crimes in the year 2010 alone. Considering these numbers, unless something is done now, the incidence of juvenile homicides in this country in the next decade could reach bloodbath proportions.

We have laws in most states that consider an offender a juvenile until seventeen or eighteen years of age. A few states use sixteen years as the legal threshold for treating violent juvenile offenders as adults. These laws accord juveniles a special status. We like to think that it is not too late for them. Our professed goal is to rehabilitate and treat them, hoping to change and reshape their lives so they can become productive members of society. But the brutal reality is that our juvenile justice system is near collapse. It has not been adequately funded for treatment, rehabilitation, and education. We are deluding ourselves to think otherwise.

Here are the facts. We know that most of the perpetrators *and victims* of violent crime are juveniles. Yet we do not have a workable system to treat most of these juveniles, and we don't have the facilities to house them all. So, what becomes of them?

In most states, offenders sixteen years of age and older who commit murder can end up being certified and tried as adults and sent to prison. They are, of course, separated from the adult population of the prison. (In California, juvenile murderers sentenced to prison go to the California Youth Authority until age twenty-five, when they are automatically released.) Many of these young offenders are already beyond help. We need to get them off the streets and keep them out of our lives.

And what about all the juvenile carjackers, the robbers, the burglars, the rapists, the gang-bangers, the drug dealers? About 99.9 percent of them get turned back to the streets because we have no programs or facilities to handle them. When I was police commissioner in Philadelphia, the entire state of Pennsylvania had only enough beds for 15 percent of the violent juvenile offenders arrested annually in Philadelphia alone.

In California, it's even worse. With overcrowded conditions

that parallel the adult prison system, whenever we send a convicted juvenile offender in the front door, we have to let someone squeeze out the back door. Youngsters who have not been rehabilitated in any way are released simply because we need their beds. They have been hardened and made more callous by the process, and they leave the system with no new skills to enable them to reemerge into society successfully. Most likely, we'll be chasing them down and incarcerating them again for more serious crimes.

Throughout the country, we have a revolving door for violent juveniles that allows them to pass through the system without needed treatment, without education, and with little or no incarceration for serious crimes. We need to recognize that a lot of juveniles are already violent criminals. When a juvenile has been involved in several shootings, in robberies, in assaults, maybe a rape or two, we might as well lock him up for a long time.

At the same time, we need to identify those younger juveniles who are at a critical crossroad in their lives. A portion of these kids *are* treatable and have the potential to become worthwhile citizens. We have to find a way to change their errant behavior when they are preteens or early teens. When we get them into custody on an early shoplifting charge or for that first small-time marijuana sale, we have to take it seriously. Whether it's a weekend or a month in juvenile hall, there must be a penalty associated with their first crime. We can't let them slip through the cracks. They should receive the professional help they need. There should be medical and psychological evaluation, counseling, and treatment.

My point is, we know that crime prevention programs for kids *do* work. We have seen proof in city after city, neighborhood after neighborhood. Combining gang-intervention efforts with emphasis on academic, vocational, arts, and sports programs has cut teenage arrests by as much as 25 percent in some regions. Reaching children with alternatives to crime is the best remedy. It is a lot smarter, more humane, and less expensive than waiting until they become adult criminals for whom we'll certainly need to build more courts and more prisons.

Most younger people become involved in crime because there is no moral leadership in the home to steer them in another direction. I don't think we can mandate a family's participation in counseling and treatment, but we should strongly encourage it. Then, follow up with the family and the youth after release.

What we are doing today, instead, when we do get our hands on juvenile offenders early on is to make a lot of excuses for them. "They just stole a bag of chips" or "They were just carrying this gun but they didn't use it on anyone" or "They sold only a little cocaine." Instead of cracking down, we let them off with a warning or probation. They should be spending a few weeks or a month in a detention facility. Perhaps they should be suspended from their regular school for a time and made to attend a special school. Possibly they should lose the right to get a driver's license until they're twenty-one or twenty-five years of age.

Most states consider the first three, four, or five contacts with a juvenile to be just that: *contacts*. They cut them loose and the kids are home before the police can finish doing the paperwork.

We are sending the wrong message. We are telling the first- or second-time juvenile offender that this infraction of the law is not important. The only real lesson they have learned is that they can beat the system and break the law without penalty. If there's not a different type of reinforcement at home or next door or through the church or at school that tells them they can't go out and do this again, a lot of these youngsters will stay involved in petty stuff until they grow older, then step up to more serious crime.

From spraying graffiti on the wall and stealing candy, it escalates to breaking into properties to steal electronic equipment. Next comes robbery, and assault when a victim resists. Then, they're stealing cars, involved in drugs, carrying weapons. Not overnight but over time, the crimes become more deadly serious. When one day they kill someone, people perplexed by such violence from juveniles ask plaintively, "How in the world did this happen?"

Some solutions are more obvious than others. For example, juveniles often commit crimes during school hours. In Philadelphia a few years ago, we increased police patrols in areas where truancy was a problem and started taking juveniles back to school. After a few weeks, vandalism, theft, burglaries, all started going down in those areas. But somebody ended up taking us to court and we were told that we couldn't do this anymore because truancy is an administrative-code violation and the police are forbidden to conduct truant sweeps. We stopped, and daytime crime went back up. There is no doubt in my mind that we need to go back to having truancy officers in this country, just like in our parents' time.

In Los Angeles, a new citywide antitruancy ordinance recently went into effect, making it unlawful for students younger than eighteen to leave their campuses on school days between 8:30 A.M. and 1:30 P.M. unless they have a valid excuse. Students receiving citations must appear with a parent or guardian before a traffic-court judge and can face up to $250 in fines and twenty hours of community service. They may also have their driving privileges suspended. Such an ordinance is a way of helping, not punishing, young people. The department would be happy with writing no citations. Our goal is strictly to make sure that our youth are safe, I explained to the community, and that they're where they should be.

I don't think the public understands the true threat imposed today by widespread juvenile crime. I think most Americans, however, want to treat our nation's children right and give them the benefit of the doubt. What we need is a major campaign to educate the public on the human and financial cost of the exploding juvenile crime rate. Juveniles commit an inordinate amount of property crime, thefts, vandalism, and burglaries. Are we as a nation willing to recognize the problem and do something about it?

We need to reconsider the arbitrary legal boundary between adulthood and childhood in terms of age. More flexibility must be allowed for us to lock up the violent juvenile offenders. Likewise, I don't think every juvenile should be tried as an adult regardless of the type of crime they've committed simply because they've reached a magic age. We must consider these on a case-by-case basis.

Frankly, I am not sure a law that automatically certifies a juvenile of fourteen or fifteen years of age as an adult is realistic. The public, by and large, does not have the stomach to sentence fourteen-year-olds to death, or even life in prison. But yet we have fourteen-year-olds who are sentencing people in our communities to death every day.

We must reexamine the various methods of treatment and levels of incarceration available for first, second, and repeat offenders. While taking the earlier offenses more seriously, we also need more programs to treat the younger offenders who may benefit from another chance. It is shortsighted to take money out of prevention and rehabilitation programs. If we spend the money it will take to reclaim juvenile offenders at this point in their lives, we will have a far greater chance of success than when they come back into the criminal justice system as repeat customers at age twenty-one, thirty-one, or fifty. By the time they're adults, we're just warehousing them at a cost of about $80,000 per year. There is no real treatment or rehabilitation of adults in the criminal justice system in America. Nothing happens to change their mental outlook; nothing affects their ability to function better in society when they come back on the street. Ninety percent of them return to prison within eighteen months of release.

If we stick our heads in the sand and dismiss our inattention to juveniles and their real problems, more of our youth every day are going to lean toward crime. Crime will only multiply and worsen. It won't matter what the police do or how many officers are on the streets.

The fix will take big dollars. Are we going to spend money now to try to remold wayward kids of twelve, thirteen, and fourteen years of age, many of whom are salvageable, before it is too late for them? As for the more violent teenagers who are repeat offenders, with our juvenile detention facilities so crowded, where do we put them?

Public safety demands that we do something now. We can't afford to be a nation living in fear of criminals.

Spending money for social services is not popular today. Quite the opposite: Funding to these programs is being slashed. Not spending the money to treat juvenile offenders, however, is shortsighted. If we don't spend money to treat juveniles early on, we will spend ten times more later. If we wait a decade down the road, we'll spend more billions of dollars constructing a new generation of prisons to house these same individuals when they inevitably grow up to become adult criminals.

Attorney General Janet Reno calls juvenile violence a "road map to the next generation of crime." I couldn't agree more. "Unless we act now to stop young people from choosing a life of violence and crime," the attorney general continues, "the beginning of the twenty-first century could bring levels of violent crime to our communities that far exceed what we have experienced."

The choice is ours.

Illegal drugs are directly or indirectly involved in at least half of the crimes committed in this country.

More so, illicit drugs are responsible for much of the increase in violent crimes. This connection first began in the mid-1980s, when crack cocaine—"poor man's cocaine"—first hit the streets of our cities.

The first category of drug offenses are all the crimes committed by addicted users to support their habits.

To finance a $300-a-day heroin habit, an addict must steal at least $3,000 worth of property every day to sell to a fence or middleman. Ten cents on the dollar is the average return a thief receives on stolen goods. A $500 television will fetch $50; a $1,000 stereo system about $100.

The initial victims are often within an addict's own family. The addict steals or cons money and property out of relatives, then moves on to friends and casual acquaintances. When they get wise, addicts turn to petty crime: shoplifting, purse snatching, thefts from automobiles. If we put pins on a map of any major city for every petty theft, then marked on the same map known areas of street-corner drug activities, they would overlap. Thefts and drug sales tend to go together so that the stolen property can quickly be converted and drugs bought right away. These crimes are a cottage industry of illicit drug traffic.

That $300-a-day habit, measly compared to the habits of many junkies, results in approximately $120,000 worth of stolen property every month—well over $1 million annually. Multiple that figure by the number of addicts in every city in this country, and you begin to understand the true financial cost of the drug trade to our society.

When a habit escalates to $500 and $600 a day, increasingly desperate addicts graduate to burglaries, carjackings, armed robberies, bank heists—crimes that often lead to injury or death of innocent victims.

A second category of drug-related crimes stems from the sales of illicit narcotics. Pushers are fond of claiming that they aren't involved in violent crime—they are simply supplying a product. "I don't *make* anyone buy it," these characters say as if they believe it.

In fact, they often *do* make sure people buy it. Someone new in the neighborhood or a new buyer from another area often gets low prices for a while. After they come back a few times, the prices go up. They are even allowed to get into debt a little in the beginning. At some point, the curtain comes down: no more drugs without cash. That begins—or intensifies—the cycle of crime as drug users desperately search for ways to raise money to buy narcotics. Not only are pushers committing a crime by selling an illegal substance, but they are also perpetrating endless criminal activity by stringing out their buyers.

Another category of drug-related crime is the often-violent battles over turf among drug dealers and street gangs. Big money is at stake at a cost of many lives.

We have no clear record how much real crime is committed through the possession, sale, and delivery of illicit narcotics in this country. There's an assumption in law enforcement that police know about and make arrests in only 10 percent of all drug-related crimes. For every one thousand arrests police make, it's fair to assume that there are another nine thousand crimes taking place that we don't know about. When one considers that up to one hundred thousand people are arrested every year in New York City for narcotics violations, the scope of our nation's drug problem becomes quite evident.

Illegal drugs are not only a law enforcement problem, they impact greatly on public health and education, the economy, and family life in America.

A lot of children come to school neglected and hungry because their parents, who may be not far removed from their teens, are high on drugs. Many babies are born today addicted to drugs. Within hours or days of their birth, they are sent home—in most cases with the parents who addicted them. What are the odds of that child one day being introduced to drugs and drifting into criminal activity thereafter?

Before long, social service agencies will be visiting that family. At least half the time, this governmental intervention will result from narcotics activity committed by family members in the street or at home. As a result, the child enters the juvenile court system. Many children in this country get their only health examination, their teeth fixed, and lice and ringworm removed because social workers visit on a regular basis to see how the children are getting along.

Our teachers and schools, already greatly overburdened,

have to be concerned about a child's health and welfare. They cannot assume that those needs are being taken care of at home. Schools give many children their only hot meal of the day—yet, at this writing, Congress is trying to eliminate federal assistance to school-lunch programs. In some case, schools even provide children with clean clothes. They have to include in classroom curricula information on the use of drugs and alcohol and on other social matters that should be, but too often are not, addressed by parents. Our schools and teachers, who should be free to concentrate on teaching our children reading, writing, and mathematics, must also become overly involved in discipline due to drug-related activities.

According to an NBC News survey, 36 percent of high school seniors in this country have used illegal drugs. The biggest problem for these teenagers? Drugs, according 32 percent of those surveyed. And 65 percent felt forced to make a choice about drugs before graduating.

On the streets, we see that nonaddictive, casual adult drug use is substantially down in the past few years. Even so, an estimated 12 million Americans use illegal drugs at least once a month.

Most disturbing is the fact that after more than a decade of reduced drug use among our young people, usage is starting to increase among teenagers. Their attitudes about drugs have changed. Marijuana use among teenagers has doubled since 1992, and six out of ten questioned in one survey thought there was no problem with occasional use of marijuana. Nearly 2 million teenagers use illegal drugs, including inhalants and LSD. These drug users are from all economic levels, from the poorest neighborhoods to the most affluent.

No dent has been made in the nearly 3 million Americans who chronically use hard-core, addictive drugs. For each one who succumbs to drugs, another steps up. About a third are addicted to heroin, which, with higher purity and lower prices, is having a comeback of sorts on the streets. The rest are addicted to cocaine (including crack cocaine). These hard-core drug users represent our biggest problem in terms of law enforcement and public health. They commit most of the drug-related crimes in this country, placing the largest burden on the courts as well as our health-care system. Through the years, various national "drug war" strategies have, to a large extent, ignored the addicted drug-user population. In recent years, more attention has been placed on these addicted users, but attempts in Washington, D.C., to find the money for more treatment programs have met with mixed results.

A former U.S. attorney general has suggested that legalizing drugs would lower crime and relieve the burden on our court system. Every few years, it seems, some reputable leader comes forth and says the same thing. I strongly disagree. I disagree as a law enforcement professional. I disagree as a parent. I disagree as an African-American.

Discussion about legalization of narcotics is brought on, I believe, by frustration with our inability to deal with the impact of drugs on our society. In legalizing drugs, we would be saying, in effect, "We give up. Nothing else is going to work. Let's give addicts access to drugs and write them off as wasted members of our society."

I have never heard it suggested that free drugs be handed out on street corners. Rather, that we make their possession and sale no longer against the law. In no way, however, would this eliminate crimes committed by addicts and users in order to obtain the cash to buy drugs.

Taking the addict who has a $300-a-day habit, if he could go into a store and buy his drug of choice at a competitive price, he would probably still have at least a $150-a-day habit. Where is someone whose mind and body are messed up by a daily intake of narcotics going to get $150 or more a day to maintain a legal drug habit? Chances are they're not going to be able to get a job that pays them enough to spend $1,000 a week on drugs and stay current on their rent, car payment, and other bills that regular working people have to pay. Addicts, whether they obtain drugs legally or not, are still going to turn to crime to get the money they need to buy drugs.

And what about all those individuals who do not use drugs because they are illegal? Today, a half million Americans die annually as the result of smoking and drinking, yet less than thirty thousand lose their lives as a result of illegal drugs. Obviously, many more people smoke and drink than take drugs. However, making drugs legal would open the door to more people using drugs and result in many more terrible addictions, deaths, and ruined lives. It would have a dramatic and long-lasting impact on the fabric of our society.

Legalization sounds nice in theory to some people, but it makes no sense at all. I agree with Jesse Jackson, who says we would be taking the management of drugs from the back room to the boardroom, from streethood to corporatehood. We'd simply be changing the bottom line.

From a law enforcement viewpoint, hallucinogens represent the greatest immediate danger to the community, the user, and the police. Otherwise law-abiding people can take a single dose of PCP and become violent and have no idea what they are doing. Often, they display superhuman strength and are impervious to pain. They will run through glass, jump off buildings, and fight with a platoon of police officers without feeling a thing. We have no idea medically, I'm told, when hallucinogens finally leave someone's system. *If* they ever entirely leave—flashbacks are not uncommon, sometimes coming years later. And there are people who advocate legalizing such drugs?

We're starting to get the message across to young people about alcohol; we're seeing a reduction in its use by teenagers today. We are also telling our children about the evils of tobacco. Suddenly, we're going to say that it's all right to use marijuana, cocaine, speed, and LSD?

The damage that would be done through legalization would be hardest felt in poor and minority neighborhoods. Those people who talk about legalization do not live in communities where drugs are prevalent, nor do their families face breakups and domestic violence as a result of drugs. Folks in our poorer and minority communities have seen and experienced more than anyone else the ravages of narcotics. Their children are already at risk. Setting up an environment that would make it easier for them and others to ruin their lives is unconscionable.

Anyone who favors legalization should visit a hospital ward that cares for babies born to crack-addicted mothers. These infants weigh no more than a pound or two and are barely being kept alive by tubes and machines. Then ask yourself how you could possibly favor legalizing the drug that causes such pain and suffering in innocent victims.

Legalization of drugs is simply wrong and shouldn't be given serious consideration in this country.

Our priorities should be clear:

- Stepped up interdiction at our borders.
- Greater focus on the illegal drug activities in our streets because this is the aspect of the drug war that most affects us and the lives of our loved ones. Arresting greater numbers of people on drug charges will mean that we'll need to build prisons that no one wants to build.
- Effective treatment and education for addicts and drug users when they are in custody—the single best way to reduce drug use in America. Again, this is going to require spending money that no one wants to spend. Although we surely will not reach everyone, those we do reach will have a greater chance of becoming productive members of society.

For the police to focus on street-level drug activities is a high priority for residents at virtually every neighborhood meeting I've attended in the past decade on both coasts. Members of police narcotics units, however, much prefer to work big-time cases that involve months of investigation and multikilo buys or seizures.

What we in law enforcement have to understand is that we can lock up a Mr. Big once a week and the public won't really care because it has nothing to do with the dealers they see on the corner selling dope to youngsters.

On the other hand, if we clear the corner once a month of dealers and addicts, our constituents will consider that progress in the drug fight because they had a few good days or nights. In effect, the quality of their daily lives was improved. If that is not the business of law enforcement and city government, I do not know what is.

The perception in many cities, particularly in poor and minority communities, is that police don't aggressively pursue white-collar, recreational drug users. It is true that these people are not arrested at the same rate as those who use and sell drugs openly on the streets of our cities. It's easier to observe and arrest someone who is out in the open than it is to conduct the extensive investigations that are required to arrest and prosecute the white-collar or middle-class drug dealer and user. The challenge to police is to pursue *all* drug offenders with equal vigor, regardless of social or financial status.

Police officers get frustrated working narcotics, and for good reason. It is a tough, dirty, dangerous assignment. When I joined the narcotics unit in Philadelphia in 1974, I replaced a sergeant who had been shot and killed during a raid. It was the one assignment I have had in my career that really worried Evelina, although she didn't tell me how much it worried her until later.

When I took over the LAPD, less than 20 percent of the narcotics unit's efforts were in "field enforcement," investigating street-level drug activities. The rest of the unit was primarily involved in larger drug operations that made headlines when a bust came down but had little or no visible impact on cleaning up the neighborhoods.

I disagree with people who say "forget the small dealers"

because someone else will soon take their spot on the corner. We have to start somewhere. And if we don't take action against these thugs, then we are giving up that corner. Where does it stop? Pretty soon we are giving up that block. Then, the entire neighborhood. Taking back our streets means fighting for every corner.

The people of Los Angeles have spoken loud and clear: They want street crimes dealt with. No community I have visited said, "Forget the small stuff, Chief. Go after the Mr. Bigs of the drug world." They have beseeched us to try to do a better job on their corners, their streets, in their neighborhoods. They want us not to forget them, to come back tomorrow and come back next week. They understand we cannot create a utopian environment overnight, but if we can improve the quality of life in their neighborhoods for a few days, a few weeks, or a few months, they would take it. Such success gives hope that one day we might be able to change it to the good forever.

I began to decentralized the LAPD narcotics unit and shook things up a bit. Today, nearly 60 percent of the LAPD's narcotics resources are assigned to field enforcement. (We had made the same shift in emphasis in Philadelphia after hearing the same thing from residents.) While it may not have been popular with all the troops, this kind of concerted effort is exactly what the residents of our various communities want from us. We are not letting the big operators off the hook, however. Far from it, we still have a major effort at shutting them down. We have no intention of letting them operate in Los Angeles without any fear of being caught.

We are following through on priorities given to us by our constituents. The community needs to establish these priorities, not law enforcement.

Government priorities should always come from the will of the people, not from the whim of its bureaucrats.

In response to America's ever-growing fear of crime, no louder mandate can be heard echoing throughout the country today than the get-tough rallying cry "Three strikes and you're out."

Three-strikes laws are on the books in more than a dozen states, pushed forth by an electorate fed up with crime. And a three-strikes provision covering federal crimes, such as bank robbery and smuggling, is in place as part of the crime bill passed by Congress in 1994.

"Three strikes and you're out" was coined in 1993 in the State of Washington when voters approved a ballot measure requiring life without the possibility of parole for third-time serious felony offenders.

In California, which has one of the nation's first three-strikes laws, any adult convicted of a third serious felony is automatically sentenced to prison for twenty-five years to life—and must spend *at least* twenty-five years behind bars. Under previous sentencing laws in the state, a twenty-five-year-to-life sentence could translate to as little as ten or twelve years with time off for "good behavior."

Clearly, the purpose of three strikes is to ensure longer prison sentences and greater punishment for those who have been convicted of serious and violent felonies. The intent of the majority of the voters in approving three strikes was to get bad people off the street—the most vicious repeat criminals who have been in and out of prison but continue to commit violent crimes. Getting such incorrigibles off the streets and behind bars makes sense. I can endorse this in principle as a voter, a father, and a law enforcement professional. Yet, in practice, three-strikes laws are not the cure-all the voters had hoped for. In fact, in some states, like California, three-strikes laws are merely misleading the public.

When three-strikes laws define the third offense as any "serious" felony rather than violent crimes, it means that the court is obligated to send the convicted defendant to prison for twenty-five-to-life even if the third offense was felony petty theft for swiping a piece of pepperoni pizza from some children. That is exactly what happened in Los Angeles to a twenty-seven-year-old man who had committed two other violent or "serious" felonies before the pizza caper. Life sentences have reportedly been doled out for such felonies as drug possession and tire theft. (The federal three-strikes law *does* distinguish between violent and nonviolent felons.)

Since our prisons are overcrowded—already over a record 1 million people are incarcerated in the United States (90 percent in state prisons and the rest in federal custody)—whenever someone is convicted and mandatorily incarcerated under three strikes, someone else is usually let out early to make room. I can't believe that the public ever meant for a pizza thief to go to prison for life and take up space that may belong to a rapist or hard-core gang-banger or even murderer who is not subject to three strikes. The ones who are being freed were either sentenced before the new law or are serving time for offenses not covered by three strikes.

In truth, three strikes is taking a harsher toll on the criminal justice system than on our criminals. Although everyone who works in the system knows what is happening—prosecutors, defense attorneys, and judges alike agree that three strikes is not working—the public has no idea that the much-ballyhooed law is so seriously flawed in many states. Well intended as it may have been, it simply wasn't thought out before being placed on the ballot in what amounted to an emotionally charged referendum against street crime.

Courts have been inundated with new defendants, many of them two-time losers facing a third felony charge and a twenty-five-to-life sentence if convicted. These individuals are certainly not going to plead guilty to a felony—they have to take their chances with a jury trial. With an increase of between 40 to 60 percent in defendants awaiting trial, district attorney offices have had to quadruple the number of prosecutors they have preparing cases for trial.

In general, judges are less inclined to lower bail for defendants awaiting trial. (Under three strikes in California, no defendant can be released on his own recognizance if bail is in excess of $25,000.) County jails, where defendants who don't make bail are incarcerated pending trial, have no more beds. The criminal justice system is simply not equipped to handle this influx of new criminal defendants resulting from three strikes. The new law has caused many thousands more defendants to be prosecuted and tried without providing any additional monies for more courts, more prosecutors, more county jails, and more state prisons.

While some judges are not comfortable dropping a serious felony to a lesser charge to remove the defendant from three-strikes jurisdiction and clear the way for a plea bargain, other judges are joining prosecutors and defense attorneys in doing just that in an effort to try to keep the judicial system from sinking under its own weight.

While plea bargains have long been necessary to keep the judicial system afloat, ridiculously lenient pleas that have become commonplace are part of the problem, not the solution. The public, rightly so, is sick of seeing offenders receive a slap on the wrist for serious crimes. In fact, widespread dissatisfaction with lenient sentencing is directly responsible for the three-strikes groundswell.

We have a system that the public wants to think is sweeping the streets of repeat violent criminals under three strikes, but it is a sad illusion. What three strikes is mainly doing is clogging the courts and jails with a huge number of nonviolent criminals—those who are facing their third "strike"—which is subverting the entire criminal justice system. Up to 90 percent of such cases had previously been settled without going to trial through plea-bargaining arrangements. Those defendants today are no longer willing to plead guilty, but would rather sit in county jail, awaiting trial. The result is an expanding jail population, swelling court dockets, and countless trial delays. Some states are having to project a doubling or tripling of their state prison populations.

In California alone, the state department of corrections estimated that three strikes would place an additional 81,000 felons behind bars over the next six years and require twenty additional prisons—nearly double the twelve prisons the state had earlier estimated (before three strikes) would be needed by the year 2000. The cost for those twenty new prisons: $6.6 billion for construction and an additional $1.6 billion per year in operating costs.

The public said firmly, "We want something done about crime," when it approved three strikes. Yet, as concerned about crime as they are, the voters haven't been willing to spend the money necessary to strengthen the criminal justice system.

Politicians, sensing the mood of the electorate, were quick to climb on the three-strikes bandwagon. But now, who is going to stand up and tell the public that it's not working as expected? Few politicians are willing to come clean with the voters on this extremely volatile issue and admit that this "get tough" law doesn't work as advertised. Serious modifications are needed, but everyone is afraid that the voters, who are already plainly angry and discontented, will end up killing the messenger. Mayors, governors, state legislators—few are willing to chance it when getting reelected is, as usual, their top priority.

It won't be easy redrafting some of the existing three-strikes laws. In California, for instance, the voters passed three strikes with a simple majority vote but included a provision that requires a two-thirds vote to make any subsequent amendments to the law.

When it comes to taking back our streets and creating a safer environment for us all, somebody has got to be honest with the public and explain that three strikes needs fixing. Someone has got to say, "We aren't delivering as promised right now, but let me tell you how we can do it and how much it's going to cost."

It is clear to me that if we are going to have three-strikes laws that make sense in this country, we need to focus exclusively on the *violent* criminal. These are the people who need to be taken off the streets and kept off for as long as possible.

Even a modified three-strikes law would result in many more defendants in court and inmates in state prisons. To handle the influx, we would have to build hundreds of new jails and prisons across the country at a cost of billions of dollars. And if we pass these laws without providing for new facilities, then the people pushed into already overcrowded prisons will only cause a faster turnaround, meaning that other prisoners will spend even less time behind bars than they presently do.

I cannot conclude that building more prisons would guarantee a lower crime rate. In fact, sociologists and other scholars have long known that the correlation between prison time and the crime rate is not a close one.

By the time you get sentenced to prison in America, you have usually been arrested at least five or six times and been convicted two or three times. Unless you commit a murder or a major felony, you don't go to jail the first time you're arrested. You don't go to jail for a first conviction for burglary or theft or robbery. Usually, the most time a defendant spends in jail is the amount of time it takes to raise bail. And often the sentence is for "time served" and probation.

From three decades in law enforcement, I can tell you that most adults who are sentenced to prison deserve to be there. By that time, the window for true rehabilitation has closed. The earlier arrests at younger ages have come and gone with little or no treatment and education. These people have continued unchecked on the criminal track, with their crimes getting steadily more serious and more violent. Many of these individuals will spend a major portion of their adult lives in state penal institutions.

I favor the death penalty for those people who have killed over and over again for the simple reason that it will prevent them from killing again. I believe we have to be judicious in using the death penalty. Clearly, there may be homicide cases in which it is not appropriate. But the only way to stop someone who has killed several times, and someone who has killed or maimed guards or fellow inmates while in prison, is to execute them. For these people, warehousing them between four walls is not enough.

In 1970, a man convicted of killing a Philadelphia police officer was serving a life sentence in prison. He and another convicted cop killer were having a meeting with the deputy superintendent of prisons about inmate demands for religious services. Suddenly, the inmates pulled out a homemade knife and attacked and killed two prison officials. I had no qualms about these inmates being sentenced to die for committing murder inside prison.

Law-abiding residents like to believe that the threat of a lengthy prison sentence is a deterrent, but everyone connected with the criminal justice system knows that a prison sentence is not a true deterrent to the hard-core criminal. People steal because they think they can get away with it. Unlike the rest of us, they aren't bothered by breaking the law. Instead, they think about ways to avoid being caught. Or after they are arrested, how to get out of being charged—and if eventually brought to court, of ways not to be convicted. It doesn't matter if we have three strikes or one strike or no strikes, we'll be dealing with these very same people and these very same issues.

Don't get me wrong: I think we have to build more prisons in this country because there are so many people on our streets today who belong behind bars. For these John Dillingers of the world and ten- and twenty-time losers, all we can do is incarcerate them to keep them from preying on other people. It's not a nice thing to have to say, and it may not be popular in some circles, but it's the truth.

I also believe that for the first- and second-time offenders who have committed nonviolent crimes, and for the younger offenders, we need to foot the bill for a massive dose of treatment, education, and rehabilitation while we have them in our custody. Again, spending money for these kinds of programs isn't very popular today. But it is their only hope and, most importantly, *our* only hope.

But even if we built hundreds of new prisons and provided tens of thousands more prison cells—a financial commitment I do not believe we are ready to make in these tough economic times—we would have to ensure that the right people are in jail to hope to have any impact. Who the right people are becomes a political and social issue. Is it the man who stole a slice of pizza for his third strike? Or is it the inmate who was sentenced to twenty years for rape and robbery but was released in two or three years to make room for the pizza thief?

Some people feel that anyone who commits a crime belongs in jail for a time, although many of those same people are opposed to paying more taxes to build new prisons. Regardless of how many prisons are built, we're still going to have many more people committing crimes than we have jail space over the next twenty to thirty years.

And no matter how many more police officers we hire in this country, we'll still be greatly outnumbered.

This is why today, more than ever before in our nation's history, it is absolutely vital for residents of every block and every town to join the fight against crime.

CHAPTER NINE

A MIDDLE-CLASS San Fernando Valley community not far from where I live was having a serious graffiti problem a while back. Private and public properties were being badly defaced. No sooner would residents sandblast, clean up, and repaint than the gang-related graffiti was back. Local property values fell, and so did the residents' spirits.

The community pleaded for round-the-clock police surveillance throughout the affected area. But with so many more pressing priorities, another solution had to be found.

We met with residents and heard them out. We let them know that the department would find a way to assist them in apprehending those responsible. In turn, the residents had to be willing to make a commitment of their own. "Work with us," we implored.

Work with us they did.

Volunteers set up a schedule of surveillance at various target locations. There was scarcely a time of the day or night that these areas weren't watched by residents from a window, a doorway, a balcony, even from atop a billboard at one location.

Whenever the watchdogs spotted anyone defacing property, they called a special number to get a message to a chase car manned with officers working overtime, who swooped in. Eventually, the main perpetrators were in custody, facing charges.

This is not something we could have done on our own. Five or ten years ago, a report would have been filed away and that would have been about it. An arrest would have been made only had a patrol car happened along at the right time. Even today, with the importance we place on responding to community concerns, we couldn't spare the manpower to stake out various locations to prevent graffiti. And this wasn't something that the residents could or should have done on their own. Yet, by working together, we solved the problem.

Another case of law enforcement and city government working effectively with residents to fight crime was the well-organized campaign undertaken to shut down a vicious, drug-dealing San Fernando Valley street gang called the Blythe Street gang.

The gang—with about five hundred members ranging in age from young teenagers to men in their twenties and thirties—had terrorized and virtually held hostage thousands of law-abiding residents who lived in the gang's declared "turf," a sprawling neighborhood of crowded apartment houses in Van Nuys. The gang ran a sophisticated drug-trafficking operation, as well as a lucrative network of chop shops where a steady stream of stolen cars were dismantled, and was responsible for a crime wave that had gripped the Blythe Street neighborhood. Heavily armed gang members used scanners to monitor police radio bands and alert one another to our activities with walkie-talkies and cellular phones. When police gave chase, gang members ducked out of sight, often forcing residents to give them refuge. At times, increased police patrols in the area resulted in numerous arrests. But when police were not in sight, gang members went back to selling drugs openly on the street and otherwise intimidating the residents.

Gangs in the West differ from gangs in the East and elsewhere. In Los Angeles, gangs tend to be dominated and controlled by grown men in their twenties and thirties—the average age for a gang member in L.A. is twenty-three years old. Gangs in the East are more often "youth gangs" headed by eighteen- and nineteen-year-olds. We've even seen situations in L.A. where fathers and sons are in the same gang, and in some cases of two and three generations from the same family have grown up in the same gang and all died at the hands of another member. The younger ones—they come as young as eleven or twelve—are used as the street enforcers. In most cases, a juvenile who kills is not treated as harshly as an adult who does. So the youngsters become triggermen. The L.A. gangs—like the Crips and the Bloods—are migratory, spreading their influence and drug-peddling to unsuspecting communities in the Northwest, the Midwest, and the South. Gangs elsewhere, whether in Philadelphia, Boston, or New York, tend to stay in their neighborhoods.

In Los Angeles, a conservative estimate would put total gang membership at one hundred thousand. Probably ten thousand to fifteen thousand members are responsible for 80 percent of all gang-related crime in the city. It's these hard-core peddlers of violence whom we're now going after with great emphasis, desperately trying to get them off the streets. As for the other, less-involved gang members, officers and community residents are working together in our Jeopardy program to get kids out of gangs and back in school. Some might say this isn't the responsibility of law enforcement. But if we don't do it, we'll be picking bodies up off the street.

Today's gangs, like the Blythe Street gang, are not as concerned as those in the sixties and seventies were in having wars over territory, events in school, or boy-girl issues. They are more concerned about controlling their narcotics trade and other illicit business operations. And like the rest of the world in the 1990s, today's street gangs find specialties: drugs, carjackings, ATM holdups, extortion, and robberies.

Addressing and solving the problem of gang violence in our communities is a challenge that requires new, different, nontraditional means. Such as: The city of Los Angeles filed a civil lawsuit (1993) against the Blythe Street gang, claiming it was an "abatable public nuisance" and charging that the neighborhood was "under occupation by an organized group of criminals involved in everything from drug trafficking to murder." It was the first time in the city's history that it had tried suing a street gang.

The resultant twenty-six-point court injunction the city won forbade gang members from engaging in a gamut of activities, many of them not illegal but often precursors for criminal acts. These conditions included banning members from using threatening words, littering public places, signaling or acting as a lookout, annoying or intimidating any persons, possessing any car parts without valid written proof of purchase, and being in a prescribed area between the hours of 8 P.M. and 6 A.M. unless they could show proof of legal residence. Even being a member of the gang was a violation of the order.

Ordinarily, such acts weren't something we could arrest and prosecute someone on.

"Round up those gang members on the corner," residents of besieged neighborhoods often appeal to us.

Yet there is little police can do unless and until someone actually breaks the law, which, in the case of the Blythe Street gang, they seldom did in front of the police. Once we had the power of the injunction behind us, however, any Blythe Street gang member committing these acts could be rounded up and prosecuted— if for nothing else—for violating the court injunction.

The city's novel efforts were opposed by civil libertarians, who claimed the rights of gang members were being violated. "Our goal is to balance everyone's rights on Blythe Street," answered L.A. city attorney James Hahn.

I couldn't have agreed more. The residents who had become prisoners in their homes and who locked themselves and their children behind security bars by night and day had rights, too. For too long, they had been denied a better life because of this violent gang. It had to stop.

The court injunction withstood the legal challenges and became a new, powerful tool in our arsenal for fighting crime on Blythe Street. As a result, a number of gang members were arrested and prosecuted, illegal drug activities declined, and the gang lost its ability to dominate the neighborhood through violence and terror.

Two years later (1995), local residents and public officials gathered at a dedication for the groundbreaking of fifty new housing structures in a Blythe Street neighborhood that had once been unfit for human habitation due to gang violence. Score one for the good guys.

In New York City, after a rash of assaults and other problems in the city's parks, police started recruiting hundreds of regular park-goers—teachers, doctors, housewives, lawyers, retired people. The only thing these folks had in common was that they used their neighborhood parks at a particular time each day. The police asked them to carry a cellular phone whenever they used the park. Hundreds of cell phones were given to the city by AT&T, with another company providing free cellular time. The only call the phones could make was to 911, which was automatically dialed by pushing a button.

These residents were delighted to work with police in fighting crime in their parks. In this way, the parks were covered almost every hour of the day by average citizens, who quickly notified police of any trouble or suspicious activity. Crime in the parks went down, and park-goers felt safer.

A revealing side note: When a New York newspaper did a story on the volunteer park-patrol program after it was already up and running, so many more people reportedly called in to volunteer that police had to turn them down.

I hope such stories provide an upbeat message for other neighborhoods and cities. Cooperation between law enforcement and residents *does* offer concrete solutions and real results.

This partnership idea should be wholeheartedly embraced by communities across the country. The old model of policing was not much interested in the views of the public. The new model—community policing, problem-solving policing, community-oriented policing, whatever name you choose to call it—

211

seeks both consultation and collaboration with the community. This philosophy stresses close cooperation between police and residents to facilitate the early identification and resolution of problems. This approach differs markedly from the tactics long practiced in Philadelphia, Los Angeles, and elsewhere, which traditionally emphasized a reactive response by police only *after* problems arose. Today, we are proactive, with the idea of *preventing* many crimes from happening.

No longer can the police alone maintain the "thin blue line" against crime. The police and public must become coproducers of the strategies designed to combat crime-related problems. The American public not only has a duty to be directly involved in crime prevention efforts, it has the right to be equally involved in policy making decisions of its police departments.

When we need the public's help, as police so often do these days, we have to be willing to ask for it. Residents of most communities, from the poorest to the most affluent, are willing to stand up and help once they have the facts and know exactly what it is they can do.

I've never believed that one model for community policing exists—one that can be made to fit anywhere with no adjustments or changes. After all, community policing means responding to what the people in *your community* want.

The residents of my San Fernando Valley neighborhood have very different policing wants and needs from residents just five miles away in Van Nuys. A police department, no matter how large the territory it covers, has to stay flexible to successfully implement community policing. Each city, and each neighborhood within a city, comes with its own cast of characters and unique set of challenges.

In Philadelphia, for example, police had long taken sick people to the hospital, a service no other big-city police department in America provides. Whether you were having a baby or suffering gas pains or needed stitches for a cut finger, all you had to do was call 911 and a police car would arrive at your door and a patrol officer would drive you to the hospital. The department was doing hundreds of thousands of these transportation calls every year.

When a citywide police-study task force asked the community which police services they valued the most, hospital transport calls ended up number one. Although this service ranked at the bottom of the department's own list for best uses of our resources, the community loved it. When it came to reprioritizing our resources in the face of a dwindling budget (the city was near bankruptcy at the time), we had to tread carefully. In transporting people to the hospital, police were providing a service the community wanted. But was it one we could afford?

When a cost analysis revealed just how many man-hours and resources were going into this service, it was clear that something had to be done. I held public meetings with residents all over the city, showing them for the first time the true cost of the service.

"If you allow us to alter the use of these resources, we can accomplish some other things," I explained. "Like increased uniform visibility on the street. Reducing our response time to calls involving crimes. Working with you on solving any number of other neighborhood problems that we don't have the ability to do at present."

Once informed, the community agreed that we needed to reprioritize our services. Like residents of other cities, they would in the future receive transportation to the hospital in emergencies by fire/rescue units. The police would be called by the fire department only as backup when necessary. The residents began to give up something that they had long received, true, but in the end they understood that they were making their police department more efficient and effective.

I don't think we could or would have altogether ended our hospital transport service without public acceptance. Any professed intention of making our customers satisfied was meaningless unless we allowed them to play an active role in developing and refining our service product.

The same process went into convincing people that they didn't need a police officer to come knocking on their door to take a stolen-car report. Shown an empty driveway or garage, all the officer could do was agree that the car was indeed gone, then write out a report in longhand. The same information could be taken over the telephone on a special dedicated line and, in fact, could be keyed directly into the computer system much quicker. The license number of the vehicle would end up that much faster on a list of stolen cars carried in all police units. In that way, a uniformed officer did not have to be taken off the street for up to an hour and made unavailable for more critical calls.

In each of these cases, it took eight or nine months to convince the public and build enough support for the changes. But in the end, people were clamoring to know when the new program was going to start in their area and why we hadn't done it sooner, since it would mean more officers on the street at any one time doing real police work.

This goes to the heart of another modern policing problem: what has been called the "tyranny of 911." There is a crying need to free patrol officers in our cities from the nonstop non-emergency 911 calls that keep them bouncing around like pinballs. I have argued for years that as long as police are tied to every single 911 call, regardless of how routine or administrative, we'll never be able to provide the level of service that people want and deserve for the amount of taxes they're paying. Ninety percent of all 911 calls are not robberies, in-progress burglaries, assaults, rapes, or any such emergencies for which uniformed police are required. Rather, they're calls pertaining to minor accidents, illnesses, abandoned vehicles, stolen cars, graffiti, loud music, and so forth. In cities big and small throughout this country, police officers spend a major portion of their time every day responding to noncrimes. Is this really what we want our police to be doing?

The public needs to understand that a uniformed police officer knocking at the front door is not required for each and every call. This is easy for me to say, but it's a challenge to convince the public to accept such a change. It can be done, as we did in Philadelphia. We were soon able to show the benefits of such a change—under the old policy of an officer responding to every report of a stolen car, for example, it had taken an average of *three hours* to get the car's license number and other pertinent information into the police national computerized system. The call didn't have a high priority, and the officer, after seeing the empty driveway or garage and writing up the report, had to return to the station to turn it in. Other more urgent calls might well keep the officer out in the field and delay things even further. By then, your car could be in a chop shop fully dismantled or on a boat headed out of the country. When we switched over in the initial test area to taking reports by telephone, we found it took an average of *sixteen minutes* to get all the vital information into the computer network.

Equally successful for us in Philadelphia had been the new specialty officers we created to deal with abandoned vehicles, deserted homes, neighborhood sanitation problems, loud music, and crime prevention. These duties could also be carried out by nonsworn employees trained to handle and *solve* a sizable portion of the nonemergency calls that clog 911 systems across the country and tie up many police resources that could be better focused on fighting crime.

In the case of an abandoned vehicle, we can get over the telephone all the vital information we need: the name of the reporting party, a description of the vehicle, and an address where it can be found. We promise the caller someone will come out in the next twenty-four to forty-eight hours. Then, we send an officer out to write up a report and coordinate with the city's towing company to have the vehicle removed.

You can have a specialized officer riding around the city writing up reports on abandoned cars or abandoned homes or sanitation violations all day, interacting with the city agency that can solve the problem and following through to make certain action is taken. Compare that to having one officer in a patrol car going to the location of an abandoned car on a 911 call to take a report that may or may not even get to the right agency. Those patrol officers' time would be far better spent catching a burglar or breaking up a street fight or simply remaining in service and keeping a high visibility on the streets. Eventually, we had twenty-five officers working full-time in Philadelphia investigating and working to remove abandoned vehicles from city streets.

There are also officers today, in both Philadelphia and L.A., working with residents to identify, seal, and keep safe abandoned houses—structures that are used by drug dealers and thieves and that breed crime within our communities.

A crime prevention specialist can meet with residents in a living room or a recreation center and talk about what a neighborhood can do to fight crime. This is the first thing to look for and the second thing and so on. "You can get ahold of me and let me know if you see more graffiti in the morning. Don't call 911. Those officers just handled a burglary or an assault or a gang fight, and they're not going to worry too much about your graffiti. But call me, and let me deal with it. I can get into the lieutenant's or captain's office, look at our resources, and come up with a plan for how to best solve the problem."

In a neighborhood where there are robberies, burglaries, assaults, and shootings every night, residents don't want the police to worry about graffiti or abandoned vehicles. They want the police to get the bad guys.

In neighborhoods where crime isn't as egregious, the residents *do* want police to deal with graffiti, abandoned vehicles, and the homeless on the corner. Those are bigger issues than crime to them, and if you handle them effectively, then you're a great police department. And if you don't deal with them, then you hear a lot of complaints: "Why don't you earn your salary and *do* something?"

The crux of community policing is ascertaining what exactly

is going on in each neighborhood, and this takes good *communication skills* and working with residents to solve the problems that concern them the most.

Some high-ranking police commanders believe that prioritizing a police department's resources should be the exclusive province of law enforcement professionals. I do not hold that view. The residents are the guiding voice for the police, and the police should always remain accountable to them.

The police-public partnership should function as a seamless one. For it to work, police officers must not be cold, isolated professionals, or worse, occupying forces oblivious to public sentiment. We need to *listen* and be willing to *change*—at times, two of the more demanding things we human beings can be asked to do.

At a neighborhood meeting in L.A. not long ago, a man stood up and complained that the house directly across the street often had loud parties. They would quiet down when police showed up, then raise the roof as soon as the black-and-white left. "Can't you put someone in front of the house to keep them quiet so we can get some sleep, Chief?" the man asked.

"Yes, I could put ten officers out front to sit there all night and make arrests for disturbing the peace," I replied. "I have the power to look over at the captain right now and order him to put ten officers on the block tonight. He may argue with me or end up putting only eight officers out there, but he'll do it. That would be four or five police cars down. As a result, other parts of the community will not get adequate policing. A lady who calls 911 when someone is trying to break down her back door may not get help in time. Is that what you want?" Obviously not, yet the man did want the loud music to stop because he couldn't sleep. That's not an unreasonable request—disturbing the peace *is* illegal—and I did ask the captain to have someone work with this resident to see what could be done to solve the problem.

I call this "cost-benefit." We have to alert the public to the choices and the cost of these choices, many of them difficult ones. That's the only way they will be able to assist us in prioritizing our services. And when we do the right thing, such as making sure the entire community is served instead of placing a squad of officers in front of a party house, they'll support our decision.

The public is not alone in needing to reevaluate what they want from their police departments in today's world. Police sergeants and lieutenants and senior staff have to reevaluate, too. They need to understand that it's okay to take some personnel off that railroad track called 911 for a shift, allowing officers to deal with problem solving and to try to devise solutions. They have to appreciate that this is real police work, too, and that in the long run the department can be more effective and efficient for it. Such a change in mind-set, in which we turn away from tradition and try something new, is the biggest challenge to making community policing work.

Unfortunately, at present, we do not have a widespread system of law enforcement in this country that supports such novel concepts. The traditional commendations for officers are for actions like breaking up robberies, catching burglars, making arrests. While these are certainly worthy accomplishments in the fight against crime, too often policing still comes down to a matter of *how many collars did you make?*

We've gotten away from counting how many tickets a traffic officer writes as a measure of his or her success, understanding that preventing traffic accidents and promoting driving safety are more important. But in so many other policing categories, we are still measuring the wrong things. On our personnel evaluation forms, there is not a space for "problem solving." There should be.

We need to change our thinking as well as our support systems. Our employees won't be motivated to do things much differently unless there is some kind of improved reward system. Demonstrating exemplary problem-solving skills with the public, for example, might result in salary bonuses, better assignments, promotions, medals, and ribbons. And, I ask, why shouldn't it?

A lot of people think that community policing means simply putting more police officers on the street. That is not by any stretch of the imagination what community policing is all about. In fact, a department can have a strong community-policing philosophy and not hire one additional officer. What is crucial is how you use the people you have.

Community policing is allowing your officers and their supervisors to try to do some problem solving on the streets without having to get authorization with seventeen stamps of approval from the chief on down saying it's okay.

Community policing is making sure your department is listening to what the public has to say, from the chief down to the newest rookie on the beat.

Community policing is being willing to redirect your department's efforts based on input from the public.

Community policing is also a style of internal management starting with who and how you recruit. Do you recruit only the John Waynes and Rambos of the world? Or do you go after a wide spectrum of different types of people who have good social skills, communication skills, and who understand that a lot of the job is going to be interacting with the public who are victims of crimes?

Community policing is making sure your people-oriented philosophy isn't just a two-hour course in the academy, but is folded into everything you do, whether it's how to interpret and enforce the laws or deciding under what circumstances to make car stops and pedestrian stops.

Community policing is communicating with your customers. In a Los Angeles that is 42 percent Hispanic, that means learning Spanish becomes mandatory in the academy. Communication means understanding, and understanding means less conflict, doubt, and distrust.

Community policing is making sure that you handpick and select your training officers so that you have only the best people with the skills to teach in that crucial position. The person who makes the most arrests is not necessarily the best training officer.

Community policing is utilizing your officers in the best way possible from the time they come out of the academy until the day they retire. Over time, they should work a variety of jobs in different neighborhoods and not be stuck in a hard-core gang area or find themselves doing little more than writing traffic tickets.

Community policing is ensuring that the men and women of a police department reflect the ethnic diversity of the community they serve.

Community policing is not just about fighting crime but also about working together to prevent it.

Community policing is changing the prevailing kick-butt-and-take-no-names policy of too many departments, assigning officers, instead, to work with residents, schools, and civic groups to resolve community problems.

Community policing is ridding the police department of sexual harassment, discrimination, and bias within the ranks. How fairly your employees are treated will go far in determining how fairly they treat the public.

As I recall, I first started hearing about community policing sometime in the early 1980s. From the beginning, I agreed philosophically with what I heard.

As a lieutenant, and then a captain, I had been running my area following many of the tenets of community policing, although we didn't have a title for it. Back then, whenever I got a few extra officers, I'd establish a foot beat in an area of heavy pedestrian traffic as a way of getting closer to the residents and solving their problems. Such an effort is more difficult when you are driving by in a police cruiser, stopping only long enough to take a report or grab a cup of coffee before going back on the road.

Even today, however, community policing is not something that a lot of veteran officers instinctively want to rally around. Some will, once they learn more about it. Others never will. This is why, almost universally, community policing isn't implemented or allowed to move forward until there is s a crisis, or maybe even a series of crises, to remind everyone why change and reform of the police department are necessary.

You seldom hear about neighborhood residents resisting community policing. And why would they? No, I don't want the police to listen to me. No, I don't want to have a greater voice in shaping police priorities. No, I don't want the police to be more committed to problem solving. It doesn't make sense.

Rather, the resistance tends to come from *within* a police department—from the officers on the beat to the highest levels of the command structure. I have seen this in both Philadelphia and Los Angeles. There will always be a group within any department who will say with great disdain, "I didn't join the department to do community policing." They joined to be Starsky and Hutch and Rambo all rolled into one.

When I went through the police academy in 1964, we were trained to go get the bad guys, write traffic tickets, make reports on automobile accidents, and get drunk drivers off the road. And we were warned not to be corrupt. That was about the extent of our preparation for the job. Within a few weeks of graduating, we all figured we had our Ph.D. in policing. We thought we knew exactly what was expected of us, and what the job entailed. Then, at some point during your police career, along comes this new chief who says, "We want you to do some different things now. We want you to act differently. We want you to treat the residents differently."

As I say, change can be difficult.

At the same time, there were plenty of old-time police officers in Philadelphia and L.A. who knew how to treat the public right long before community policing came into vogue. These officers could catch the bad guys and at the same time treat members of the community with the respect they deserve. I would be honored to have each and every one of these officers in my department today.

The claim that community policing is soft on crime is one rap I have often heard from the ranks. In truth, it is resolving crime in a more long-lasting way. Still, there are officers who see it as soft, liberal, and namby-pamby because they might have to say hello to a resident and actually listen to a "civilian." It all goes against their grain—someone who views himself as a cop's cop doesn't think he should have to bother with such social niceties.

In Philadelphia after the MOVE bombing, newly appointed commissioner Kevin Tucker at first tried to change the department over to community policing from the bottom up, which didn't work. We had a number of programs and pieces in place—crime prevention officers, victim witness officers, substations, and various patrol-level strategies—but there had been little training or preparation of the majority of senior commanders for the major shift in direction and philosophy. This wasn't done intentionally but simply in the rush to get results. These commanders resisted letting go of their traditional power and authority and chafed at the idea of having to go out into the community to find out what type of police services residents needed and desired.

What we needed, what any community-policing department needs, is *decentralization*, which can be threatening to those already in charge of an office or a station or a district. We needed the chief inspectors and inspectors to let the captains make more decisions and run more things without having to go upstairs for approval. We wanted the captains to let the lieutenants do the same thing, and the lieutenants to allow the sergeants to make more decisions. Decentralization must filter down to the patrol officer, who has to feel it is okay to go out of service for a while to try to solve a problem that, if left unsolved, would only result in more 911 calls and other units responding again and again. The officer needs to be supported and encouraged in this endeavor, even if it doesn't mean getting a "collar."

We soon realized that you cannot change an organization from the bottom up because the authority to do new things comes from the next level above. Without training and reinforcing the middle- and upper-level supervisors, the newly indoctrinated patrol officers who go out on the streets with their new tools will soon become frustrated. They're going to be inhibited because their sergeants and lieutenants don't have a clue as to what they're doing. The supervisors won't be evaluating and rating the officers in areas that have become important: Naturally, the officers are going to feel frustrated. This can lead to wholesale distrust and confusion, and a breakdown in the entire program. And that's what occurred in Philadelphia.

So we had to start over. We sent more supervisors and managers to more schools—including Harvard—and training programs to learn how to share their authority and power with subordinate personnel and with the community, to learn how to solve problems differently from how they had done it while coming up through the ranks. They needed to look at the organization as a whole rather than separate parts, and to manage better with what was a continually diminishing budget at that time in Philadelphia's municipal history.

Only then, by opening doors instead of closing them, by really listening to the community, and by beginning to decentralize an age-old military-style command structure, did we take the path to true community policing.

Perhaps more than any other major police department in the nation over the last thirty or forty years, the LAPD had operated largely independent of the community it served.

The department coveted its militaristic image, which began in the 1950s under Chief Bill Parker, who set out to create the "professional police officer." Parker wanted officers with military bearing and training who did not get too close to the public and therefore remained corruption free. (Today, some top police commanders still worry about their officers getting too close to the public for this very reason—a dynamic that works decidedly against community policing.) Indeed, a hallmark of the LAPD over the past four decades is that it has been one of the most corruption-free departments in the history of modern policing. This achievement is something that all police agencies in the country have known about and admired.

The LAPD under Parker was viewed, at the time, as the ideal model for a "modern" police force. Many departments strived to emulate the mighty LAPD, which became well known to the entire nation through popular television shows, like *Dragnet* and *Adam 12*.

For its part, the Los Angeles community left the LAPD alone to run itself and make sweeping dictatorial decisions about the type of services it would and would not deliver.

What began to hurt the LAPD was that as the community's needs and wants evolved, the department didn't change with them. The LAPD kept recruiting, hiring, and training the way it always had and stubbornly stuck with the same style of policing it was famous for.

Residents still wanted police officers who responded quickly, arrested the criminals, and made the streets safer, but they also came to want something more. They wanted officers who had compassion, and who understood and accepted and were representative of the cultural diversity of the community. Minority neighborhoods with high crime rates were afraid to ask for more police because some officers didn't seem able to tell the difference between law-abiding residents and criminal suspects of the same color. Interestingly, many of the same views about overbearing police were held in poor white neighborhoods. In other words, while these residents longed for safer streets, they didn't want police harassing them endlessly.

As the Christopher Commission had concluded, the department was too militaristic in structure and failed to embrace the community because it was too inwardly focused. Historically, then, the LAPD was the antithesis of community policing. Not surprisingly, bringing community policing to Los Angeles in the 1990s has not been easy. We've succeeded better in some areas than in others. It's a process that will take several years to fully implement.

The shift to community policing in Los Angeles is working, albeit slowly. Frankly, it is happening much slower than I would have liked, and I'm sure slower than the community would like, too.

It took a frustrating two years just to get some senior management staff working with some cohesiveness on the change in direction to community policing. I became distressed to find that some of my upper-level managers whom I saw and talked to quite regularly weren't always carrying my message back to their subordinates. I found, much to my surprise, that even good news that could help department morale—such as the purchase of new vehicles for our patrol fleet—was often bottlenecked at the top and didn't filter down. I decided to increase my personal communication to large groups of officers, at roll-call sessions and through periodic video briefings, to get the word out about the changes and improvements we were making.

Next, we focused on the midlevel managers—the captains and lieutenants. To date, we haven't as yet targeted much on the rank and file. Again, you have to start at the top and work down. In an organization as big and entrenched as the LAPD, any major change is going to take time and effort.

Still, some progress can be measured:

- Community police-advisory boards were formed in eighteen different areas of the city in early 1994. These groups, made up of community leaders and other neighborhood volunteers, meet regularly with police officers and supervisors, including area commanders. We don't just talk *to* them, but listen, *really* listen. These grassroots volunteers have a strong voice in determining how fair and effective police service is delivered in their communities.

- We have opened more than thirty-five "stop-in" centers throughout the city where residents can report nonemergency matters to officers. The idea in giving residents this kind of close personal contact with officers is that when something goes wrong, they will be more likely to talk to the police. Such contacts build trust and respect.
- We have opened a number of substations for patrol officers working in cars as well as those assigned to foot beats. Also, neighborhood "community service centers" where officers can phone in and prepare written reports without having to drive five or ten miles back to the main station. In this way, officers remain in the field where they are needed rather than disappearing inside headquarters. We are encouraging them whenever we can to get out of squad cars and into the neighborhoods to talk and work with residents.
- The LAPD has instituted the Community Police Academy, where residents of different sections of the city go through a ten-week night-school training program that offers the same instruction on department rules and regulations as is given to police cadets in the academy. They learn a bit about the law, and why we can and cannot do certain things. They hear from officers, prosecutors, even a judge. They get a chance to ride along on patrol and appreciate the difference between having to make instantaneous decisions and being a Monday-morning quarterback. Graduates receive a certificate, and much more: a better understanding of how the department operates and the reasons behind our policies. They return home as ombudsmen who can set their relatives and neighbors straight next time they start talking about the LAPD.

Our first Community Police Academy graduating class

came from South Central L.A. and included some long-time critics of the department. "We're not here to be backslappers," one woman announced on the first day. Ten weeks later, a classmate observed, "Now I know why officers can't just sweep the corner when I call because there are a bunch of kids hanging out. I still don't like it, but I understand."

- In some neighborhoods, there is beginning to be a break-through in the trust factor. This is especially true in areas where there are strong community-based organizations such as block-watch clubs, homeowners groups, etc. I think there's a new realization among these residents that the LAPD is *their* department. In these neighbor-hoods, we're getting a little closer and feeling more com-fortable with each other.

In other areas, there is less visible progress. In some of these neighborhoods, there has been a traditional dis-trust of police—a lot of it founded on real experiences. It's difficult to say to them convincingly, "We're a com-munity-based police organization now and we want to talk to you." They want to see what exactly is different, if anything. For them, the proof is in the pudding. And unfortunately, many of them have not yet seen a change in the police officers who patrol their neighborhoods. After hearing me go on about community policing at a neighborhood meeting—I attend at least a dozen around the city every month—they might say, "Yeah, the chief wants to change things. If he comes out and answers my next 911 call, I'll feel better." Their reality, however, can be that when the next black-and-white pulls up on their street, out pop two unsmiling cops wearing dark aviator glasses with their arms folded across their chests. "So what's changed?" these residents must wonder.

When the officers on the beat respond and act differ-ently, when their supervisors respond and act differently, and when the managers of the LAPD respond and act differently—only then will the public begin to acknowledge any real change.

If a citizen's complaint against an officer is handled in a proper manner, then the resident will go away feeling as if justice has been rendered and may begin to think that this community-policing stuff is working. If the complaint is mishandled or swept under the rug, then the resident will walk away even more distrustful of police.

We also have parts of the city where almost entire police districts are made up of first-generation immigrants who don't speak English. This makes our communicating with them that much more challenging. However, we're now paying bonuses to officers who are fluent in Spanish and other needed languages, and we're continuing to teach Spanish at the academy, as well as recruiting more Hispanic and other minority officers. Long-range, I have no doubt that we will reach every neighborhood in Los Angeles.

- Our appeal to L.A.'s corporate community has worked, especially after we began to manage the LAPD more like a business that was accountable to its customers. We also got the attention of business when we talked about changing the image of Los Angeles after the riots, and when they saw our preparations for the two trials that everyone thought would result in more rioting. The business community has a vital interest in ensuring a safer Los Angeles and, to this end, in seeing that the LAPD is strengthened and improved.

When it became clear that the city could not afford the purchase of a computer network for the LAPD—unbelievably, the LAPD was still paper-driven in today's era of computers, with officers estimated to be spending as much as 40 percent of their day completing paperwork—the mayor, and a group of business leaders, and I succeeded in raising the $15 million necessary to install computers departmentwide. This new system is expected to save the LAPD more than 640,000 hours annually—putting the equivalent of 368 officers back on the streets where they belong.

If the proof is indeed in the pudding, we do handle a multitude of things very differently today than the old LAPD did.

Not long after I arrived in L.A., an LAPD officer shot and killed an eighteen-year-old Hispanic gang member near Pacoima out in the Valley.

Police had been called to the scene by the man's mother after she and her husband had been unable to subdue her son, whom they described as "acting strangely." He had used a broomstick to break a front window of his mother's house and smash the windshield of her car.

Ordered by the officer to drop the broomstick, he charged instead, swinging and jabbing it at the officer, who, fearing for his own safety, took out his service revolver. He shot a number of times to stop the rampaging suspect. The coroner later found a high level of the hallucinogenic drug PCP in the man's blood at the time of his death.

Though our internal investigation would rule this an "in-policy" shooting and rightly so—facing a suspect on PCP is every cop's worst nightmare because the drug gives increased strength, causes bizarre behavior, and often makes the user impervious to pain—there was naturally a loud outcry at the time from residents in the neighborhood.

LAPD's Foothill Division in Pacoima was the scene of angry protests. A few hours later, police units had to protect L.A. firefighters, who were pelted with rocks and bottles as they put out a fire at a nearby school.

I went out to the northeastern end of the Valley and, along with the deputy chief in charge of the Valley and a local congressman, met with more than thirty people, including gang members, teachers, and community activists. At another community meeting a few days later there were some two hundred people, and about forty or fifty were gang members.

A lot of my officers and commanders were of the opinion that the chief of police had no business talking with gang members. No doubt previous chiefs would have avoided such encounters. I cannot say that such stonewalling would have led to increased tension and outbreaks of violence in the community. But I do know that had I not gone, it would have meant that I was giving little more than lip service to changing and reforming the department. Community policing means, as much as anything, going to these difficult meetings, looking angry people in the eye, listening to their concerns, and being straight and candid with them.

I was stern when I had to be at these meetings. While promising a full and prompt investigation, I made it clear that I was not going to allow any lawlessness and craziness on the streets. If people broke the law, no matter what the reason, they would be arrested. I solicited the residents to work with us, not against us, in finding out what happened, and in helping to defuse tensions in the community.

In the end, that's exactly what happened, although everyone—the man's mother, his friends and neighbors, and certainly the officer who pulled the trigger—could only feel remorse at this tragic death.

Three summers later, I was out of the country on vacation when an officer-involved shooting took place in the Lincoln Heights section of East L.A. that resulted in the death of a teenager. The boy, fourteen years old, was shot and killed on a dark street when he pointed a powerful semiautomatic weapon at officers working the gang detail. The loaded weapon was found not far from the boy's body.

Two days of street unrest by rock- and bottle-throwing youths followed, with the department going on tactical alert. Informed by telephone, I cut short my trip and returned home. By the time I got back to L.A., the unrest had subsided. A number of things had happened in my absence.

Not only had the department dealt firmly and fairly with the lawbreakers and demonstrators, arresting the most violent, but a citywide meeting had already been held with Hispanic leaders from all walks of life, and they had been given a full briefing. An LAPD captain, along with a member of the clergy, had set up meetings with the local street gang that the dead youth had belonged to as well as another gang—both were rumored to be ready to retaliate. Liaison between the department and the city council had also been strong, with elected representatives kept apprised of all events. The department had disseminated correct and detailed information to the media, in the hope of avoiding inaccurate and sensationalistic coverage.

I was proud of the way the department had responded—operationally and philosophically. They had done so without the chief in town, which made me feel even better. Upper- and middle-level management had not been afraid to act, and each step had been the right one.

"Ten years ago, maybe even five years ago," one of my senior commanders told me, "this whole thing would have been handled very differently. The department's main response would have been to line up the troops, hand out the helmets and shields and whatever else was necessary, and meet the threat in the street."

Instead, what had happened was that some very enlightened commanders at headquarters and at the scene in the Hollenbeck area had orchestrated a strong and measured show of force to stop the brick and bottle throwing—there were no serious injuries—then turned their attention to the public at large. They disseminated the facts of the shooting to community leaders, ministers, business and civic people, and anyone else who had a stake in the incident. Simultaneously, they also made sure that a full investigation was launched.

Upon my return, I met with some of the same groups and leaders. Although we were together because of the shooting, some people soon turned their attention to secondary issues. They

231

wanted to see more police in the area, they told me, and better curfew enforcement and increased effectiveness in handling gangs. It turned into a community-policing opportunity—we were able to hear what the neighborhood needed and find out how we could provide them with better police services.

Following through and solving some of their problems would be like saving money for a rainy day. The next time something happened and we needed to count on the community's goodwill, we could make a withdrawal.

In the fall of 1994, some two thousand students from a dozen San Fernando Valley schools took to the streets to demonstrate against a controversial state ballot proposition, which subsequently passed, denying public services, including medical benefits and education, to illegal residents of California. (Most chiefs of police in the state, including me, had come out in opposition to the measure. It was, we had concluded, bad for some local governments and could lead to increased crime and victimization that would go unreported.)

In Los Angeles, it is illegal to demonstrate or march in the streets without a parade permit. If you stay on the sidewalk, fine. The second you step into the street, you are subject to arrest. This law had been used in past years to break up many demonstrations and arrest the participants.

Although the demonstration was well organized, with students from eleven different Valley middle and high schools boycotting classes and leaving their various campuses en masse at noontime, no one had bothered to take out a permit.

We took the protests, and the possibility for trouble, seriously. I ordered a tactical alert to keep officers on duty in case the protests grew violent. We dispatched more than two hundred officers to protest sites.

In Van Nuys, there were isolated incidents of vandalism—sporadic rock and bottle throwing and minor theft from stores. One patrol car's window was smashed by unruly demonstrators.

Once again drawing on our "unusual occurrence" training

from prior to the second King trial, the department's response was well coordinated and appropriate.

Not looking for an excuse to make arrests, we escorted the students down the middle of the street for several miles, trying to keep them from breaking laws and being run over while maintaining public safety and the safe flow of traffic.

Another day, another time, something else entirely might have happened—a confrontation, perhaps, that could have ended up on the front pages of newspapers across the country.

Most of these kids were not being violent or looking for trouble. As one teacher put it, "They're out here getting a civics lesson." So we let them march. We never boxed them in but always gave them a "back door" in the event they wanted to turn around or disperse.

We brought up buses and kept them in the rear. Finally, when the students felt they had made their point, they willingly boarded for rides back to their schools.

There were no injuries or arrests.

The point is, this type of situation can easily be mishandled with overly aggressive policing. Legally, each and every one of the students marching in the street could have been arrested. But my officers and I knew whom and what we were dealing with: impassioned children of our city making a political statement. They were not criminals and did not deserve to be treated as such.

The students that day, and many demonstrators before and since, could thank a man they had never heard of, Inspector George Fencel, who more than any other law enforcement professional in America showed the way for the proper and appropriate police control of demonstrations.

In Philadelphia, the Civil Affairs unit, which handled any civil unrest and large demonstrations, had been the most sought-after assignment in the department. Formed in the late 1960s by Inspector Fencel, one of the most famous and respected commanders in department history, the unit grew out of the need to keep order during marches and demonstrations against the Vietnam War and in support of civil rights. From the beginning, it was a unit of hand-selected veteran officers who worked only in plainclothes and handled any type of demonstration, march, or activity that brought people out into the streets. They would only call in uniformed officers as a last resort if there were serious problems. Amazingly, four or five Civil Affairs officers could handle a march of five hundred people or more.

I had commanded the unit for a year in 1987 when I was inspector. By then, Civil Affairs had a reputation as being unbiased and impartial. Ninety-eight percent of the people who were going to demonstrate in Philadelphia would call Civil Affairs ahead of time, let us know their plans, and we'd tell them what they could and couldn't do. If they wanted to "take an arrest" to get their point across, we would coordinate with them the best way to accomplish that. "You can't block that intersection—we won't let you over there," we'd explain. "If you want to be arrested, stand over here."

The unit was made up of officers from all walks of life and was a sought-after assignment because it was viewed as special. You had to be a special officer to get there. You were not heavily supervised. You wore a suit and tie. You were respected by members of the community and the department alike. While some officers wanted into Stakeout (SWAT) and the bomb squad because they liked the action, the waiting list for the fifty-member Civil Affairs unit was always the longest at any time— 150 to 200 officers.

In an incident such as the May 1992 shooting in the Twenty-fifth District of Philadelphia during the L.A. riots, it was important to get the Civil Affairs team knocking on doors and telling residents—in conjunction with the Neighborhood Advisory Councils—exactly what had occurred. Just standing back and letting the rumors run their course would guarantee trouble—so would waiting for some interpretation of the incident to be reported by the media. Even if what you had to tell people was bad news, it worked better knocking on doors and providing information than waiting. The message, "This is what occurred and this is what the commissioner and the department are doing about it," left residents with the impression that the police were being responsible and fair-minded.

Working large demonstrations, however, was where Civil Affairs had earned its national reputation. The year I commanded the unit we had a major event celebrating the birthday of the Constitution. We had about half the U.S. Senate, a third of the House of Representatives, the entire Supreme Court, the president of the United States, and about one hundred foreign ambassadors in town for Fourth of July. Along with all this media attention came the demonstrators. You name it—pro-this, anti-that—we had a demonstration. Civil Affairs coordinated with organizers for groups involving from fifty to two thousand demonstrators.

One group protesting racial intolerance insisted that they were going to walk through police lines, and that they weren't going to cooperate with us. They insisted on placing an empty coffin on the steps of Independence Hall, which was in our "safe and secure" zone close to where all the luminaries would be sitting. We found ourselves in a stalemate with this group. They started a rally around city hall, then began the nineteen-block walk to Independence Hall and our police barricades.

I dispatched my captain and twenty-five Civil Affairs officers to walk with the thousand demonstrators and try to work out a last-minute compromise with their leaders en route. I was kept posted by walkie-talkie. Finally, the captain reported ominously, "Inspector, you better get the horses ready if you're going to hold the line. They're coming."

Of course, various federal protective services were on the scene in force, including the Secret Service. I advised them of the threat, and they warned that if any demonstrators passed through the barricades into the secure zone, they would be arrested and thrown in jail.

If that happened, I knew we would have a big fight on our hands. "You guys can go home tomorrow," I pleaded, "but we have to live here."

Finally, with not much more than a block to spare, we worked out an agreement. We would allow three demonstrators to carry the coffin—once it had been checked out by "bomb dogs"—up to the steps of Independence Hall. The remainder of the demonstrators would go down to the park where they had a permit to gather.

Everything worked according to plan. They placed their coffin on the steps, made a five-minute speech, then went back across the line.

Later that night, there was a big gay and lesbian demonstration. Everything was going peacefully, and we were standing down, relaxing for a spell. We had been working since 2 A.M. and it was then around 5 P.M.

With no warning, an intoxicated woman suddenly jumped over a fence that the demonstrators were supposed to stay behind. Before I could react, a uniformed Philadelphia police officer picked her up and tossed her back over the fence. She landed with a thud. I just about had a heart attack.

Several of my Civil Affairs officers went over the fence with me to see if she was all right and to try to defuse things. The dazed woman was, of course, hollering "police brutality." I ordered the uniformed officers back a distance so as not to further provoke the crowd.

The next thing I knew, about a hundred angry demonstrators were charging us, with the intention, no doubt, of scaling the fence and challenge the uniforms. We stood our ground calmly, and they stopped. Their leaders came up and asked what had happened. I told them and added that I didn't think the officer's reaction was appropriate. "We'll follow up on this and investigate it," I promised. Because we were Civil Affairs and because they had found us to be fair this day and in other similar situations, they backed off and we were able to calm the moment.

The LAPD has a history of handling demonstrations with uniformed personnel. The Metro unit has been trained to handle demonstrations, large or small, similar to the way we handled them in Philadelphia with our special plainclothes unit, following many of the same policies, rules, and guidelines. Today, Metro is fully outfitted with all our less-than-lethal tools, such as shotguns that fire rubber bullets and pepper spray.

In L.A., too, there is advance communication with group organizers. We find out if some people are going to want to "take an arrest" for publicity's sake. Everything is well coordinated.

During the past few years we've had major demonstrations in front of the federal building in Westwood and also downtown, and nothing has ever gotten out of hand and no one has been seriously injured.

As I said, we can all thank George Fencel.

We read in the newspapers these days:

"U.S. Crime Rate Dips Three Percent, FBI Says." "3rd Straight Drop in Homicide Rate in U.S." An 8 percent drop in the national homicide rate last year (1994) marked the third straight year it has fallen.

"Crime Rates Drop Again in California." Crime in California dropped 7 percent during the first six months of 1995, with double-digit decreases in homicide, rape, and robbery.

It's true, in Los Angeles and across the country, that crime—*statistically*, at least—is on the decline.

Figures collected by the U.S. Bureau of Justice Statistics suggest that more than 90 percent of Americans are safer today than they have been during the past two decades. The alarming exception to this trend is our teenagers, especially minorities, whose violent-death rate has been on the rise for a number of years.

In Los Angeles, crime has been dropping since 1992, including an 11 percent decrease in 1994. Homicides were down 21 percent; robbery, down 20 percent; rape, down 12 percent; burglary, down 14 percent; auto theft, down 16 percent; and theft from person, down 26 percent.

Police need to be extremely careful when it comes to calling a press conference to take credit for lower crime-rate figures. In L.A., we have mounted an aggressive campaign against crime, and some of the things we are doing might well be working—such as hiring more officers, increasing uniform visibility on the streets, emphasizing the arrest of violent gang members and career criminals. I hope they are. But other factors unrelated to law enforcement can cause variations in these statistics.

For instance, it is believed that a major reason for the decline in homicides is a dip in the young male population (under twenty-five years of age), who fall victim to homicides more than any other age group. Such a population cycle will undoubtedly correct itself one day, causing the press to report a "sudden rise" in homicides.

Also, measurable crime rates only reflect *reported* crimes. We don't know how many crimes are occurring that aren't reported, and we have no way of knowing whether these numbers are up or down.

Another factor that shouldn't be overlooked is the unacceptably large percentage of crimes nationally that remain unsolved. In the case of burglary, we only solve 20 to 25 percent of all reported cases. Every robber we arrest is probably responsible for at least four or five other robberies that remain unsolved.

Anyway, if police departments are going to share responsibility for crime-fighting with their communities, then the residents should be equally credited with any real reduction in crime. In fact, by creating better community partnerships, such as block clubs and neighborhood watch groups, residents may be doing as much as or more than police to prevent crime.

Another headline might read:

"Safer Streets, yet Greater Fear."

Numbers aside, the fear of crime is on the rise. One of the reasons is that crime today tends to be more violent than it was ten or twenty years ago. We've always had people stealing cars, but up until the last five or ten years, we didn't see car thieves put a gun to your head in a parking lot, force you from the car, and before driving away shoot you because you didn't move quickly enough. We have always had bank robbers—bank robbery used to be one of the least violent crimes in America because robbers usually just walked in with a note and maybe a hidden gun and the money was handed over. Now, they go in waving semiautomatic weapons, ordering everyone to the floor, and are quick to start shooting to get their point across. Armored cars are another example. No one ever went after an armored car before, but today, armored-car drivers have probably one of the most dangerous jobs in the country. We see three or four armored-car shoot-outs every month or so in southern California. Armored-car people shoot and kill robbers, and robbers kill them.

All this makes news. The way crime is reported by the nation's electronic and print media is another reason for the increased fear of crime. It's sensationalized and out of proportion to the coverage of other human events. A violent carjacking in L.A. doesn't just make the news locally, it becomes a national story. Stories about crimes involving young people either as the perpetrators or the victims raises the level of fear another notch.

Fear is immobilizing, not empowering. The paralyzing fear that the spreading cancer of violent crime will end up on your front porch is a terrible weight to live with. The reality of living with some level of crime in the community isn't much worse; importantly, you can do something about it by finding out what precautions to take for yourself and your family, by organizing with neighbors, by working with the police.

As long as people don't feel safe, there could be zero crime in their neighborhood and they would still lock themselves behind closed doors and not go out unless they have to. When people don't feel safe, they want to flee to some other "safer" place. That sanctuary, however, may not be as safe as Los Angeles or Philadelphia, both of which are among the safest major cities in the United States.

Philadelphia has for years ranked lowest in major crime among the nation's ten biggest cities. Los Angeles is ranked among the top one hundred cities in the country that have the most crime—but in the bottom half of this ranking even though it is the second-largest city behind New York. Yet, if you polled one hundred people and asked them what they thought were the most dangerous cities in America, ninety-five of them would probably have Los Angeles among the top five.

Fighting fear of crime is a major responsibility of city government and the police department. While we hope that increased uniform visibility on the streets will deter crime, we know for certain that a strong public safety entity on the street makes most law-abiding residents feel safer and, as a result, better about their city.

I know that my job as police chief is to deal with the reality of crime, first and foremost. But I've also learned how important it is to deal with perceptions.

In Philadelphia, I placed uniformed officers outside some subway stops at commuting hours because people were concerned about being robbed and panhandled. Because we had an officer on the street, people felt great. Now, the crime rate didn't change—it really hadn't been that bad at these locations to begin with. But there was a strong *perception* that crime had gone down, and more people began using the subway and stopping to shop at stores.

The LAPD is known for its "To Protect and To Serve" emblem on all its black-and-whites. It's important to me that this isn't just a slogan. Huge responsibilities come with it. The majority of officers in the department join me, I know, in taking them very seriously.

I tell the police officers in the field that to protect and serve means that we have the job of reducing crime and the fear of crime in the city's neighborhoods.

We have a responsibility to protect the young, many of whom are scuffling every day to get to school and back home safely.

We have a responsibility to protect the elderly; the generation that nurtured us and got us to adulthood now needs our help.

We have a responsibility to serve all the people who live in our communities regardless of ethnicity, sexual orientation, and political or personal preferences.

We may be called upon to serve the public in nontraditional ways. In addition to getting the robber or the burglar or car thief off the street, we might serve by talking in our elementary schools about the evils of drugs in programs like DARE.

It is our responsibility to work with health and human services people to try to get the mentally ill in hospitals instead of just throwing them in jail when they commit minor infractions.

We may be called to serve by walking a foot beat or riding a bicycle or standing outside a school or subway stop. The sun may be blindingly hot one day, and it may be pouring rain the next. But we will do it because we wear the badge of a police officer—

—and because we promise "to protect and to serve."

CHAPTER TEN

A MONTHS-LONG investigation by LAPD vice officers working with Beverly Hills police and the FBI ended in June 1993 with the arrest of Heidi Fleiss for felony pimping, pandering, and narcotics charges.

The complex investigation revealed that Fleiss operated a highly sophisticated prostitution ring where call girls made as much as $1,500 an hour catering to an exclusive clientele that included well-known figures from the entertainment world. She was arrested at her Benedict Canyon mansion about an hour after four of her employees were picked up in a vice sting at a swank Beverly Hills hotel, where hidden cameras filmed the women dispatched by Fleiss to entertain four police officers posing as Japanese businessmen celebrating a deal.

Fleiss was indicted by a grand jury three months later. In December 1994, she was convicted of three counts of pandering. The jury deadlocked on two other counts and found her not guilty of supplying cocaine to an undercover officer. She was sentenced to three years in prison.

The press had a field day with the "Hollywood Madam" story. From the beginning, the media sought to name names from Fleiss's so-called black book, which had been confiscated by police. Reporters scurried about trying to find out which movie stars and producers, rock stars, and other famous clients were listed. Fleiss herself periodically joked about releasing her client list. Hundreds of stories were published with as many lurid details as reporters could find about the high-priced prostitution ring and its madam.

I'll always think of this case as being joined at the hip with another unrelated case that received even *more* publicity: the investigation of pop singer Michael Jackson for alleged child molestation.

In August 1993, two months after the arrest of Heidi Fleiss, I received a phone call one evening as I was enjoying a backyard dinner with my wife and some friends visiting from back East.

I took the call on the patio, listening intently for ten or fifteen minutes and jotting down a few notes. When I finished, my good friend James Golden, who had been one of my top aides in Philadelphia, said, "Something's up. I can tell by the way you handled that call."

The news I had received concerned a complaint made to children's services officials by the parent of a youth who was said to have spent time at Jackson's Santa Barbara ranch. The young boy asserted that the singer had sexually molested him. Our investigation would be conducted by the department's Sexually Exploited Child unit.

My concern at this point, having already seen the media bedlam surrounding the Heidi Fleiss story, was to be certain that everyone in the department was clear on our protocol. Simply put, the case would be handled with the same confidentiality as any other child molestation complaint. We would not elaborate on it in any way.

The LAPD had investigated some four thousand child abuse reports the previous year, when nearly 3 million reports of child abuse were made nationwide. Of those we investigated, about 40 percent were substantiated, resulting in twelve hundred arrests. As these types of investigations went on by the thousands every year in L.A., it was premature to judge the singer or the credibility of the boy's report.

Inasmuch as stardom and the entertainment world are news unto themselves in Los Angeles, I braced for what I knew could be another onslaught. Even forewarned by experience, I was still incredulous at the extent of the coverage given this case.

More than three hundred stories about Michael Jackson appeared in the *Los Angeles Times* between August (1993) and the end of the year. No doubt that figure could easily be multiplied by the hundreds if you take into account the national and international press. One local media critic described the resultant chase by the press to cull information from dubious and so-called legitimate news sources alike as "Forget the facts, we want the story!" The most offensive aspect of this out-of-control coverage, from my perspective, was the disclosure, repeatedly, on local TV of the boy's identity.

A civil suit was filed against Jackson by the boy, claiming child molestation and seeking monetary damages. Jackson's civil attorney subsequently sought a six-year delay in proceedings until after the statute of limitations for the alleged crimes had expired.

For its part, Jackson's team of criminal-defense lawyers and private investigators went public with attempts to discredit the boy and his feuding, divorced parents and our investigation.

In a televised public statement in December 1993, the singer denied the allegation against him and described as a "horrifying nightmare" having parts of his body, including his genitalia, photographed by investigators.

His comments implied, I thought, that he had been terribly wronged, that we had set out to intentionally humiliate him because he was Michael Jackson.

It is always difficult to react at the time to such a statement and explain what you are doing while at the same time protecting the rights of both the child and the accused. We also do not want to give away our case before it is ready for prosecution.

Listening to Jackson that day, one could have drawn the erroneous conclusion that it was the first time that investigators had ever photographed someone's body in such a case. In thousands of cases where a child claims an adult has committed some type of sexual abuse, we have acquired a search warrant to take the photographs after receiving some indication that the child might be able to identify certain bodily characteristics. The point is, how would the child know these details unless something had occurred? This can be powerful corroborating evidence to support a child's word against an adult's.

Jackson eventually reached an out-of-court settlement in the civil matter with the boy and his parents. Jackson himself described the settlement as "less than $15 million." When the boy's attorney subsequently indicated that his client was not prepared to testify, no criminal charges were filed against Jackson. Without the main complainant, you don't have a case. In this situation, forcing the boy to testify could backfire.

Jackson, of course, has resumed his high-profile career. In a 1995 TV interview watched by 60 million people, he claimed that the boy who had accused him of sexual molestation had not been able to back up his charge by describing markings on Jackson's genitalia. "There was nothing that matched me to those charges," he declared.

I know that the LAPD and the other agencies involved in the investigation did their job correctly in the Michael Jackson case. I monitored it closely, and I know what evidence was gathered and how it was collected. Although I am not free to go into detail, I will say that Jackson's comments on TV were not all correct and were inconsistent with some of the evidence in the case.

Although some media have reported that Jackson was cleared of molestation charges, that is not true. The case is still open to this day. The investigation is currently suspended until somebody comes forward. It remains a prosecutorial decision as to whether charges will be filed before the statute of limitations expires.

Frankly, I had never experienced close-up anything like the media feeding frenzy that went on around these two "Hollywood" cases. I kept thinking, *There are so many more important things happening in this city and in the country that get little or no media attention.* I realized that I hadn't really known what a high-profile case was until I came to L.A.

How could it possibly get any crazier than the Hollywood Madam and Michael Jackson cases?

Little did I know.

Shortly after midnight on June 13, 1994, a passerby walking in the 800 block of South Bundy Drive in Brentwood found Nicole Simpson's body sprawled on the steps of the walkway in front of her town house. The body of Ron Goldman was found a few feet away. The throats of both victims had been slashed.

Police were called and the area was cordoned off so as to preserve the crime scene. Detectives from our West L.A. station were dispatched to the scene.

With little delay, the case was handed over to Robbery/Homicide, an elite investigative division based downtown. Not only did the unit have more resources to handle a crime of this magnitude, it also had some of the most experienced homicide detectives on the LAPD, which is why it traditionally worked the more complex murder cases from all parts of the city.

By that afternoon, evidence had been gathered at two different locations: the murder scene and the home of O. J. Simpson. The detectives had also preliminarily talked to Simpson for a few hours downtown upon his return on a commercial flight from Chicago around noontime that day.

Some hours later, I was at Los Angeles International Airport myself, heading to Philadelphia. I had been subpoenaed to testify the next day in a civil suit pertaining to a personnel matter from my days as commissioner. A civilian employee I had fired in 1990 for not doing his job had sued the city, the department, and me personally for damages. Although we would prevail in the trial, it turned out that I was stuck in court the remainder of the week.

During courtroom breaks and well into the evening, I spoke many times a day with my two assistant chiefs. Whether it was a shooting, a robbery, or a personnel matter, I stayed on top of what was happening in L.A. I also spoke with my chief of detectives and was kept fully abreast of what was being developed in the double-murder case. From experience, I knew that most homicides that aren't solved within a week or two have less chance of ever being solved. I was aware also of the LAPD's solid track record of clearing nearly three-fourths of all homicides with arrests.

Within a few days, the evidence clearly led to one and only one suspect. On Thursday, I was told that Robbery/Homicide detectives felt there was sufficient evidence to ask the district attorney to file a warrant for the arrest of O. J. Simpson on two counts of first-degree murder. I asked for a review of the evidence and information gathered, after which I concurred that it was time to go to the DA.

Simpson's lawyer, Robert Shapiro, promised to surrender his client the next morning, an arrangement that is commonly done every day with suspects throughout the United States, and one that we had even negotiated with Shapiro in other cases. Previously, he had always turned over his clients as promised. Also, in Simpson we were dealing with someone who had voluntarily returned from Chicago when we called him, and who had come in and waived his rights and submitted to three hours of questioning without his attorney. We did not give any preferential treatment to Simpson because of his notoriety. Nothing indicated he would be a flight risk. However, an hour before he was to surrender, Simpson disappeared with a friend.

At the time, the department was second-guessed for the way it had arranged to pick up Simpson. Even my predecessor condemned the LAPD for not arresting Simpson "days earlier." I can only point out that had we locked up Simpson on Monday, we would have had to release him on Wednesday, as police can't hold someone for more than forty-eight hours without a filing. The DA may well not have filed within the first forty-eight hours because we hadn't yet developed enough information and evidence to support a filing of two murder charges. How would we have looked then?

I was asked, some days later, by Bryant Gumbel on the *Today* show, whether or not we had treated Simpson special because of who he was. I denied it then, and I deny it now.

I could only shake my head in bewilderment later whenever Simpson's legal defense team thundered in court about the LAPD's "rush to judgment." Had we rushed to judgment, we would indeed have arrested Simpson days earlier, when detectives first followed the trail that would eventually connect the crime scene and Simpson's home. Instead, Robbery/Homicide was methodical in pursuing all leads and gathering a great volume of physical evidence.

When police units located Simpson riding in his friend's white Ford Bronco on an Orange County freeway late Friday afternoon, I was having dinner in Philadelphia (where it was three hours later) at the home of my successor, Police Commissioner Richard Neal, after another long day in court. The house was staked out by local TV and print media hoping for some comment by me on the breaking Simpson story.

From the moment the Bronco was located, I was on an open line to Parker Center. In addition to making some decisions, I asked lots of questions. Can we talk to him by cell phone? Are SWAT and the hostage-crisis negotiators ready to roll? Do we have his ex-wife's place covered? Where are the two children? I was gratified to find that most of my areas of concern had been anticipated and already taken care of. Yes, we had him on the phone. SWAT is ready. And the children were covered.

When it came to strategy, I affirmed that based on what we knew—Simpson was reported to be suicidal and holding a gun to his head—police units shouldn't force a stop on the freeway. With so many other people and cars around, that was not a situation we could fully control. If shooting began, innocent bystanders as well as police officers could be hurt or killed. At the same time, we had no intention of letting the Bronco off the freeway so it could get lost in city traffic. In what was a tricky tactical operation, chase cars were positioned near every exit. If the Bronco pulled off the freeway, their orders were to block it at the foot of the off-ramp.

Eventually, it became apparent Simpson was heading home. That was fine—we could better control the situation there. We would let him go, and we'd be ready.

From my old friend's family room I watched the chase live on CNN, like millions of Americans. It would be reported later that two-thirds of the nation's households had their TVs tuned in to this odd "slow-speed" chase along the Los Angeles freeways. We might wonder, just what were the other one-third doing?

I watched as the Bronco pulled into the driveway at Simpson's home. My thoughts at the time were that if something went horribly wrong, the department would be living with the impact for years. If Simpson seriously injured someone or if we had to shoot and possibly kill him, we'd be damned until the end of time. And there I was—watching it on TV from 2,800 miles away.

Our crisis negotiators went to work—always in control, very relaxed, never forcing the issue, keeping an open dialogue with the armed and depressed suspect. Never showing fear or nervousness, they were in every way consummate professionals, and I was proud of them.

When it ended, I breathed a sigh of relief, as I'm sure the men and women of my department did. Later that night, I was told, Simpson's attorney thanked the LAPD, and me personally, on TV for the peaceful resolution.

I would hear for weeks from other law enforcement professionals around the country, who wrote and telephoned their congratulations. The consensus was that this arrest had been the LAPD at its finest. Even the local and national media jumped on the bandwagon. Rush Limbaugh, a day or two later, exulted, "Kudos, kudos to the LAPD for a job well done!" And a *Los Angeles Times* columnist wrote, "Give [the LAPD] a pay raise— they deserve it." (The lengthy labor dispute between the city and the police union, which had resulted in two thousand officers marching in protest on city hall and illegal "blue flu" epidemics with hundreds of officers calling in sick at the last minute, had reached a pivotal point and would *finally* be resolved in a matter of days.)

I guess I could be accused of letting my department take its bows whenever and wherever possible in this vexing case. To the charge, I plead guilty. The point that so often got lost, or at least badly obscured, during and after the long trial was that the Los Angeles Police Department did some very credible police work here.

Our investigation did not stop with Simpson's arrest, of course. We still had physical evidence to gather and review, and countless interviews to conduct. As I told the media that night, "We would be beyond the greatest police department in the world if we could close a homicide case in four days. Everybody expects this case to be a slam dunk, and no homicide case is a slam dunk."

Eventually, the strategy of the Simpson legal defense team became apparent. They intended to focus attention away from their client and the mass of incriminating evidence in the case and put on a kind of scorched-earth defense. They would implicate and put on trial the entire system that had brought their client to the bar of justice. They would contend that the entire LAPD took part in a grand scheme to frame their client, or was terribly incompetent, or both when it suited them. All the scientific testing procedures, even those done by the FBI and outside labs, would be found wanting—inaccurate, slanted, and biased. Importantly, they would not have to prove any of this because only the prosecution, not the defense, must prove its case. They could score points just by asking the questions and planting the seeds of doubt. It was, they must have believed, the best—and maybe the only—way to divert the attention of the jury, thereby making it more difficult for the prosecution to meet its burden of proving guilt beyond a reasonable doubt.

This tactic was really nothing new. Defense lawyers throughout the United States had been attacking police for decades in an effort to put anyone and everyone on trial except their clients.

251

I remember it happening to me back in the 1970s when I was a young detective testifying in court. On cross-examination, one of Philadelphia's most famous trial lawyers, Cecil Moore, went up one side of me and down the other. I no longer recall the nature of the case, but he attacked the way I had read the Miranda rights to the defendant, he attacked how I had handled the evidence, he attacked my credibility and virtually everything I did, trying to put in the judge's mind—it was a nonjury trial—that I had really messed up.

During a court recess following my testimony, I was standing out in the hallway, feeling a little shaken.

The defense attorney came over to me. "You did a good job, kid," he said, smiling kindly. "You're going to make a good detective someday."

I realized then that it wasn't anything personal. It had been all business for him—the business of defending his client. If it came at the expense of me or other police officers or the department itself, too bad. I came to learn through the years that even when you did everything right, you could expect to be attacked in court. That's just the way the game is played.

In most cases, however, it unfolds in a nearly empty courtroom with a judge, lawyers, sometimes a jury, and a few onlookers. The difference in the Simpson case, after the judge's decision to allow cameras into the courtroom, was that the entire world would be watching.

I have been asked, in light of the Simpson case, how I feel about cameras in the courtroom. Would I favor restricting live coverage of criminal cases in the future?

I am a strong defender of First Amendment rights. If we're going to err on the side of caution, I'd rather err by having a more open society and learning how to live with all the ramifications. So I'm not opposed to cameras in court—I think the judicial system should be open for public review.

The biggest problem, as I see it, is some of the interpretation that's done during the breaks and after the day's session by reporters, news anchors, and so-called experts. These inter-preters of the news can make lasting impressions in telling the public and an unsequestered jury—or in the case of a sequestered jury, the pool of prospective jurors for a second panel in the event of a hung jury the first time around—what has supposedly taken place. This analysis is completely subjective and sometimes bogus, yet it is passed off as gospel. Still, I'd never advocate keeping cameras out of the courtroom. Long term, I think such openness does much more good than not.

In California, cameras are allowed in state courts at the dis-cretion of the judge. The California Judicial Council is presently examining the wisdom of allowing cameras in the courtroom. In the meantime, I think some judges will try to anticipate the level of sensationalism that may result from live coverage and decide, accordingly, if cameras would be a hindrance to a trial. I expect they will be called upon to make some tough calls.

In the Simpson case, I didn't want to respond to rumor, innu-endo, and statements to the press by the defense lawyers prior to trial. But inwardly, I chafed at the defense lawyers' public cam-paign to discredit the department. They were clearly hoping to plant seeds of doubt in the minds of some of the people who might become jurors. I also knew that such garbage had to be taking its toll on the rank and file, which was already suffering from low morale. Finally, in September (1994), four months before the trial began, I decided enough was enough.

"Very unfairly, the defense has decided to target my depart-ment," I said on the *Today* show, my first TV interview since charges were filed in the case. "Individuals have been attacked, their morals, their values, their skills. The organization as a whole has been attacked. I think a lot of it has been to divert the public and the people who will sit on that jury from the real facts in the cases."

Bryant Gumbel asked if "police leaks" hadn't help foster the "media circus" that surrounded the case.

"I absolutely disagree. A lot of 'leaks' are only rumors, or orchestrated 'leaks' to the press by the defense, or outright fantasies made up by the media," I said. "Just go back to June and the 'bloody ski mask.' "

Inside the LAPD, we had known that no bloody ski mask existed, yet in the days following the murders, the media reported such evidence, pinning the report to unnamed "police sources." The national and international press ran the story. A month or two later, during a pretrial hearing on the case, the prosecution's complete list of evidence was made public. Of course, it did not include a ski mask. (It did list a black watch cap, which did not contain any blood evidence.) The defense well knew there was no bloody ski mask, but playing the moment to the hilt in open court, a defense attorney had said, "Your Honor, I've read about this bloody ski mask. Can the DA tell us where it is?" Predictably, this "news break" became headlines.

"The press acted as if a piece of evidence had disappeared rather than acknowledging that no bloody ski mask ever existed," I pointed out to Gumbel. "Anyone close to the case knew there was no bloody ski mask. That means the reporter who broke the story didn't talk to anyone in the police department who was on the case—if he or she even *did* talk to someone at LAPD. But talking to just anyone in uniform over coffee doesn't make for a credible source. That's not a 'leak'—it's no more than a rumor."

In covering the Simpson case, the media was like a school of sharks in a seafood store. There were numerous examples of the press hurrying to report on evidence that didn't exist, statements that weren't made, and nonexistent laboratory reports. I don't mean just the supermarket tabloids, either, but responsible media outlets that got caught up in the chase for the next Simpson scoop. The department could not respond to such reports— we could not talk about what evidence existed and what didn't.

Another issue I was asked about was the dispatch of an inexperienced forensic criminalist from the LAPD's Scientific Investigations Division (SID)—along with a more experienced criminalist—to the crime scene. Although this woman had been fully trained, she was new to SID. The defense was implying publicly that the LAPD had badly erred in giving her this important assignment, although again, they didn't have to prove now or ever that she had in fact made mistakes. (As far as I'm concerned, she did a first-rate job.)

Gumbel wanted to know why we hadn't sent only the most experienced criminalists, given the fact that we were dealing with O. J. Simpson and a potentially huge case.

This was the opposite tack from that taken by the same interviewer three months earlier when he had hit on whether we had given Simpson any preferential treatment when we had arranged with his lawyer for his voluntary surrender.

"What kind of signal would it send to John and Mary Q. Citizen who don't play football or aren't famous?" I asked. Somehow, I didn't think residents would appreciate it if they thought they were getting the crime lab's "second team" because our more experienced lab techs were saved for cases involving celebrities and those who would get more news coverage. "I don't think we want to work that way."

I was also asked about Mark Fuhrman, whom the defense was already targeting. I was not willing to discuss anything confidential from his personnel jacket. "One thing I can say: In evaluating Fuhrman's work at the crime scene the night of the murders, I've found nothing to suggest that he did anything but the appropriate job of an LAPD detective."

In his opening statement to the jury in January 1995, defense attorney Johnnie Cochran Jr. described the department as having bungled the case and also alleged a nefarious LAPD conspiracy to plant evidence on the night of the killings and frame Simpson for the murders.

With the defense's trial strategy now "on the record" in court, I opened up my own aggressive offensive in defense of the hardworking men and women of my department who were being beaten up daily.

"It is unconscionable to paint a picture where detectives, police officers, civilian lab people, and others decided to plot against Mr. Simpson, carry it out, all keep quiet, and not have anyone break it," I said at a news conference the next day. "It's too fanciful to imagine."

In those wee hours of the morning we had at least eight to ten patrol officers from Traffic controlling the perimeter of the crime scene. We had homicide detectives from our local station in West L.A. We had civilian laboratory technicians from SID. We had Robbery/Homicide detectives from downtown. And because it was a double murder, the command staff began showing up in short order to oversee things. And of course, the media, which monitors police scanners, arrived in droves. One officer could not have pulled it off alone. A number of these officers, some of whom had never met before that night, would have had to say, "Hey, this is O. J. Simpson's ex-wife. Let's move some evidence over to his house and frame him for her murder."

They would have had to do this between three-thirty and four o'clock in the morning, prior to going over to Simpson's estate. They would have had to do this without knowing where Simpson was at the time of the murders, whether he was in town or not, or even whether he was alive or dead. Suppose he had an airtight alibi or was out of town? Would the scheming officers then *unplant* the evidence and move it back to the crime scene to save their own necks?

Then, at some point, someone involved in this perfect plot would have had to know that Simpson would voluntarily submit a blood sample the next day, go back to the scene of the crime, as well as to Simpson's house, smear it around the scene, at his house, in his car, and on other evidence. However many were involved in this frame-up would all have had to concoct it quickly, agree to do it, then keep it secret.

"It's outrageous, it's fantasy, it's something that belongs in Disneyland," I concluded.

The police-conspiracy theory didn't wash, but it really didn't have to. The job of the Simpson defense team, which it undertook with great relish, was to keep throwing wet spaghetti at the wall and see how much of it stuck. Any innuendo that worked to cloud the minds of the jurors was a win for them and placed their client one step closer to walking—this in a brutal double-murder case with an overwhelming amount of physical and circumstantial evidence that all pointed to his guilt.

Early on in the Simpson case, it had become clear that the defense team had decided to attack and destroy the credibility of the Los Angeles Police Department. They made the decision to attack the department at all levels: patrol officers, detectives, lab people, and the leadership. They had months before the trial to sharpen their attacks and plant their stories, all in an effort to influence the population from whose ranks the jury would come. And the media, not to law enforcement's surprise, sucked it right up. They fell for it hook, line, and sinker. They reported every rumor, every innuendo, every veiled allegation as if it were fact, from the bloody ski mask to the existence of an organized police plot to frame their client. The defense in any case has a right—in fact, an obligation—to question the actions and tactics of police. That's fair, and I defend and support defense attorneys, including Simpson's, to proceed accordingly. But there's an ethical line that I believe the defense in this case crossed. They did an awful lot of showboating at the expense of my people. They didn't care how many capable, honest, and conscientious officers and civilian employees of the LAPD they smeared.

As the trial progressed, I seldom had an opportunity to watch live coverage. I did try to sneak glimpses whenever our investigators were testifying. In the snippets of testimony I managed to see, I thought detectives Tom Lange and Philip Vannatter were particularly strong. If anyone ever wanted to make a movie about what a real detective is like and what it means to work homicide in Los Angeles, all they had to do was watch these two pros on the stand.

As for Vannatter carrying the vial of Simpson's blood around with him for three or four hours before turning it in to the lab, I am convinced he committed no improprieties. Detectives all over America carry pieces of physical evidence around during the day as they work an investigation and book it in when they return to the station from the field. If they had to drive to the station every time they came across some shred of evidence, they'd spend more time stuck in traffic than working their cases.

This is not to say that I didn't hear some things in this case that I thought could be improved upon—ways that we could do something better or differently next time. Of course, I've felt that way about most cases in my thirty-two-year police career. Like anyone in any profession, we should not be afraid to learn and improve. In fact, it's more important we learn from our mistakes than from our successes.

Few jobs in the public sector come under the constant, consistent scrutiny that law enforcement does. This applies to the entire profession, sworn personnel as well as civilian employees, from the newest rookie cop on the beat right on up to the chief of police. The larger the city, the more intense the scrutiny. People will examine the actions of the fire department after a big fire—could it have been put out quicker and with less loss of life or damage to property?—then go away. People may look at the streets department after a major disaster—how quick was it to rebuild damaged roads?—then go away. But in law enforcement, because we have constant contact with the public—70 percent of the time we are dealing with countless small crises and the rest of the time with major crises—someone is always watching. The scrutiny comes from such diverse groups as the local political leadership, the media, and community groups—often, *all* at the same time. So, scrutiny is nothing new for us. In Los Angeles, however, from the first day I arrived, I had the feeling that we were operating not under a microscope but under the Hubble Space Telescope. I don't want to sound overly paranoid, but I'm pretty sure there's this big telescope somewhere out in

space that just waits to flash images around the world of everything we do.

The LAPD crime lab has long been viewed as being in the top
10 to 15 percent of police labs in the country. To try to get away
from all the incriminating evidence in the case, however, the
Simpson defense desperately had to cast the LAPD lab as being
filled with hopeless bumblers who don't know the business end
of a microscope. After much innuendo, critical testimony by
highly paid hired guns for the defense, and plenty of artful
phrasing of questions by defense lawyers, in the end *not a shred
of evidence proved that our crime lab in any way negatively
impacted the quality of the scientific evidence in this case.*

This is not to say that SID's proficiency can't regularly be
improved with more and newer cutting-edge equipment and
additional training. No technical lab in the world is immune to
the need for modern enhancements, least of all those supported
by municipal taxpayers in today's economy.

Every year at budget time, I've requested increased funding
for the lab—to buy new equipment, to step up training, to hire
more technicians, etc. The lab has never once received the level
of funding requested. For five straight years the department
sought major increases in the lab budget. Each year from 1990
through 1995 these requests were denied almost in total. One
year, for example, I asked for more than $750,000 for lab
improvements. The city government, allocating the sparse
resources of a city strapped for cash, approved less than 10 percent of that amount. I intend to diligently keep pursuing more
resources for the crime lab. Perhaps the attention placed on the
lab during the Simpson case, and the recognition of just how
crucial scientific evidence can be in criminal cases, will help.

In late August, the Simpson trial took a terrible turn. For the
first time since he stepped down from the stand five months earlier, Mark Fuhrman's voice again filled the courtroom. This time,
his "testimony" came by way of taped interviews conducted in
the mid-1980s with an aspiring screenwriter. He bragged about

police brutality, boasted of fabricating evidence against suspects, and used the word *nigger* time and again, contradicting his earlier testimony that he had never used that hurtful epithet.

A week later, Fuhrman, who had retired from the department the previous month, returned to the stand after a series of witnesses had portrayed him as a hate-filled racist. This time, with his attorney at his side, he answered every question he was asked with the same monotone response: "I wish to assert my Fifth Amendment privilege."

It was chilling to see a police officer evoke his right against self-incrimination in a criminal trial. It was chilling for local residents and for the nation as a whole, and it was chilling for us in law enforcement who had done our job properly and ethically for decades.

Although only a few excerpts from the Fuhrman tapes were heard by the jury, America heard much more. Decent people of all races everywhere recoiled at the former detective's seething racism and sexism—his attitude about women in policing didn't even belong in the twentieth century. On one tape, Fuhrman complained about all the "niggers in L.A. city government— and all of 'em should be lined up against a wall and [expletive] shot." At the time he mouthed those ugly words, that would have included city council members and police commissioners, city department heads, and the mayor of Los Angeles.

Whether all of Fuhrman's hideous bragging about his tailored brand of sickening street justice turned out to be true or not— and I *did* intend to find out how much of it actually happened— I knew that his hateful words were going to haunt the Los Angeles Police Department for years to come. Every time I thought morale had fallen as low as it could go, and as soon as I thought we'd done something positive to start back on the road to recovery, something else was layered right on top. Never in my life had I seen a police department go through such a series of divisive incidents as LAPD had, beginning with the Rodney King beating in 1991 and extending to Mark Fuhrman in 1995.

I had long thought that the tape of the King beating had done the most damage imaginable to the image of the LAPD. But now, whatever that shocking videotape had failed to destroy, the Fuhrman audiotapes laid waste to.

There was still a double-murder case being tried in the criminal courts building across the street, and I didn't forget that for a second. At the same time, I had to be concerned about where the LAPD went from here. I would not stonewall the public, the media, or members of my own department on the Fuhrman issue. We could not duck it because it was painful. We had to take a long look in the mirror, even if we didn't like what stared back at us.

In a taped video message to the department in late August that was shown at every roll call, I said, in part, "During the past week, we, the men and women of the LAPD, have found ourselves once again being painted with a broad brush of accusations—this because of the comments of one of our former members, Detective Mark Fuhrman.

"I am here today to call upon each and every member of the LAPD to stand up and let his or her fellow employees, plus the men and women of our great city, know that those of us who wear a badge and carry an ID card as members of this department are not racist and are not sexist. It is up to us to say, 'Enough is enough. We do not condone, we do not accept, and we do not tolerate racism and bias and sexism in our midst.'

"We must look in the mirror. We must each turn to our fellow employees and say, 'If you're part of the problem, stop it. If you can't stop it, get out of the LAPD and make room for an employee who will treat our city's residents and other employees with the respect and dignity they deserve.' "

I was extremely concerned to see every hour, twenty-four hours a day, on the national and international news, that the LAPD was being portrayed as racist, sexist, anti-Semitic, brutal, and capable of planting evidence.

I was interviewed that week by scores of TV and print media outlets. "We have zero tolerance for racism, sexism, anti-Semitism, and any type of discrimination in the LAPD," I said. "That is a nonnegotiable issue."

I also pointed out, every chance I got, that there was no proof—and still is none to this day—to indicate any planting of evidence in the Simpson case. Think for a minute about the defense's scenario of Fuhrman removing the glove from the crime scene and taking it to Simpson's house. How could he have known that those were special gloves, only two hundred pairs made and that two pair of them had been bought by Nicole? Like so many of the defense's theories in this case, it didn't compute. And don't forget, four or five other police officers and investigators testified to seeing only one glove at the crime scene early that morning. And again, Fuhrman would have had to remove the second glove at a time when he didn't know *where* Simpson was during the murders.

We immediately undertook a "biopsy" of Fuhrman's entire twenty-year career. Soon, five LAPD detectives—and eventually eleven—were working full-time, interviewing his former partners and young officers he had helped train, examining virtually every case he had handled as a detective and patrol officer. We were doing this for two reasons: damage control within the department—to what degree had Fuhrman infected our ranks?—and to keep the public fully informed. There was a very real possibility that if Fuhrman had broken any laws for which the statute of limitations had not run, he could be prosecuted.

In nearly every interview, I was asked the same question: "Are there other Mark Fuhrmans in the LAPD?"

"Yes, there are other Mark Fuhrmans on the force," I answered with a heavy heart. "They're a small but significant number."

I estimated that perhaps two hundred to three hundred members of today's LAPD might share Fuhrman's warped views. Although we did not have a list of names, we knew they existed in our ranks, just as any large company or agency, public or private, has to face up to the fact that a small percentage of its people are racists or sexists.

But even if we knew who all the other Mark Fuhrmans were, we could not automatically fire them. We do have ways to keep them off the street and nail them to a desk job, but that is only a partial solution. We and other police departments should be able to fire any officer for being a racist, but it doesn't work that way. The reality is that given employee protections under civil service regulations and the city charter, it will take time to move them all out. And Los Angeles, by the way, is not the only major police force in the country with this problem. I don't know if this will be considered "the good news," but ten to fifteen years ago racist police officers were more numerous in the United States, and much less shy about letting their true feelings show, both in the locker room and on the street.

Today, we are sending a strong message to the Mark Fuhrman types of the LAPD, one that the rank and file, the supervisors, the managers, and the chief must deliver simultaneously: *You are not going to do it and get away with it if we find out. And those people who know about it and cover it up and say nothing because of the old code of silence are going to be held just as liable.*

I watched the announcement of the Simpson jury verdict in my office with one of my deputy chiefs and my adjutant lieutenant.

As we waited for the verdict to be read, I knew that no matter which way it went, segments of the media and the public would dump on the department. If there was a guilty verdict, we would be accused of planting evidence and framing an innocent man. If it was a not guilty, we would be accused of doing such a poor job in the investigation that our efforts resulted in a guilty man going free. It was a classic no-win position for the LAPD.

Although part of me hoped that the jury had seen the preponderance of evidence that I saw and quickly voted guilty, I was uneasy about the extremely short time they had spent deliberating. After a nine-month trial with a mountain of evidence and tens of thousands of pages of testimony, they made up their minds in under *three hours?* Another part of me figured that it would be easier to vote not guilty than guilty with such limited effort.

When I heard the verdict, I was surprised but not over-whelmed. After more than three decades in law enforcement, there aren't many things left in the world that can truly shock or amaze me anymore. I was equally prepared, I think, for any result. That is not to say, however, that I wasn't sorely disappointed.

The mayor had asked to see me after the verdict, but before I went across the street, I went directly downstairs to the third floor and Robbery/Homicide. Although probably forty to fifty detectives and civilian employees were sitting around televisions, the room was stone silent. I spent more than an hour there, speaking words of encouragement and letting them know, as a group and individually, that nobody blamed them and that they did the best they could.

"We're not going to let the world dump on this department," I said. "There's not going to be any massive turnover or change in Robbery/Homicide. But we do have to live with this verdict. We have to go on. We're cops and we're professionals."

I met with Lange and Vannatter alone for a while. They were very down, of course. The thing that bothered them the most was the minuscule amount of time the jury had taken to deliberate. Obviously, a majority of jurors had their minds made up ahead of time and had just gone through the motions. But as the true professionals they are, Lange and Vannatter knew they had to move on. Any police officer with more than five years on the force has experienced the exact same thing. You conduct an investigation, you arrest someone who you'll absolutely believe until you go to your grave was guilty of the crime, and then you see him walk. It's tough. "But you know, Chief," one of the detectives said, "we've got other homicides to work. We're going to go out and do the job that the people pay us to do."

The worst violation by the Simpson defense team, I had felt, had been to lump Vannatter and Lange with Mark Fuhrman. The two veteran detectives, who, again, had never met Fuhrman before the night of the murders, were right about how darn sorry they were that they had *ever* met him.

The fact that Fuhrman was on duty for West L.A. detectives that night was another stroke of bad luck for the department. No other officer on the case had his background or was as open to attack. I had a feeling then, and nothing has changed my mind since, that Mark Fuhrman, after two decades with the LAPD, probably doesn't have ten friends left in the department.

It's still my belief, based on the evidence that was gathered, that we arrested the right person for the murders of Nicole Brown Simpson and Ronald Goldman.

Like Lange and Vannatter, the LAPD had to move on. In the same week of the Simpson verdict, several people were found guilty of murder based on successful investigations by the LAPD. Around that same time, I handed out Medal of Valor awards to a dozen earnest, hardworking, and professional officers who had taken that extra step to put themselves in harm's way to serve the people of their community. Whether they arrested a robber or rescued people from a burning car or crawled through a collapsed apartment house looking for survivors, I find these men and women to be the truest reflection of the LAPD today.

This doesn't mean we are complacent in any way. One of my highest priorities since assuming command of the LAPD has been to rid the department of bias based on race, gender, and sexual orientation. Now that we have all seen the damage that unchecked prejudice can cause within our ranks, perhaps I have everyone's attention more than ever.

Last year, I instituted a "zero tolerance" policy for officers who would follow the code of silence and not report inappropriate behavior by their fellow officers. In not speaking up, they will henceforth be considered an accomplice. We still need to follow up with changes in the disciplinary system, such as reworking civil service guidelines. In my view, officers like

265

Mark Fuhrman must be as easy to dismiss as officers who are caught taking kickbacks from drug dealers or who stole and robbed.

The unfortunate perception from the Simpson case that many LAPD police officers are racist is simply not true. This doesn't mean there are no bad apples in the department, any more than it means there are no bad apples among the sixty thousand peace officers in California. Of course there are. But today, more is being done in L.A. than ever before to screen out and evaluate police candidates, and to identify and deal with rogue cops. That we have a few hundred people in the department who reflect Fuhrman's views on the job *will* change. Already, I suspect, they are less inclined to say certain things on the street or commit certain acts than the Mark Fuhrmans of the department were a decade or two ago.

In fact, personnel complaints filed by officers against other officers—which, interestingly, have been running significantly higher than complaints filed against LAPD officers by residents—were down 20 percent in 1994 (878 complaints). My interpretation of this is that our employees are realizing that they are now more likely to be held accountable for inappropriate actions; therefore, they are thinking twice.

Continued diversity within the ranks of the department will help eliminate racism and sexism. Along those lines, great strides are being made. Fifteen years ago, only 22 percent of the LAPD were nonwhites and women. Today, just over half of the officers on the force are women and minority.

The LAPD is nationally renowned for being corruption-free. It's probably one of the greatest strengths we have. When we become nationally renowned for not tolerating biased views and for not beating up suspects, then we'll have closed the gap that we find ourselves still living with.

In the summer of 1995, I fired an officer for sexual harassment of a female employee. He was a training officer, with five or six years on the job. It was his first major transgression, but the act that he committed was so significant that I felt he should be dismissed. That didn't happen four or five years ago for this type of behavior. He would have received a slap on the wrist, maybe a few days off and a transfer. The message wasn't there earlier. It is today.

This message overlaps with how officers treat residents. As a direct result, citizen complaints are down 12 percent (638 complaints). Use-of-force complaints are also down, from 238 in 1992 to 168 in 1994, with 81 complaints in the first eight months of 1995. Another barometer: Between 1980 and 1992, the amount the city paid to settle police-misconduct lawsuits increased more than twenty times, to $19.7 million. In the three years since, settlements have declined about 80 percent—down to under $8 million for 1995.

As 1995 came to an end, the LAPD was in the middle of the first stage of change and reform begun in mid-1992. There are people, both in and out of city government, who expected the department to have the entire process wrapped up by now, so we could go on to whatever was next. The fact is, true reform of this or any major police department will probably take ten to twelve years.

It will take a decade of accountability, openness, and progressive leadership from the LAPD to show minority communities in Los Angeles that the earlier era—call it the era of Mark Fuhrman—has passed. It will take that long to overcome because it went on for too long.

I intend to continue to be an instrument for reform, which I know will not always make me popular with everyone. To date, many of the 150 specific recommendations of the Christopher Commission have been implemented. There is still a lot of difficult work ahead, however. Not to address the quiet cancers of racism and sexism and other intolerances that eat away at the fabric of a police department would be derelict on my part. My goal is nothing short of mobilizing and inspiring the LAPD to be better and fairer, every day, than we were the day before.

To be successful ultimately, we will need the continuous attention and support of the people in our community. The window of opportunity that opened for police reform in Los Angeles with the Rodney King beating five years ago is still open.

How much longer it will be open, I do not know.

WHAT WE ALL CAN DO

IN THE 1990S AND BEYOND, we're going to have to learn to live and survive in a society that is not always nice. We're going to have to live with bad folks roaming the streets who don't belong there. We're going to have to survive the threat of serious crime, even violent crime, present throughout our lives on a regular basis. Accepting these harsh realities of modern life doesn't mean we have to give up. Far from it.

However, for residents to help save their community or just their block, they have to be willing to draw a line in the sand. They have to learn how to join with neighbors and police in fighting crime where it affects us all the most: in our homes and on our streets.

I have seen through the years that there comes a time when most residents will jump up and do what needs to be done to help fight crime. That time often comes when they are fed up, when they are ready to become part of the solution. Only then do good things start happening.

Community policing is at work in cities large and small across America, from Los Angeles to New York City, from San Diego to Portland, from Philadelphia to Miami, with ordinary residents and police forming partnerships to reduce and prevent crime and make their homes and neighborhoods safer. It can be done!

Here are some actions the average citizen can take:

- *Good neighbors protect each other.* Most thieves and other criminals will not go where they think there's a chance of being reported or apprehended. They will look for easier pickings, of which there are plenty in any city in the country. Get organized. If there's already a neighborhood watch program, become a member. If there isn't, get together with your neighbors and start some type of neighborhood crime-prevention group. In getting to know each other and working together, you and your neighbors *can* reduce crime on your block.

- *Get involved and stayed involved.* Crimes are solved by ordinary people coming forward and being good witnesses. Learn to recognize and report suspicious activities. Don't keep walking or turn your back or pull down your living-room shade when you see a crime being committed. Remember, next time the victim could be you.

- *Identify the problems.* Research your neighborhood's crime problems. Are they burglaries and thefts, or vandalism and graffiti? Don't be overwhelmed by all the possibilities— make a list of priorities and attack the worst problems first.

- *Expand your personal space.* The block you live on is as much your world as your porch or front lawn. Consider the entire block your space, not just your house or apartment. Become invested in it by knowing your neighbors. Care about them and their homes and their loved ones, too. Criminals are most successful when they are able to divide and conquer law-abiding residents.

- *Don't let teenagers take over.* Adults have to take some chances and let their views be known to the young people in the neighborhood. Start with your own home and children, then expand to your neighborhood. Let the kids know you're not going to tolerate certain things. Let young people know that you're not going to accept their sitting outside at midnight and one o'clock in the morning playing radios, drinking, smoking dope, cursing, and carrying on. Let them know you'll talk to their parents or whomever they live with. If they live alone, make it clear they're going to have to deal not just with you but with all the neighbors.

- *Volunteer at the local police station.* Help out by giving your time, energy, and any special expertise, such as computer literacy. Typing, filing, helping with graffiti cleanup programs, or becoming a reserve officer—in the end, all of it frees that many more officers to be out on the streets doing real police work.

- *Show that you intend to take back your block.* Make sure your community takes part in the National Nite-Out program, where once a year in the summer all over America people come out of their homes in neighborhood after neighborhood and take back ownership of the streets. In Philadelphia, neighbors had everything from barbecues to picnics to fairs. People would make sure the shut-ins were invited. Young people would make a point of introducing themselves to the elderly to lessen the fear some older people have of all teenagers. For a night, the bad guys disappear and the rough corners are cleared. Residents come away realizing how powerful they are when they unite.

- *Improve your home security.* Complete a home security survey, available at many police departments, checking windows, doors, garages, and making sure outside landscaping and lights will deter, not aid, burglaries. Make sure home security is maintained when you're not home—set lights on timers, leave drapes and shades in their normal position, keep valuables out of sight, etc. Do a home inventory of all your valuables: make a list with description, cost at time of purchase, replacement cost, etc. Take pictures of valuables. Marking property will not, in itself, completely prevent its theft, but when done in conjunction with other crime-prevention steps, it can be a deterrent. (The best identifying mark is your driver's license numbers because it provides the easiest way for police to trace stolen property.)

- *Learn how to stay safe on the street.* Whether you are taking a Sunday stroll or walking home from your bus stop on a work night, follow well-lighted, well-traveled streets. Travel with companions, especially after dark. Stay alert and have your key ready to open your home or car quickly. If someone follows you, cross the street and head for bright lights and people. Avoid wearing expensive jewelry. Carry a small penlight to help you see in the dark. Don't overburden yourself with packages and groceries that block your view. Do not enter your home if something seems different or suspicious. I generally do not recommend Mace or other sprays for the average person—it can be difficult, if not impossible, for an untrained individual to aim, spray, and hit the attacker. However, noise-making devices such as whistles, shriek and other personal alarms, and Freon (compressed-air) horns can be effective at chasing away a would-be attacker. If you find yourself the victim of a crime, try your best to stay calm, and remember, if facing a weapon, do as you're told—it's far better to give up your purse or wallet than your life.

- *Get the information you need.* Your local police department is the first and best place to start in a search for crime-prevention materials and information.

You can also contact these organizations:

National Sheriffs' Association, 1450 Duke St., Alexandria, VA 22314, 800-424-7827. Provides information on the neighborhood watch program to law enforcement agencies and citizen groups.

National Association of Town Watch, P.O. Box 393, Wynnewood, PA 19096, 800-NITE-OUT. Sponsors National Nite-Out every August and promotes other local crime-prevention activities.

National Crime Prevention Council, 1700 K St., NW, 2nd Floor, Washington, D.C. 20006, 202-466-6272. Provides written material and offers assistance on crime prevention to community groups.

*   *   *

In turn, police departments and city governments can initiate actions and programs to encourage community participation in the fight against crime.

These include:

- *Listening to the community.* Sending police specialists into the community to work with residents is really the quickest and most visible way a department can show it is listening to its customers. Also an effective way to begin community policing, bringing needed specialists in is an opportunity for police to show they understand what the residents want and are committed to finding solutions.

- *Provide leadership.* Even the most dedicated community volunteers need direction, and that's where law enforcement comes in. Whether helping to organize a neighborhood or attending community meetings, police must get across that they are willing to work with, not apart from, the residents in preventing and fighting crime.

- *Be creative in problem solving.* Police must work with other city agencies to find novel ways of attacking crime, such as the city's filing a court injunction against a street gang; this has been done successfully not only in Los Angeles but in two other California cities: Burbank and San Jose. I am sure these city attorney's offices would be willing to provide representatives of other cities or police departments with information.

- *Decentralize from the top down.* Everyone has to be willing to give up some power and control, from the chief of police down to the newest patrol sergeant. Giving people at various levels the authority to solve problems helps to untie bureaucratic red tape, making the police department more efficient and more effective.

- *Changing our reward system.* Find ways to reward officers for solving problems and otherwise excelling in community policing rather than just for making collars.

- *Creating an employee-friendly environment.* Community policing is not just how we deal with residents but also ow we deal with our own employees. We must provide adequate training, equipment, counseling, and be fair and consistent in our discipline. Sensitizing your employees to race and gender issues within their ranks should help make for that much more understanding on the streets.
- *Expand recruiting.* The more a department reflects the makeup of the community, the more the officers understand the needs and wants of the people they police. Reach out in recruiting efforts to all segments of the population, women as well as minorities, college-educated as well as ex-military, etc.
- *Make patrol home for the best and brightest.* No assignment in the department should be more important than patrol. Patrol is any department's front line in the fight against crime and represents that part of the department that the public sees and deals with the most. Uniformed crime-prevention officers should be right up there with patrol in terms of emphasis and importance.

Forging true partnerships between police and the public empowers both and is the best and perhaps only way to successfully fight today's crime. Only by working together do we outnumber and outmuscle the criminals.

Think of the possibilities.

In memory of the honored police officers who were killed in the line of duty during my watch:

Los Angeles Police Department

Police Officer Gabriel Perez-Negron, Nov. 4, 1995
Police Officer Charles Heim, Oct. 22, 1994
Police Officer Christy Hamilton, Feb. 22, 1994
Police Officer Clarence Dean, Jan. 17, 1994
Police Officer David Schmid, Dec. 16, 1992
Police Officer Ray Messerly, Oct. 22, 1992
Detective Edward Kislow, Aug. 22, 1992

Philadelphia Police Department

Police Officer Daniel Boyle, Feb. 6, 1991
Police Officer Freddie Dukes, Dec. 25, 1990
Police Officer Joaquin Montijo, June 14, 1990
Police Officer Winfred Hunter, June 4, 1990
Police Officer Albert A. Valentino, Oct. 23, 1989
Sergeant George Hall, Jan. 30, 1989

They are a source of pride because they made a difference that will never be forgotten.

They are our heroes.

INDEX